Climbers' Guide to Central & Southern Scotland

A Comprehensive Guide to Low-Lying Crags

JERRY HANDREN

THE SCOTTISH MOUNTAINEERING TRUST

First published in Great Britain in 1986 by
The Scottish Mountaineering Trust

Copyright © by The Scottish Mountaineering Trust

ISBN 0 907521 17 7

Front Cover — *First ascent Dunker's Delight: Climber Duncan
           McCallum. Photo: Rab Anderson.*
Rear Cover — *Snowwhite. Dumbarton Rock. Climber, Ken Johnstone.
           Photo: Gary Latter.*

Graphic reproduction by Arneg, Glasgow
Typeset by Gray & Dawson, Glasgow
Printed by Brown, Son & Ferguson, Glasgow
Bound by James Gowans, Glasgow

CONTENTS

THE EASTERN OUTCROPS

THE OUTCROPS OF THE SOUTH WEST

FOREWORD

It used to be accepted that the SMC produced guides to mountain crags and was happy to leave it to others to produce guides — usually slim, low budget affairs — to the quarries, boulders, bridges, railway walls and sea cliffs in the Lowlands.

My own 1967 Creag Dubh and Eastern Outcrops guide was followed by another, with the title reversed, from Highrange Sports. The West has been covered by Ken Crocket's 1975 Western Outcrops published by Nevisport and by Glasgow Outcrops Vol. I & II from Highrange Sports.

Explosive activity screamed out for a new Guide and Jerry Handren responded with the brave decision to collate all the information about climbing in Central and Southern Scotland. It was too big a task for any one person and Jerry was greatly helped by not only those who are credited with having written sections but by many, many other climbers who offered help, advice and constructive criticism.

After months of hard work the manuscript was beginning to take shape and, in November 1983, I was asked if the Scottish Mountaineering Trust would be prepared to undertake publication of the guide.

The Committe of the Scottish Mountaineering Club was consulted and instantly recognised and accepted the dramatic change which has taken place on the rock climbing scene in the last decade. It willingly gave its support to the publication of this volume.

Late in 1984 a rather rough and incomplete manuscript was circulated for comment. It was agreed that the final manuscript should be submitted early in 1985 and that an Addendum be added at the end of the summer '85 so that production could proceed over the Winter with a view to publishing very early in 1986.

Handren, disconcertingly, kept disappearing to the United States in search of surfing and a more relaxed lifestyle. Some of us gave up all hope of ever seeing the manuscript again.

On one of Jerry's rare visits home, Bob Duncan had been press-ganged-into seeing the manuscript through to publication but despite letters and 'phone calls to the States, there was no manuscript and no response. Eventually, late in 1985, the manuscript turned up having been sent Surface Post from the United States. Two valuable months had been lost.

Bob Duncan in the East and Ken Crocket, ably assisted by Tom Prentice, in the West, agreed to see the manuscript through to publication and slaved over the Christmas and New Year period to make up lost time. The fact that this guide exists at all is due in no small way to their efforts.

The Scottish Mountaineering Trust exists to give assistance to Scottish mountaineers but without the assistance of mountaineers it cannot fulfil its task. The Trust gratefully acknowledges the efforts of all who contributed to making this guide possible.

Graham Tiso
Convener — Publications Sub-Committee
Scottish Mountaineering Club.

INTRODUCTION

The outcrops of south and central Scotland have seen an explosion of activity in the last few years. Completely new crags have been unearthed and extensively developed, while the guides to many established areas have long been rendered obsolete by the volume of new routes climbed. This development has transformed a hitherto relatively obscure area into a major climbing ground. The ease of access from the cities of Glasgow, Stirling and Edinburgh, the year-round climbing possible on many of the crags, and the sheer quantity of climbs would in themselves be enough to ensure the popularity of these outcrops; the quality of much of the climbing which has come to light must surely place the importance of the area beyond doubt. It is hoped that this guide will allow many more climbers to enjoy what to date has largely been the privilege of the few.

Such is the variety encompassed by the guide that any generalisations about the nature of the rock or the climbing would be virtually useless. The rock types include sandstone, limestone, dolerite and granite, while the situations vary from quarries to sea cliffs.

The guide has been divided into four separate sections: the Western Outcrops, the Central Outcrops, the Eastern Outcrops and the outcrops of the South West. Many of the areas have appeared in various private publications, but a majority, especially in the Central, Eastern and South West sections, are appearing in print for the first time. The authors have tried to be as consistent as possible, but, especially as this is a first edition, there are bound to be occasional errors. Information would be welcomed on any of these, as well as on any new routes. for inclusion in future editions of the guide.

ACKNOWLEDGEMENTS

THE WESTERN OUTCROPS

This list of contributors will almost certainly leave out some names. This is not intentional and we apologise in advance for any such error. To write such a wide-ranging guide would be impossible without the efforts of many people. For assistance of various kinds we thank: Ronnie Bruce, John Christie, Dave Cuthbertson, Roger Everett, Mark Garthwaite, Colin Gilchrist, Martin Hind, Andy Kirk, Bish McAra, Alan Shand. Tom Prentice should be singled out for much hard work, as should Rab Anderson and Duncan McCallum for help with illustrations. Gary Latter supplied the second half of the history. Those responsible for particular crags are acknowledged below. Finally, the contribution of earlier guides should be acknowledged. These are 'The Western Outcrops' by Ken Crocket (Nevisport: 1975), and 'The Glasgow Outcrops' by various (Highrange: 1975).

CENTRAL OUTCROPS AND EASTERN OUTCROPS

Many people have contributed to the production of these sections. The following list is hopefully complete, but, due to the way the guide has evolved, may be slanted towards those who have helped in the latter stages of preparation of the manuscript. My sincere apologies if there are any significant omissions. So, my grateful thanks to the people below for providing information, advice, technical help, comments on the manuscript and/or moral support and assistance: Rab Anderson, Derek Austin, Dick Baker, Jamie Cameron, Nicky Campbell, Calum Fraser, Murray Hamilton, Jimmy Hewit, Kevin Howett, Craig Macadam, Duncan McCallum, John 'Spider' McKenzie, Jimmy Marshall, Neil Morrison, Graham Fedley, Ken Spence and Andy Tibbs.

The contribution of the original guides to the climbing on several crags in the Eastern section should be acknowledged. These guides are the 1967 guide to Creag Dubh and the Eastern Outcrops (G.Tiso and authors) and the Highrange guide to the Eastern Outcrops and Creag Dubh (S.A.Brown, Highrange Sports).

THE OUTCROPS OF THE SOUTH WEST

I would like to thank the following people for their help in producing this section from the rock to the page: Derek Austin, Bob Duncan, Andrew Fraser, Donald Gibson, Jerry Handren, George Macadam, Moira Macadam, David Todd, William Todd, particular thanks go to Valerie Macadam for her hard work on the diagrams.

NOTES ON THE USE OF THE GUIDE

Gradings

Because of the number of contributors to this guide there are minor differences in the grading systems used for various crags. For most areas the standard adjectival grades have been used, as follows: Easy, Moderate, Difficult, Very Difficult, Severe, Hard Severe, Very Severe, Hard Very Severe, Extremely Severe.

The Extremely Severe Grade has been sub-divided, using the open-ended E-grading system, into E1, E2, E3, E4, E5, etc.

Technical pitch gradings have been given for climbs of Very Severe and above. Consideration of the technical grade in conjunction with the adjectival/E.grade will give an indication of the degree of seriousness of a pitch, how strenuous and/or how sustained it is, etc. As a rough guide the following technical grades equate to these adjectival grades:

4b	Mild Very Severe	5b	E1
4c	Very Severe	5c	E2
5a	Hard Very Severe	6a	E3
		6b	E4, E5.

Generally speaking a technical grade lower than that expected from the adjectival grade would indicate a very sustained or poorly protected route. A higher technical grade would indicate a short and usually well-protected crux.

In a few areas variations on this system are used. For shorter, boulder problem-type routes technical grades alone have generally been given. These can go down as far as 2a, rising through 2b, 2c, 3a, 3b, 3c, 4a, etc.

Many of the routes described have been repeated very rarely, if at all, while a large number of newer climbs were extensively cleaned and inspected on abseil prior to leading. Grades are for on-sight ascents, but for the above reasons should be treated with caution. although an attempt has been made to upgrade routes where doubt existed.

A further hazard is that many of the quarry climbs get dirty very quickly, effectively raising the grade, so care should be exercised in this respect.

Pegs

The use of pegs is discouraged, as they damage the rock. Pegs used for runners should be left in-situ, unless it is possible to climb the route without. The use of pegs on routes which have been climbed without is not acceptable.

Bolts

Climbs utilising specifically-placed protection bolts have not been excluded from the guide (although only one is recorded at present), but it is hoped that this practice will never become widespread. There is a great tradition of bold climbing in Scotland, and it would be a great pity if this was to be destroyed as a result of the thoughtless actions of a selfish minority. It is hoped, therefore, that responsible attitudes will prevail and that no potentially controversial actions will be taken without due consideration.

Left and Right

These refer to a climber facing the cliff, except where otherwise specifically stated.

Recommended Routes

A three star system of recommendation has been used. A consensus has been sought where possible, but stars should not be taken too seriously. One man's meat is another man's poison! A lack of stars does not imply that a climb is not worthwhile.

Finding the Crags

For each outcrop an O.S. 1 50.000 series sheet number is given, along with a six-figure Grid Reference. Most areas include detailed access notes.

Litter

This guide includes some extremely attractive areas, as well as some better suited to the gymnast than the aesthete. Nonetheless, litter should not be dumped, but disposed of carefully, irrespective of any consideration of the particular beauty — or lack thereof — of the crag in question.

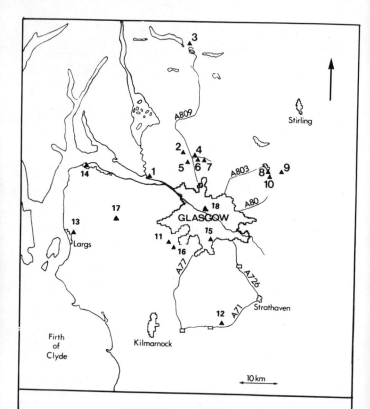

THE WESTERN OUTCROPS

1 Dumbarton Rock
2 The Whangie
3 Ben A'n
4 Craigmore
5 Craigton
6 Pillar Crag
7 Dunglas
8 Auchinstarry Quarry
9 Cowden Hill Quarry
10 Jackdaw & Lower Girnel
11 Johnstone Quarry
12 Loudoun Hill
13 The Quadrocks
14 Craigmuschat Quarry
15 Court Knowe
16 Neilston Quarry
17 Craig Minnan
18 Kelvinbridge & Finnieston

INTRODUCTION — THE WESTERN OUTCROPS

From Highland Ben A'n in the north to Loudoun Hill in the south, from The Quadrocks in the west to Auchinstarry Quarry in the east, the various and varied outcrops of Scotland's Western Central area cater to all tastes and abilities. The rock types include metamorphic schist, intrusive basalts and trachytes, with surroundings as diverse as introspective quarries and the panoramic Firth of Clyde.

All of the outcrops are accessible for an evening's climbing. Only Ben A'n and The Whangie demand more than a 20-minute walk and then only just, while Dumbarton Rock and Auchinstarry Quarry are of immediate access. The rainfall in the West of Scotland is obviously higher than parts further east, though much lower than mountainous regions. To offset this the climate is milder, and given dry rock, climbing can be had at any time of the year.

The countryside enfolding Glasgow includes some of the most beautiful in the country — to find enjoyable rock climbing as well is a bonus. Climbers must be aware of the fragility of the whole system. Leave no litter. Protect wild life. Allow other users to enjoy the sites in their own ways. Respect local Bye-Laws and private property. Preserve the crags for the next generation of climbers.

Ordance Survey maps covering this area are Sheets: 56, 57, 63, 64, 65, 70, and 71.

HISTORY 1890's - 1950's **by Ken Crocket**

'A precipice 20 feet high does not sound very serious, but there may be more fun and real climbing in getting up or down such a place than there is in ascending the 4,406 feet of Ben Nevis . . . A quarry face is by no means bad fun, if one can either find a place free from onlookers, or can turn a deaf ear to their somewhat personal remarks about the sundry coppers missing from the shilling . . .

This comment about outcrop climbing was by Gilbert Thomson, one of the founder members of the Scottish Mountaineering Club. It was published in January 1892, by which time various rock athletes from that club - themselves young at some point in their lives - had scurried up quite a few crags. On Saturday, December 12 1891, the day following that Club's Third Annual Dinner, a team of hard men paid a visit to The Whangie. This was the third visit to that crag, the party on this day consisting of: Horace Walker, President of the Alpine Club: Professors Ramsay and Veitch; Messrs Maylard, Munro, Naismith, W.A. Ramsay, and Thomson. Despite snow on the moor and ice-filled cracks, some time was 'very enjoyably spent in various pieces of fancy climbing.'

The following July, Maylard, Naismith and Thomson attacked the Whangie with two 40-foot ropes; joining them together and climbing the isolated pinnacle now known as The Gendarme by techniques dubiously modern. Crag climbing had arrived in Central Scotland. In September 1892 the crags saw the first climbing accident, also on the Whangie, as loose rock precipitated a climber off the top of the ridge. He lived, thanks to his roped companion.

Other crags were being visited at this time; Craigton, Pillar Crag, the Salisbury Crags glowering over Auld Reekie, Loudoun Hill in Ayrshire. About this time also, in the mid-1890's, started the east-west rivalry which in one form or another persists to this day. Ben A'n in The Trossachs came under siege in May 1896, by that crag-rat Thomson, H.C. Boyd and his brother the Rev Arnold Boyd. The lower rocks appeared too steep and difficult, the party tackling instead two vegetatious gullies. These remain vegetatious, the cleaner, steeper rocks in the interim having given many enjoyable routes.

Thomson and his friends thus recorded the first route on Ben A'n with the 30m Left Hand Gully (Very Difficult). The other gully, on which they failed that day, was climbed two years later by Naismith, Douglas and Maclay, on New Year's Day, 1898. On January 22 1898, Harold Raeburn and J.S. Napier visited the crag and recorded the Oblique Crack, a Very Difficult on the upper tier of rocks.

Loudoun Hill meanwhile had been visited by Naismith as long ago as 1895, when he had attempted to solo a route up the Central Wall. Returning alone by cycle in April 1896, he managed to reverse his line, finding great difficulty climbing in the rain wearing cycling shoes. His route, more of a scramble, starts under The Edge and traverses up and right.

The rocks at Dumbarton Castle were known of by those pioneers, but footwear then was too inadequate for the technical gems waiting to be found on the Boulders. Outcrops in any case were regarded by most as a convenient means of obtaining fitness with amusement at the same time, an attitude which persisted for over 70 years. This early, casual approach to the crags has inevitably led to a dearth of recorded history. With a few exceptions, most of the routes climbed before the 1970's have no sure claimant. Only since the early 1970's has a section of climbers attached more importance to the outcrops; recording routes in minutiae, leading or soloing routes and problems previously top-roped, freeing aid routes.

The initial phase of exploration by the SMC died out during the first three decades of the present century; only with John 'Jock' Nimlin in 1930 can we put a date on the renaissance. In that year W. White led the Ash Wall on Ben A'n, graded then as an 'Amiable Severe'. Nimlin that same year recorded several other excellent routes, including the Birch Wall, The Last 80, and The Rent, the latter Severe or Very Severe, depending on one's jamming abilities.

With mass unemployment in the 1930's great numbers of young people took to walking, the cheapest sport available. For some, climbing naturally followed, many new clubs forming. Jock Nimlin from Glasgow was the force behind the Ptarmigan Club, while Andy Sanders formed the Creagh Dhu. The Lomond M.C. also came into being at this time. Nimlin recorded his climbs on Ben A'n, but on the lowland crags nobody bothered, being intent on a friendly spirit of competition.

With the end of the Second World War the Whangie especially took a beating, the talents of the Creagh Dhu and the Glencoe M.C. being prominent. Hamish MacInnes left a visiting card with several peg routes; to be freed many years later. Craigmore was also visited by the Creagh Dhu - this area was where they first explored the outdoors after all - but not being accustomed to digging for their routes they soon left that future crag in peace, though not without in all probability first climbing the prominent Craigmore Corner. John Cullen edited the first outcrop guide to appear with the Whangie, in 1950; significantly, that crag already appeared mature, with some 76 routes. Loudoun Hill seems to have slumbered along as usual since Naismith's visit in 1895; only with the late John Jackson and members of the local Strathaven Climbing Club did activity pick up, in the late 1950's and into the 1960's. The Quadrocks were being developed round about the 1960's, with members of the Greenock M.C. prominent, 'Big' Bill Skidmore recording the lines in an interim guide.

1960's - 1980's by Gary Latter

At the same time, probably as rock boots began to find their way over the channel, Dumbarton Rock began development. The leading light there was the late Neil Macniven, killed in the Alps in 1963 at the age of 21. His brilliance at the 'Rock' led to ascents of such face routes as Stonefall Crack, Stonefall Crack Direct, and the aid route Chemin de Fer. Macniven also climbed about half of the boulder problems, including Pas Encore, Route Royale (with Brian Shields), Suckers Slab, B.N.I., and Nemesis.

Brian Shields, Michael Connolly and others climbed the remainder of the Dumbarton routes in the early 1960's, Shields being responsible for recording them. Climbs put up by Shields included: Longbow (with Jimmy Houston, using 7 pegs and 8 wedges); Windjammer Crack; Monsoon Gully, the latter seeing a failed attempt on a direct finish by Macniven and Shields. Many of the boulder problems fell to Shields, including: Short Notice; Skint Knuckles (one sling); Switch Direct (in vibrams). Shields was also responsible, with Connolly, for the big aid route Requiem, the finish up the headwall requiring expansion bolts. The other aid route from Shields was The Big Zipper, with A. Baillie.

This wave of activity passed on its way too, though the comparative trough was to be short-lived, as a new group of climbers was spawned at the 'Rock'. The 'Dumbarton Boys', whose core included 'Big' Ian Nicolson, Rab Carrington, John Jackson, 'Wee' Ian Fulton and others, found newer and harder boulder problems, some of which took weeks to work out. They also repeated the face climbs, finding some additions. All this was at the end of the 1960's and into the 1970's. Shields had two more routes to record however, with the aid route Cyclops, and with Desperado. Court Knowe in Glasgow's suburban south was explored by the Crocket brothers in the late 1960's, Wullie's Crack and other routes being soloed. The family washing line was taken along but used for abseiling fun only!

At the beginning of the 1970's a visiting gritstone climber, Steve Belk, began to investigate the 'Rock'. This led to; Bobtail, the first free ascent of Longbow, and the top rope ascent of Grey Wall. On January 3 1971, Belk and Ken Crocket started up Requiem, pegging the first pitch and placing the bolt belay on the grass ledge below the corner of Cyclops. They climbed part of pitch two, the monster overhanging crack, before nightfall called a halt. This was done to the strains of a wind-up gramophone, brought along by an acquaintance. Returning the next day they prusiked up the fixed ropes and finished the climb, Belk making a superb lead on tied-off blade pegs at the top of the wall, where the wide crack fades. No signs of any bolts were found on this ascent, supposedly the third.

Craigmore began to have its concealing cover of turf removed in secret, the diggers being an expatriate Welshman, John Kerry, and Gordon Jefferies. The latter had climbed on Craigmore in the late 1960's. John Mackenzie was also living in Glasgow at this time, his enthusiastic explorations finding many lines on Craigton, Pillar Crag and Dunglas, the latter with Colin Garthwaite. Craigmore was such a well-kept secret that it was not included in the first outcrop guide to be published for this area - Ken Crocket's 'Western Outcrops' (Nevisport,

1975). This beat the rival 'Glasgow Outcrops' (Highrange,1975) into print by about six months.

Auchinstarry Quarry was rediscovered in 1975 by Ken Johnstone. It was included in a second volume of the Glasgow Outcrops. Johnstone recorded the first routes here with Trundle and Mascarade. Kerry soon homed in on this old quarry, finding such popular routes as Spirogyra, Thumbalena, and Red Lead. Pete Greenwell found Knife Edge, while Willie Todd climbed the thin arête Nijinski employing a runner on the neighbouring route Promontory Crack, having first top-roped the route. In 1982 Dave Cuthbertson cleaned the arête by abseil then made the first lead with no side runner. Deep Throat by Johnstone was top-roped then lead.

Westwards Ho! to Dumbarton, with Andy Kelso recording Ciamar a Tha Sibh and a short aid route, later freed by Todd to give Snowhite. Two fine arêtes succumbed; Nick Colton's Fever Pitch, Todd's Gaucho. Johnstone was also busy here, with ascents of Slainte, Drizzle, Rough Sea, and the fine crack of Antigrav, using two aid points. This was later freed by Todd, with several yo-yos. Modern attempts to free the classic aid routes saw Murray Hamilton climb The Big Zipper with two bolts. At this time too (1977), Kerry and Johnstone put up most of the routes on Cowden Hill, while the latter produced the first route on Girnel Quarry with Obelisk and most of the routes on the West Face of Craigmuschat.

The boulder problems at Dumbarton, the 'black Fontainebleu', were gradually being added to in 1978, with Mark Worsley on Supinator, Greenwell on Gorilla, and Todd on Good Nicks. Auchinstarry saw further developments from Rob Kerr with Power Play and Soft Machine. Two years on, both top-roped routes on the Trundle Slab were soloed to give Walk on the Wild Side and Midas Touch.

In 1981 Tom Prentice, Callum Fraser and Dave Cuthbertson visited Johnstone Quarry, Cuthbertson leading Tom's Crack. Two years on saw much activity at Auchinstarry, with Jerry Handren producing The Dream Machine, Blade Runner, and Death is the Hunter. Ben Masterton boldly climbed Balance of Power while Gary Latter made a two-day ascent of Carouselambra. Duncan McCallum solved 'the last great problem' in the quarry with his ascent of the blank-looking wall of Surface Tension. The latest route in the area was in Jackdaw Quarry, where Tom Prentice climbed The Dispossessed in 1985.

It somehow seems appropriate to conclude this abbreviated and of necessity incomplete history of the Glasgow and West of Scotland outcrops, with a mention of some of the latest deeds at Dumbarton Rock. On the boulder front, Latter added Mestizo, Toto and Physical

Graffiti. The old peg problem Pongo was freed. But the big guns were aimed at the aid routes of the face. Cuthbertson worked hard in the spring of 1980, recording Woops, an alternative, fingery start to The Big Zipper. The same climber also succeeded in freeing Chemin de Fer, over the course of several evenings, ropes and runners being left *in situ* overnight. Kerr climbed Datura at the far right of the West Face.

Cuthbertson returned in 1981, freeing the uncompromising corner of Cyclops, taking successive falls on to a pre-placed peg runner. Two years later Masterton made a Direct Start to Requiem, while Latter climbed the excellent Rock of Ages, and made the first lead of Grey Wall. Latter went on to free the two aid bolts on The Big Zipper, taking six day's work spread throughout the summer.

The last great problem on Dumbarton Rock was the great Requiem crack. This fell at last to Cuthbertson after an heroic struggle encompassing six weeks of humid climbing in the summer of 1983. At the time of climbing, this was Scotland's hardest pitch. Finally, in the spring of 1984 Latter climbed Rising Power and Samora.

The art and practice of outcrop climbing has travelled far and hard since Gilbert Thomson's days. Long looked on as a useful adjunct to bigger things, many now find much pleasure in the short, but difficult problems described in this volume. It is hoped this guide will help climbers of all abilities to continue to find pleasure in these rocks.

Map: O.S. Sheet 64 G.R. 400 745

DUMBARTON ROCK

INTRODUCTION

Dumbarton Rock is 22 km WNW of Glasgow, 1 km South of the A814. A site of strategic importance since the Fifth Century A.D., its volcanic plug projects abruptly from the alluvial plain of the River Clyde at the mouth of the River Leven. It rises to a height of 73m, composed entirely of intrusive basalt which is fine-grained and sound. Climbs are either on the very steep or overhanging faces or on the massive boulders lying below the NW Face. There is very little vegetation and the rock dries within hours. The face climbs include several old aid routes, now free, along with others also of a high technical standard. The boulder problems require rock boots only and are of great training value. They also provide much pleasure, on rock which is virtually unique amongst the outcrops.

Routes on the main NW Face may finish within the Castle grounds. Dumbarton Rock is an Historic Monument, open to the public at certain times only and then by payment of a small admission fee. Discretion should be excercised at all times if climbing is to be allowed to continue on the faces — it is a privilege, not a right.

ACCESS:

Travelling by the A814 from Glasgow, take the second road on the left after Dumbarton East railway station (Victoria St.). Follow this to the Rock and a parking spot. Behind this a path leads under the North Face, arriving in about 100m or so at the Boulders and the Main NW Face. The train provides a convenient service between Queen St., Glasgow and Dumbarton East.

The first section of routes is on the North face, adjoining the access path. Routes are described from left to right. The grassy slopes above some of these routes can be hazardous, especially if wet. Descent by abseil may be preferable in some cases.

DUMBARTON ROCK — THE FACE ROUTES

North Face

1   Alpha   20m   Hard Very Severe   5a
High on the left-hand end of the face can be seen a series of short
cracklines. Gain and climb twin cracks up the left edge to a belay well
back.

2   Beta   20m   E1   5b   ★
Start directly below the central crack. Climb sloping rock to reach the
crack and follow it to a belay well back.

3   Gamma   20m   E1   5c
In essence a left-hand finish to Uisge Beatha, taking the steep crack just
left of the ramp on that route. Climb sloping rock to the foot of the crack
and follow it throughout.

4   Uisge Beatha   27m   Hard Very Severe   5a
The leftmost of two rightward sloping ramps. Climb sloping rock for 7m
then follow ramp, stepping right at the top.

5   Rising Power   36m   E2   5b   ★
Start as for Uisge Beatha, but follow the obvious rightward slanting
fault line to the foot of the crack on Antigrav. Climb crack a short
distance to good hold, continue traversing right to join Crackerjack and
finish up that route.

6   Bohert   30m   Hard Very Severe   5a
Start beneath the rightmost of two sloping ramps. Climb sloping rock
for 8m, follow the ramp to finish up a crack.

7   Antigrav   30m   E3   6a   ★★
A fine pitch with a short, technical crux, well protected by Friends. Start
directly below the hanging crack. Climb wall to crack, up this with a hard
move to gain slab. The continuation crack is then climbed to a belay well
back.

8   Slainte   30m   E2   5c   ★
Right of Antigrav are two hairline cracks. This route climbs the
right-hand crack. Climb wall to crack, up this by turning small overlap on
right.

9   Crackerjack   30m   E1   5b   ★
A fine route, climbing the excellent finger crack high on the face. Start
immediately below the crackline. Up wall to gain small ledge at about
8m. Step left from here and follow the crack and its continuation to top.

10   Drizzle   30m   Hard Very Severe   5a   ★
Another good route. Start below the leftward slanting crackline. Follow
easy crack then make an awkward move to gain the sloping ledge
above. Follow corner for a few moves before moving left to arête.
Continue to top.

11   The Neilweg   30m   Hard Very Severe   5b   ★
An early line on this face, taking the shallow corner above the start of
Drizzle. Gain the corner and follow it to ledge and possible belay. The
crack above provides an airy finish.

12   Big Ears   33m   E1   5b
Right of The Neilweg and above the ramp can be seen a shallow
grooveline. Pull on to shelf directly below the short groove. Follow this
and the thin crack in the headwall above.

13   Boulevard   30m   Very Severe   5a   ★
Another of the early routes, taking the rightward sloping shelf.
Difficulties on the initial section and on the grassy finish. Gain the shelf
from the left and follow it to a nut belay at the top (old peg). Either
continue up grass or descend by abseil.

14   Hailstone Climb   30m   Severe
On the wall left of Monsoon Gully is a faint grooveline. Climb this to a
small ledge, step left and continue up broken ground to a grassy finish.
Not recommended.

15   Left Edge Route   30m   Very Severe
Takes a line up the left edge of Monsoon Gully. Start at the middle of a
short wall and follow a direct line, aiming for the arête above. Climb
arête until a steep section forces a move out left to a finishing crack.

16   Monsoon Gully   33m   Severe   ★
An interesting gully of near-Victorian character. Often damp and greasy,
the finish is on steep grass. At the top of the gully move left to gain the
grass.

17   Monsoon Gully, Direct Finish   10m   Hard Very Severe   5a
Climb the steep crack on the right wall at the head of the gully.

18   Nameless Crack   24m   Very Difficult   ★
Start 10m right of Monsoon Gully. Climb pleasant, slanting crackline to join gully near the top.

19   Alleyway   24m   Very Severe   5a
Starting at the same point as Nameless Crack is a narrow, sloping shelf. Gain it awkwardly and so up to a grass. Step left and up mixed ground to finish.

20   Sunset Groove   30m   Very Severe   4c
At the rightmost end of the face is a loose, broken groove. Climb groove and continue up broken rock above.

21   Angel's Pavement   90m   Very Severe   5a   ★★
The low-level girdle of the face, usually less than 3m up. The crux is the section at the foot of Boulevard. An excellent training route.

Gully Wall

This is the steep, west-facing wall some way up the open grassy slope. It is recognised by the large mass of ivy on the left. Descent is by traversing right from the top and so down by the obvious, steep path. The cliff is approached by scrambling up the grassy slope.

22   Ganglion Grooves   18m   Very Severe   4c   ★
Just right of the ivy is a bulging groove. Climb this for 5m then, using a dubious flake, pull right on to a slab. Continue up the groove and crack to the top.

23   Ciamar A Tha Sibh   23m   E1   5a   ★
The shallow corner high on the face, poorly protected in the middle section. Follow Ganglion Grooves for 5m, then up the narrow slab diagonally right to the short corner. Enter corner and up this until forced left to the arête. Finish up this.

24   Snowwhite   20m   E1   5b   ★★★
A superb pitch, taking the fine crack in the centre of the wall with gradually improving protection. Step left on to a slab, then back right to the base of the crack. Follow this to the top.

25   Rag   16m   Severe
Climb the groove right of Snowwhite.

26   Tag   15m   Hard Very Severe   5a
Up and right of Rag can be seen a series of short, discontinuous cracks. Start below the twin, left-hand cracks. Climb the cracks and the wall above to finish up the groove on the left side of the block overhang.

27   Bobtail   12m   Hard Very Severe   5a
At the far right-hand end of the face is a short crack leading to a groove. Climb the crack and make an awkward move to gain the continuation groove, up this, stepping left at the top.

North-West Face
The face overlooking the Boulders — one of the most spectacular, overhanging faces of any outcrop, giving some of the best and hardest one-pitch routes in Scotland. Descent following a route is by abseil.

28   Route Three   20m   Hard Very Severe   5b   ★
Start directly beneath the left-hand of the overhang. Climb straight up to an old peg in the corner. Continue as for Stonefall Crack.

29   Stonefall Crack   21m   Hard Very Severe   5a   ★★
Start beneath the crack on the right. Follow crack a short way then the leftward-trending line of holds which lead to an old peg in the corner. Undercling the roof rightwards and finish up the left wall of the chimney.

30   Stonefall Crack Direct   20m   Hard Very Severe   5a   ★
Start as for Stonefall Crack. Climb the crack direct. Protection is poor in the middle section.

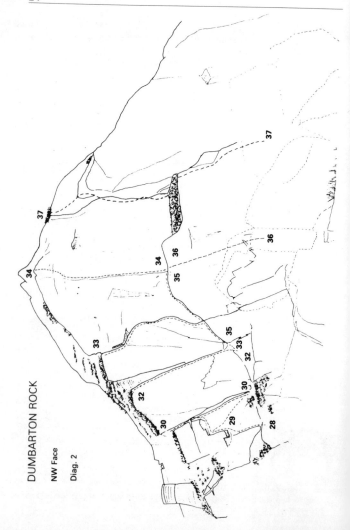

DUMBARTON ROCK

NW Face

Diag. 2

31   Woops   10m   E4   6a   ★
This short and overhanging finger crack provides a fine variation start to
The Big Zipper corner. Start 1m right of Stonefall Crack. Climb the crack
to gain the obvious traverse line leading into the corner. Finish up this.

32   The Big Zipper   30m   E4   6c   ★★★
Start below and left of the line of old bolts, directly below corner.
Mantelshelf on to ledge and up wall with difficulty to gain small ledge at
foot of corner (no hands rest). Continue up the corner, strenuous. Belay
well back.

     The Big Zipper Variation   E3   5b   ★★★
Climb Stonefall Crack Direct until possible to traverse out right round
arête (serious and unprotected) to a belay at foot of the corner.
Continue up corner.

33   Chemin de Fer   31m   E5   6a   ★★★
Perhaps one of the finest crack pitches in Scotland. Start at faint
crackline at foot of slab. Climb slab to gain crack proper. Climb crack,
hard moves at bottom, middle and top, the latter probably the crux.
Belay well back.

34   Requiem   46m   E7   6c   ★★★
A very hard route, requiring powerful and determined climbing. From
the bolt belays at the foot of the overhanging crack (gained by either of
the two lines described below) enter the crack. Where the crack peters
out take a rightward–trending line of holds up the headwall. There are
two in situ nuts near the top, the crux being the last move below the
top.

35   Rock of Ages   17m   E3   6a   ★★
This follows the rising traverse line leading to the bolt belay at the foot
of Requiem. Start as for The Big Zipper. Climb across to, and follow the
'flake', crossing Chemin de Fer en route. One peg runner in situ.

36   Requiem Direct Start   17m   E3   5b   ★
A bold and serious pitch climbing wall direct to turn small overlap on
left.

37   Cyclops   42m   E4   5a   6b   5a   ★★
Start beneath a series of ledges at the right-hand end of the slabby wall.

1.   20m   Up ledges and wall above, bypassing a large, dubious block
to reach bolt belay on grassy ledge.

2.   13m   Difficult bridging leads to a good protection peg at 5m. Make
a few moves on left wall then regain corner to follow this and crack in
right wall to a block belay.

3.   10m   Step left and up short groove to a nut belay well back.

Continuing right from Cyclops, the West end of the NW Face is
reached. This compact buttress is just past the Boulders and has
several excellent routes. There are two prominent, dark grooves;
Longbow is the left-hand one, with an overhanging right wall. For all the
routes good nut belays are available some distance back. Descent is
either by abseil, leaving a sling at the finish of Cyclops, or by scrambling
down rightwards into the Castle and down the gully just right of Pinky
and Perky.

38   Fever Pitch   32m   E4   5c   ★
A serious pitch climbing the left arête of the buttress. Start just right of
the arête. Climb straight up until a move left brings a resting place at half
height. Move up past the overhang and finish by moving slightly
rightwards up the wall above.

39   Longbow   32m   E1   5b   ★★★
The left-hand groove, giving steep and well-protected climbing with an
exciting finish. Climb the groove, hard move right near the top.

40   Gaucho   32m   E2   5c
Start just left of Windjammer Crack, below a shallow groove. Climb
groove to join Desperado. Move diagonally left to the arête then
diagonally right to the lowest part of the small overlap. Go up 1m then
move left underneath a large overhang to finish at the same point as
Longbow.

41   Desperado   32m   Hard Very Severe   5a   ★★
The central, hanging grooveline. Protection is scanty in the middle
section. Climb Windjammer Crack for 10m to a sloping ledge. Traverse
left into the groove and follow this past old pegs to the top. A variation

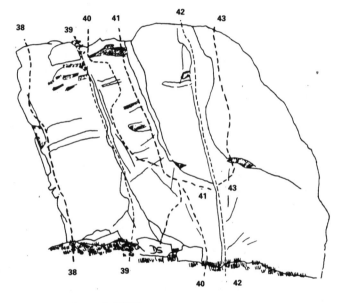

Diag. 3   West end of NW Face

start is possible to left of original line. Climb overhanging rock until a swing right is possible to gain the groove of Gaucho. Finish up Desperado (5c).

42   Windjammer Crack   32m   Hard Very Severe   5a   ★★★
A superb pitch, climbing the right-hand groove of the buttress. Follow the groove, the overhanging flake at the top being turned by a layback.

43   Rough Sea   32m   E1   5a   ★
The arête right of Windjammer Crack. Follow the latter to its junction with Desperado. Traverse right to the arête on hollow flakes and climb the wall on the right to the top. A serious pitch.

West Face

This is the continuation of the face past the arête right of Windjammer Crack. The face looks down the Clyde and starts above the waterline. The rock is much rougher than elsewhere on the Rock and dries quickly. About 18m right of Windjammer Crack is the overgrown scoop of West Face Gully. Descent is by the gully right of Pinky and Perky. The first route climbs the obvious chimney left of West Face Gully.

44   Dumbarton Chimney   30m   Very Severe   4c
An unpleasant route on poor rock. Start below the chimney. Gain and climb the chimney, exiting left to continue up broken rock and grass to finish.

45   Silly Thing   40m   Hard Very Severe   4b   5b
The rightmost corner in the wall left of West Face Gully, by which it is reached.
1.   25m   From the gully traverse easily left to the foot of the corner and follow it to a block belay at the foot of the steep crack.
2.   15m   Climb the crack above to take a belay well back.

46   Frendo   30m   Very Severe   4c   ★
Climbs a slab on the left wall of West Face Gully. Bordering the slab is a narrow ramp. Climb this ramp for 10m or so, then after a short section of mixed ground make a short right traverse over loose blocks to gain another slab. Finish on good holds.

47   Grey Slab   25m   Very Severe   5a
Above and right of Frendo is a steep slab, near the finish of the gully.
Climb the slab direct to finish up Frendo.

48   West Face Gully   30m   Severe
The overgrown gully, 18m right of Windjammer Crack. Start directly
beneath the gully. Above a bramble thicket climb the deep chimney in
the right side of the gully. At the top, move right and continue up
Plunge, or traverse left to the corner formed by the rock and the Castle
wall and finish up this.

49   Plunge   28m   Difficult   ★★
A good route, taking the rib which rises from the beach to the Castle
wall. Start by traversing in from the left. Follow the rightward-trending
rib, traverse right at the top and climb the Castle wall.

50   Red Slab   8m   Hard Severe   ★
Just right of Plunge is a slab topped by a bulge. Climb the slab.

51   Old Socks   9m   Very Severe   4c
Some 7m right of Plunge is a crack leading up to an overhang. Climb
both directly.

52   Poison Ivy   9m   Very Severe   5a
7m right of Old Socks is a steep red slab, topped by ivy. Climb the slab
centrally, delicate but rough rock.

53   Pinky   12m   Very Severe   4b
On the small crag up and right of Poison Ivy. Start just left of the small
central overhang. Climb up to gain the shallow groove and finish up this.

54   Perky   12m   Hard Severe   4b
Start just right of Pinky, below a groove. Follow the groove, passing to
the right of the overhang.

   About 18m right of and above Poison Ivy there is a small crag below
the Castle wall. A dark groove splits the crag. The next six routes are
found on this crag.

55   Banana Rib   15m   Very Difficult
Climb the rib on the left-hand side of the crag.

56   Banana Groove   15m   Very Severe   ★

This route climbs the dark groove, moving right at the top to finish.

57   Banana Slide   13m   Hard Very Severe   5a

An eliminate line up the left side of the wall. Start just right of the groove. Climb the wall until forced left on to the arête. Make a few moves up the arête then traverse right to finish.

58   Grey Wall   13m   E4   5c   ★

A serious pitch up the centre of the wall, the crux near the top having no protection. Follow a vague line of holds, using a hanging flake at about half-height.

59   Datura   12m   E3   5c   ★

Similar climbing to Grey Wall. Start at the right-hand end of the wall, below a small, downward-pointing flake. Climb the wall direct, past two ledges.

60   Samora   12m   E3   5c

A surprisingly independent line up the right-hand edge of the wall. Start a few feet right of Datura. Follow an obvious line of holds to gain ledge at rightmost end and finish directly.

61   West Face Girdle   140m   Very Severe   4c   ★★

This traverse lies between the foot of West Gully and the park railings on the South side of the Rock. The route is usually less than 5m above the beach. For most of its length the traverse is about Difficult; midway there is an 11m stretch containing the crux. Objective dangers include interesting animal life in every crack, and high tide. Other bits of rock can be found on the West face, giving short stretches of up to Severe standard.

The Boulder Problems

Some time after the last retreat of the Loch Lomond Glacier, a massive rock fall must have taken place from the main face of Dumbarton Rock. The fall has left eight solid blocks of black basalt beneath the NW Face, boulders that might have been designed by some cosmic climber, so ideal are they for climbing. They range in size from the massive Boulder A (Eagle Rock), to the tiny Boulder H.

It is important to bear in mind when attempting a boulder problem, that to use a hold on any neighbouring route is not legitimate, as the

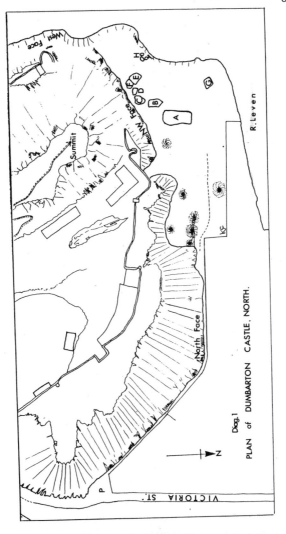

Diag.1

PLAN of DUMBARTON CASTLE. NORTH.

standard is then usually lowered. On the other hand, once proficiency is gained, holds can be missed out and eliminate lines climbed. The technical standard of many of the problems is high by any system. Though many of the problems are strenuous, the climbing is also surprisingly delicate. As the only equipment necessary is a pair of rock boots, the boulders are recognised as one of the most useful of training grounds in the West of Scotland.

Boulder A (Eagle Rock)

The large, slabby East face of this boulder greets the arriving climber. Descent is by the easy arête facing the Castle. Routes are described moving right, starting with two just left of the descent route.

1   The Blue Meanie   5c   ★★
Just left of the descent route are two blue paint marks. Start at the smaller mark and climb straight up the overhang.

2   P.T.O.   4c
The short wall and overhang above the larger paint mark.

3   Left Edge   Very Difficult
Climb the slabby face just right of descent route.

4   Rankin's Bajin   Very Difficult   ★
Start about 1m right of Left Edge. Climb straight up the slab on good holds.

5   Soixante-Neuf   4b   ★
Start about 2m right of Left Edge and climb straight up the slab.

6   Pas Mal   4b   ★
Straight up the slab, just left of No.1 Route.

7   No.1 Route   Difficult
The easiest route on the slab. Climb on good holds up a shallow leftward-slanting groove.

8   Left Direct   4a
Start at the ledge of No.1 Route and climb straight up on good holds.

9   Centre Direct   5b   ★
Midway between Left and Right Directs. Delicate, with few holds.

10   Right Direct   4b
Climb to the left of the flake on No.2 Route.

11   No.2 Route   Difficult
Climb on good holds to the large flake and follow this to top.

12   Pullover   5a   ★
Start about 1m right of No.2 Route, pull over a bulge and continue
directly.

13   Zig-Zag   5a   ★★
Right of Pullover is a flake hold. Pull up on to a stance and step left
(delicate). Continue directly on traverse left and continue up Pullover.

14   Tam's Route   5c   ★
Right of Zig-Zag is a line of holds up overhanging rock.

15   Gorilla   6b   ★★★
The first route on the sea face. Start below layaway at the lip of the
cave. Gain this by a leap and swing left to a good hold on the lip. Pull
over this and finish up slab.

16   Cautious Lip   6b   ★★
Similar to, but harder than, Gorilla. Climb as for Gorilla to the layaway
then go straight up to the slab and finish up that.

17   Supinator   6a   ★★
The thin overhanging crack in the centre of the sea face is climbed, with
a hard exit move on to the easy slab above.

18   2HB   6a   ★★
Start just left of the tree at an undercut hold. Climb overhanging wall to
finish up easy slab above.

19   Girdle Traverse   4a   ★
Start up the descent route and traverse the East face at mid-height. Either finish up No.2 Route, or continue by descending as far as possible down the North arête then traversing along the sea face to regain the descent route.

Boulder 'B'

There are three excellent routes on the wall facing the water.

20   Friday's Fill   4a   ★
The broken crack on the left. At the top is a long stretch and a strenuous pull.

21   Friar's Mantle   5b   ★★★
The central line. Climb a bulging mantelshelf, surprisingly delicate.

22   Ungava   5a   ★★
The wall on the right. Avoid using the right edge.

Boulder 'C' — Home Rule Boulder

On the side facing the Castle are three bulges. The arête which descends towards the Castle is both the line of The Beast and the easiest descent route. The first route is just left of this arête.

23   The Beauty   5a
Climb wall over an overhang on good holds.

24   The Beast   4b   ★
The arête facing the Castle. Pull up, turn nose on left, follow arête to top.

25   The Brute   5a
The wall just right of the arête, gained from the smaller of two rocks.

26   Valkyrie   5a   ★
Step off the smaller of two rocks, at a small diamond-shaped wall, pull up and step right on to the slab. Continue diagonally right to top.

27   Pas Encore   5b   ★★
From the larger rock pull over bulge directly. Strenuous.

28   Mugsy   6c   ★★
Start directly below shallow groove, just left of arête. Climb imposing wall to a good incut on left, pull right into groove and so to top.

29   Mestizo   6a   ★★
The arête and groove above. Start below arête, gain good hold high on arête and move left to finish up a shallow groove.

30   Physical Graffiti   6b   ★★
Bold and fingery, climbing the wall direct.

31   Home Rule   6a   ★★
The original way on this face. Start just right of Physical Graffiti, climb to good flat holds, traverse right and finish up arête.

32   Home Rule Direct Finish   6a
Mantelshelf on to the handrail, pull over top avoiding holds on arête.

33   Presence   5c   ★
The right arête.

34   Route Royale Direct   6a   ★
This is on the face behind Boulder 'B', looking down to the water. Start in the centre of the lichenous wall and climb the weakness direct. The original route traversed in from the left.

35   The Whip   5b   ★
Start below the blunt arête right of Route Royale. Take a series of small sloping ledges to shallow depression on right, up this to top.

36   The Switch   5a   ★
Climb a sloping shelf on the left of Valhalla.

37   The Switch Direct   5b
Instead of veering left at the top, climb the bulge on the right.

38   Valhalla   4c   ★
In the centre of the face is a shallow fault. Climb this to an awkward move at the top.

Boulder 'D' — Suckers Boulder

There are four slab routes on this Boulder, at the V-junction between Boulders 'D' and 'F'.

39   Mosca   Very Difficult
Climb the left arête on small holds.

40   Antimatter   5b   ★★
This thin eliminate line goes immediately right of the arête.

41   Suckers Slab   5a   ★★★
Climb straight up the centre of the slab on faith and friction.

42   Volpone   Very Difficult   ★
Climb straight up the thin crack.

43   P.S.   5a   ★
A short and strenuous jam up the angle between Boulders 'C' and 'D', on the side facing the water.

44   Toto   6b   ★
The short, left slanting crack just right of P.S., eventually joining that route.

45   Snooker Shelf   5a   ★★
Start at the right end of the face, pull up on small holds to gain sloping shelf and follow this leftwards until possible to climb easily up wall above.

Boulder 'E'

A few metres left of Sorcerer's Slab a cave-like passage leads under Boulders 'E' and 'F'. The next route begins at the East entrance.

46   Skint Knuckles   5b   ★★
Using a small sidepull on the right wall pull up to gain a good layaway. Gain a standing position on the sloping ledge using the edge above.

47   Pongo   6b   ★
A short and very hard problem up the overhanging crack, gained by swinging in from the left.

48   Sorcerer's Slab   5a   ★
This route and the two following climb the slab right of the fast-growing tree. Pull on to the slab and follow a left trending line.

49   Magic Wand   5b
Climb straight up from the start of Sorcerer's Slab.

50   Slant   5b
Just right of Magic Wand is a black groove. Climb the groove.

51   Nemesis   5b   ★
This route and the five following lie on the face right of the slab. An easy groove is gained with difficulty.

52   Narcosis   5b   ★
Start just right of Nemesis and climb up and left to gain a short, shallow groove in the arête. Follow groove and arête above.

53   Lunik   5b
Start at the same point as Narcosis but climb rightwards to gain the arête.

54   Cheddar Direct   4b   ★
Start below the arête. Pull on to it from the right to finish up it.

55   Hard Cheddar   5b   ★★★
Just left of the rightmost of four bulges on this face. Delicate. Pull up and step left into an easy groove.

56   Juggie   4b   ★
The rightmost bulge. Pull up on two small holds and continue in a straight line to the top.

Boulder 'F'   B.N.I. Boulder

The Boulder hard under the Windjammer Face. The initials B.N.I. reputedly stand for 'Bloody Nigh Impossible'. Descent is either by reversing Astronomy or by jumping from the top on to the ledges on the main face. The first routes are on the wall left of the hanging slab.

57   Harvester of Eyes   4a
The open groove on the left of the face.

58   Astronomy   4a
The blunt rib in the centre of the face.

59   Deo Gratis   5b   ★
On the wall left of the B.N.I. slab, facing the docks. Climb the wall, with
a hard move at half height.

60   Imposter Arête   5a   ★ ★
Climb the left bounding arête of the B.N.I. slab on small but good holds.

61   B.N.I. Direct   5c   ★ ★
Start below arête. Step right on to slab and climb straight up, avoiding
holds on the arête.

62   B.N.I.   6a   ★ ★
Traverse right from the start of the Direct and climb across then up to a
semi-detached flake. Mantelshelf on to the top. A delicate route.

63   Good Nicks   6a   ★ ★
Start below and right of slab, at foot of thin undercut crack. Climb this to
niche, swing immediately left on to rib and up this to top.

64   Pendulum   4c   ★ ★ ★
Climb on to a ledge and face into a series of bulges on the left. Pull up
and swing round, using a jug, on to the sheer slab. Mantelshelf on to the
flake or finish on small holds. A delightful route.

65   Pendulum Variation Finish   5a   ★
From halfway along the flake reach right into the short V-groove and
finish on good holds.

66   Chahala   5c   ★
Difficult for those of less than medium height. Start just left of Skint
Knuckles below a trio of good incut holds. Gain the first by a leap and
follow them until possible to pull right to finish.

Boulder 'G' — The Sea Boulder

The isolated Boulder by the water's edge. The first route described is the hardest, found on the East wall, facing the access path.

67   White Streak   6a
On the centre of the wall is thin streak of white paint. Follow this directly, without recourse to either arête.

68   Steptoe   4c   ★★
Climb the left arête of the face looking over the river. Large holds at top. The inserted lump of lead is not to be used.

69   The Red Streak   5b   ★★
Just right of the arête of Steptoe is a streak of red paint. Follow this directly, avoiding holds on adjoining routes.

70   Chowbok   4c   ★
Climb the centre of the sea wall.

71   Erewhon   5b   ★★★
The right arête of the sea wall. Good holds high up, difficult to gain them.

72   Tuesday Treat   5b
Moving right to the face looking down on the Firth, climb the wall just right of the arête of Erewhon, avoiding using that arête.

73   Commercial Route   4b   ★
Climb the small corner right of the arête of Erewhon and continue to top.

74   Wednesday Wail   4c
This eliminate line goes up just right of the small corner, avoiding holds on adjacent routes.

75   Silver's Route   4c
Climb the slabby wall using sidepulls to start. Either move left and up or finish more directly.

76   Gardner's Girdle   5a   ★★
Circumnavigate the Boulder until tired.

Boulder 'H'

A small trio of Boulders, below Boulder 'E'. There are three routes.

77   Short Sight   4a
Climb short wall left of Short Notice, facing East.

78   Short Notice   5b
The nose of rock facing the Distillery. Step on to slab below nose and pull up.

79   Long Reach   5c   ★
Just right of Short Notice is a scoop topped by a small arête. Pull into scoop avoiding the right arête and finish directly.

THE WHANGIE

INTRODUCTION

This unique outcrop is to be found on the NW flank of Auchineden Hill. The rock is an olivine basalt, dark green or black when fresh, weathering to a red. Near the tops of the faces and at many other points suspect holds will be met. Routes range in length from 5m to 15m. It is advisable to top-rope, though belays are in some cases difficult to arrange. Any sun will be on No.1 Face from noon till sunset, with a memorable view over the Loch Lomond Hills.

ACCESS

From Glasgow take the A809, Glasgow-Drymen road to Queensview car park. The Glasgow-Drymen bus passes Queensview several times daily, leaving Buchanan St Bus Station. From Queensview car park the path climbs about 100m then contours round the north side of the hill, reaching the rocks in about 35 minutes. The estate is under sheep and dogs are not permitted.

Approaching from the north, the isolated wedge, or 'whang' of rock known as The Gendarme is first met. Further south, No.1 Face looks out to Loch Lomond, with No.2 Face on its reverse. On the flank of the hill is the overgrown No.3 Face. Finally, the largest fallen rock before No.1 Face has several interesting problems centred around an overhang.

The Gendarme: Diagrams 1 & 2

1 Spider Slab 4m Severe
Climb slabby wall at north end of The Gendarme. The few holds present slope awkwardly.

2 Blaeberry Crack 4m Very Difficult
Climb crack direct, easing above.

3 Mossy Slab, Right 4m Severe   ★
A deceptive route, climbed mainly on small holds.

THE WHANGIE:

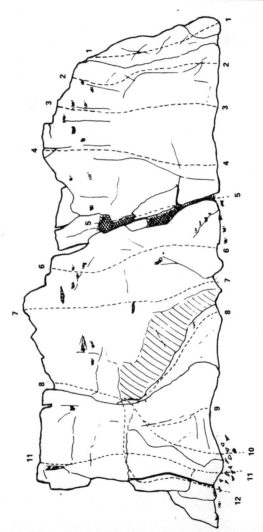

The Gendarme: Inner Face

4   Mossy Slab, Left   4   Difficult   ★★
Straightforward and pleasant.

5   Staircase Crack   4m   Easy
The convenient descent route.

6   The Bulge   4m   Severe   ★
The small bulge left of Staircase Crack. Climb direct or more easily to
either side.

7   Bird's Nest   5m   Very Difficult   ★★
Follow a series of good holds, including a 'letter-box'.

8   Red Crack   5m   Very Difficult
This climbs the corner closely.

9   Red Slab   5m   Very Difficult
Climb up and left on red polished holds. Finish as for Red Crack or more
directly above for a Severe finish.

10   Windswept Wall   5m   Severe
A harder variation start to Red Slab.

11   Upturned Flake   5m   Hard Very Severe   5a   ★
Start immediately left of the edge. A few thin moves lead to a good
undercut after which follow the thin crack above.

12   Upturned 'L'   6m   Very Difficult
Climb corner then traverse right to finish up Red Crack.

13   Angel Corner   7m   Hard Very Severe   5a
Climb the south arête of The Gendarme.

14   Angel Direct   6m   Very Severe   4c   ★
An alternative and strenuous start to Angel Corner.

15   Heartbreak Corner   5m   Hard Very Severe   5a   ★★
Climb shallow corner, move right and up to finish. Strenuous.

16   Knife Edge   5m   E2   5b
Climb arête immediately left of Heartbreak Corner.

THE WHANGIE:

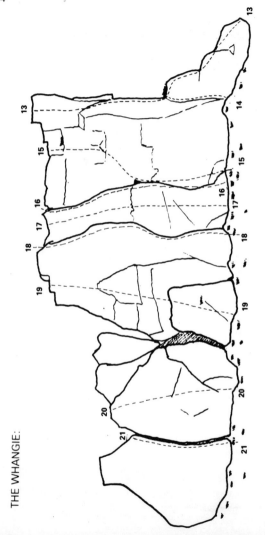

The Gendarme: Outer Face

17   Hangover Overhang   5m   Severe
Climb the strenuous rib on the left of Heartbreak Corner.

18   Whodunnit   5m   E2   5c
Climb steep wall just right of Trench Wall.

19   Trench Wall   5m   Very Difficult   ★
Up detached flake and pleasant slab.

20   Barrowland Bulge   4m   Very Difficult
The bulging wall to the left of the gap. Climb direct.

21   Backsnapper Crack   4m   Severe
Loose rock requires care.

Number One (The Loch Lomond) Face — Diagram 3.

22   Triangle   3m   Very Severe   4a
At the north end of the face is a small triangular boulder. Find a finger hold for a strenuous pull up.

23   Thin Crack   4m   Severe   ★
Climb directly the corner crack on the right of Triangle.

24   Finger Exercise   8m   E1   5b
Climb blunt arête to finish just left of Recess Route.

25   Recess Route   8m   Severe   ★
A good, exciting line, though with loose rock. Gain obvious recess, swing left and up.

26   Cave Crack   9m   Very Severe   4c
Follow chimney, which narrows to a crack. Climb gently overhanging wall then finish more easily.

27   Grim Wall   9m   Hard Very Severe   5a
From the lowest point of the wall climb up and right to a ledge. Gain the arête then swing left and climb poor rock to top.

THE WHANGIE:

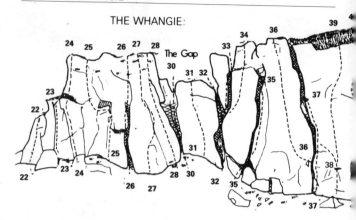

28 Sou'West Rib   9m   Very Difficult
Climb the rounded arête at the end of this section of the face. Loose rock abounds.

29 Cave Chimney   9m   Very Difficult   ★★
To the right of the arête. The chimney widens to a small cave then narrows again. Climb direct.

30 Easy Chimney   8m   Difficult   ★
This open chimney at the left end of the gap provides pleasant footwork.

31 Easy Wall   7m   Very Difficult   ★★
Climb short wall by any chosen line.

32 Easy Groove   7m   Moderate   ★
A useful beginner's route, or use for descent.

33 Vampire Crack   9m   Very Severe   4c   ★
Begin as for Easy Groove then continue awkwardly up jam crack.

34 Vampire Rib   9m   Hard Very Severe   4c
Begin as for Easy Groove then as soon as possible swing right on to rib which follow to top.

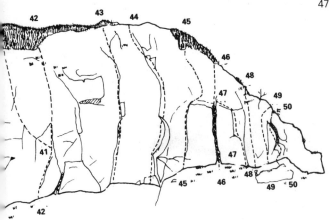

35   Ivy Crack   10m   Severe   ★★★
A popular route. Layback to a resting place then follow crack to a
through route.

36   Ivy Rib   10m   Very Severe   4c   ★
Climb first few moves of Backstep Chimney then traverse left to follow
rib to top.

37   Backstep Chimney   12m   Severe   ★★
A classic. Either climb the lower crack direct, or throw a foot backwards
on to the triangular hold on the left wall. Above, climb the chimney
finishing by a through route, easy for the slim.

38   Backbreak Wall   13m   Very Severe   4c
Named after the obvious penalty clause. Mantelshelf on to sloping
ledge, climb bulge then continue as for Backstep Chimney.

39   Horror Route   14m   E1   5a
Climb bulge of Backbreak Wall then continue directly.

40   Bluebottle   14m   E2   5b   ★
Start just right of an edge, faint arrow. Climb directly on small holds,
strenuous.

41   Sudden Death   14m   E3   5c
Follow Slim Crack for 4m then out left to reach high jug. Up crack line, past sapling to loose rightward finish. Bold and sustained.

42   Slim Crack   14m   E2   5b
About 6m right of Backstep, and left of a large flake. Follow a thin curving crack, originally pegged.

43   Hedgehog   14m   E2   5b   ★
Another old peg route. Follow obvious crack, passing old pegs.

44   Curving Crack   15m   Hard Very Severe   5a   ★★★
An excellent route. climb obvious corner to striking curved crack. Step right on to white rib, up to ledge, then move left and up bulge to finish.

45   Sloping Ledge   13m   Severe   ★
Climb slab and crack above, using an expanding flake. Exit up loose rock.

46   Overhanging Cleft   10m   Hard Very Severe   5a   ★★
An interesting problem in jamming and bridging up the bulging crack.

47   Toenail Traverse   12m   Very Severe   4c
Climb ledges on small holds, move left to finish as for Overhanging Cleft.

48   Angew's Wall   9m   Very Severe   4b
Start as for Toenail Traverse but climb right trending crack to holdless slab. Finish up bulging wall.

49   Rowan Rib   8m   Very Severe   4c   ★★
Left of a recess is a small bulging rib. climb it on small holds then move up and right below a small tree.

50   Sunshine Crack   8m   Very Severe   4a   ★★
A deceptive little problem. Enter recess and climb crack above.

Number Two Face — Diagram 4.

To compensate for the sunless and gloomy nature of this face, it does contain most of the best rock and climbing at the Whangie.

51 Be-Bop 7m Very Difficult ★
A short way in from the south end of the passage climb a short wall on good holds.

52 Monk's Wall 7m E1 5b
Steep wall left of Ladybird Layback, climbed to sharp pocket then up leftward.

53 Ladybird Layback 8m Very Difficult ★
Climb the obvious right sloping ramp.

54 Ladybird Direct 7m E1 5b
This climbs the left arête of the large overhung recess, finishing as for the normal route.

55 Militant Tendency 7m E1 5b
Climb back of 1st recess to roof, pulling out left to join Ladybird Layback.

56 Nocibur Wall 10m Very Severe 4b ★★
A good interesting route. Where the passage is narrowest opposite the second recess, climb the No.3 face or bridge up for 3m or so, then commit to the No.2 face and climb to top.

57 Ruth's Route 10m Very Severe 4a ★★
Another good route. Immediately right of the second recess a line of holds leads to a thin crack. follow the holds, step left, then up.

58 Whippenwoof Wall 10m Severe ★
Climb shallow groove to ledge, continue up wall.

59 Gremlin Groove 10m Very Difficult ★★
The obvious groove 4m right of the second recess. Pleasant.

60 Mantelshelf Wall 10m Severe ★
Climb broad rib, with an interesting move on to a large hold a few moves up.

61 Varsity Groove 10m Very Difficult
Start as for Mantelshelf Wall, follow shallow groove right to a grass ledge then up wall.

THE WHANGIE:

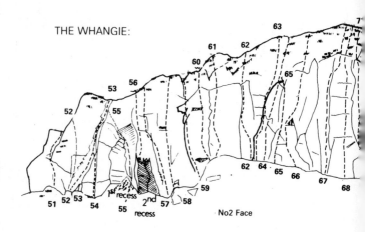

62   McBains Wall   10m   Very Severe   4c   ★ ★
Start at vertical crack immediately left of Rowan Tree Groove. Hard
move off ground, gain handhold, swing left on to slab, continue up past
spike. This is a harder variant of the original line which begins a short
distance left.

63   Rowan Tree Groove   12m   Difficult   ★
The obvious right trending groove on the left side of an arête. Good
holds.

64   Fallen Tree Arête   12m   Very Difficult   ★
Start below right facing arête, make difficult move on to arête then
continue more easily.

65   Fallen Tree Groove   12m   Severe
Climb corner immediately right of arête, awkward at top.

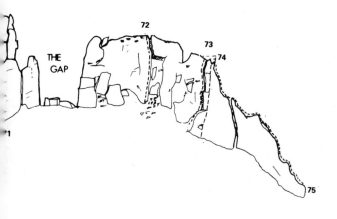

66   Young's Route   12m   Severe   ★
Start below nose of rock, climb slabby wall to left of nose, step right and finish up wall.

67   Allison's Route   12m   Very Severe   4b   ★★
Immediately left of the Ripple Wall climb steeply on good holds, moving right at top.

68   Ripple Wall   12m   Very Severe   4c
Climb series of smooth ripples starting with a finger hold.

69   Long John's Wall   12m   Hard Very Severe   5a
Climb wall on small holds, sustained.

70   Hutch's Route   8m   Severe
Right of Long John's Wall the angle eases. Climb wall easily.

71   Needle Route   7m   Moderate
Climb arête left of descent route from Backstep Chimney.

THE WHANGIE:

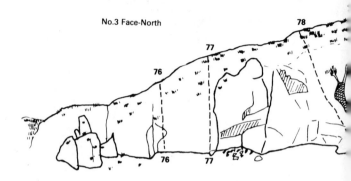

No.3 Face-North

72   Novice Overhang   6m   Difficult   ★
Rib left of prominent recess. Steep but good holds.

73   Novice Crack   6m   Moderate
The easy crack on left side of arête.

74   Jughandle Arête   7m   Moderate   ★
The prominent arête right of the recess. A pleasant line with good holds.

75   Arrowhead Arête   16m   Difficult
Start at the north end of the whang and follow arête easily.

Number Three Face — Diagrams 5 & 6

This face is the longest, wettest and most loose. A long stretch of the most uninteresting section is omitted from the diagram. The first six routes face the Gendarme and are shown on Diag. 5.

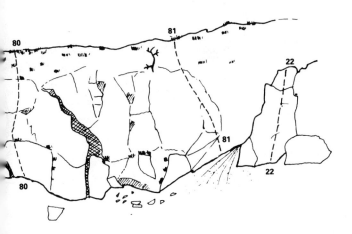

76   Heather Wall Scoop   5m   Severe
The short, loose recess at the left end of the face.

77   Heather Wall Overhang   6m   Very Severe   4c
Climb the bulging rib on the right of the recess.

78   Nonchalant Route   10m   Hard Very Severe   5a
Start up slab, then up and left on rib.

79   Manky Crack   10m   Severe
A gardener's delight. Climb loose rock on left of vegetatious crack, step right into heather, and somehow finish.

80   Suicide Wall   12m   Hard Very Severe   5a
A suitable companion route to Manky Crack. Climb wall right of dirty crack.

81   Bolsyn   10m   Very Severe   4c
Climb wall opposite the start of Arrowhead Arête.

THE WHANGIE

No.3 Face-Centre & South

82   Jungle Groove   12m   Very Difficult
Just left of Weed Groove is a green, slimy corner. Climb this finishing
up a turf overhang.

83   Weed Groove   13m   Severe
Opposite Novice Overhang. Climb groove and arête left of a rock fall.

84   Gnomie Arête   12m   Very Difficult
Opposite the south end of the gap is a loose arête. Start on the left side;
swing on to and up arête. Replace any holds removed!

85   Gnomie Arête Variation   12m   Severe
Climb steep corner-crack on right of arête to join the arête just above
half-height.

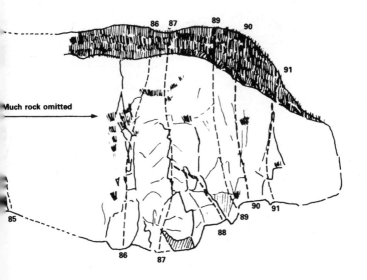

86   Garden Wall   12m   Very Difficult
Opposite Ruth's Route is a prominent corner, just left of the arête at the
bend in the passage. Follow line of luxurious ferns, curving rightwards
below the top.

87   Earthquake Arête   12m   Severe
The blunt arête at the narrows of the passage. Start left of the edge;
move on to the arête; finish up dubious rock.

88   Slantin' Crack   6m   Severe   ★
On right of arête is a slab recess. Climb crack at top, moving left on
excellent holds to gain arête.

89   Charity Arête   6m   Severe
Short, steep arête opposite Ladybird Layback. Becomes progressively harder and looser. Start on right of arête. Step left and continue up arête.

90   Rotten Rock Route   6m   Severe
Climb loose wall immediately right of Charity Arête.

91   Cancer Wall   6m   Severe
Some 6m in from the south end of the passage is a white-speckled wall. Climb up on dubious rock.
   The remaining five routes are traverses, useful for strength training. Most of the climbing is at low level and is fairly obvious.

92   Gendarmerie   25m   Severe   ★
Attempt to circumnavigate the Gendarme, going clockwise from Spider Slab at the north end.

93   Snowy Traverse   12m   Severe
Start at the foot of Sou'West Rib; go left.

94   Flakealong   10m   Severe   ★
Start at the foot of the large prominent flake just left of Hedgehog; go right.

95   Tidemark   45m   E1   5a   ★
The girdle of No.2 face, split by the gap. Start at either end.

96   The Grand Traverse   60m   E1   5b
The traverse of No.3 face, between Nonchalent Route at the north end and Cancer Wall at the south. A feat of strength.

BEN A'N

INTRODUCTION

These mica schist crags begin at 300m on the south flank of Ben A'n (464m), overlooking Lochs Achray and Katrine. The rock is dangerously greasy when wet. Most of the climbing is pleasantly easy, with some variation possible on most routes. The rocks are in three tiers, with heather in between.

ACCESS

Ben A'n is about 8km north of Aberfoyle, where the bus from Glasgow stops. From Glasgow by car take the A81 to Aberfoyle then the A821 over the Duke's Pass. Shortly after the turn-off for Loch Katrine and 100m before the Trossachs Hotel turn right into a car park. Opposite this the approach path follows a fence before heading into the woods. The first rocks are reached in 25 minutes or so, the path arriving at the foot of the first rocks, split by an open gully. Routes are described from left to right, tier by tier.

1 Ash Wall 30m Severe ★★★
About 12m left of the open gully splitting the first tier of rocks is an ash tree. Behind the tree is a polished flake. Gain the top of this and step into the groove on the wall. Climb the corner to reach a slab and climb this for 13m or so to reach a rib on the left edge. Follow the rib for 10m to finish just right of a prominent tree.

2 Twilight Groove 20m Very Severe 4a ★★
The wall right of Ash Wall becomes steep and undercut. 5m right of Ash Wall a shallow, undercut corner marks the only line of weakness. Enter the corner awkwardly, then follow it directly on improving holds to slab above. Climb the slab to finish.

3 Jughandle Wall 13m Difficult
On the left wall of the open gully, looking up, and opposite the finish on The First Thirty, a diagonal fault trends right. Climb it.

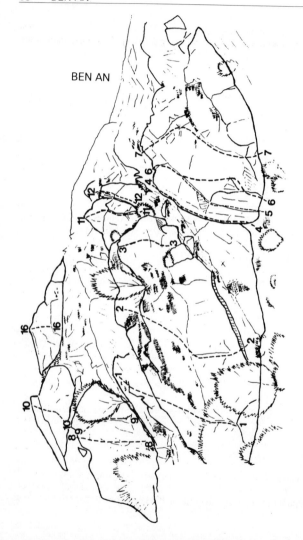

BEN AN

Band One

4   The First Thirty   10m   Difficult   ★★
At the gully entrance is a small, compact crag. This route climbs the gully wall following polished but good holds.

5   Club Corner   12m   E3   5c   ★
The short corner just left of the lowest point of the crag. A hard and strenuous bridging problem. Exiting right to finish as for The Edge. Serious.

6   The Edge   13m   Very Severe   4a   ★
Start at the lowest point of the crag at an edge, make a strenuous move right on to a slab. Climb this then follow crack up and right, or move left on to edge.

7   Preamble   13m   Severe   ★
Starting just right of the lowest point of the crag climb a small overhang. Finish as for The Edge, or more easily by moving right.

8   The Hook   10m   E2   5b   ★★
Ash Wall finishes at a birch tree, behind which is a small crag and two good routes. This route starts up a rusty wall just left of an obvious corner. Climb straight up the wall, strenuous. On a wall behind the finish is a superb spike belay.

9   Birch Wall   13m   Severe   ★★★
The obvious corner just right of The Hook, and behind the prominent tree. Enter the corner by a short traverse, deceptively steep, and climb it to exit left on excellent holds. Belay at metal spike.

10   Rowan Rib   10m   Difficult   ★★
This route begins directly above Birch Wall, at the metal spike. Pull over the small overhang and continue more easily to belay at a large boulder.

11   The Hanging Crack   10m   Very Severe   4a   ★★
This small crag is in effect the back wall of the open gully splitting the first rock band. It is recognised by a steep crack with a small bush at its start, a few metres above a niche. Gain the niche, make an awkward move past the bush then layback up the crack. Finish directly up a small wall.

12   Diagonal Groove   10m   Severe
Start as for The Hanging Crack, but continue up and right on an awkward ramp, passing a small rowan.

Band Two: This second tier of rocks lies left of and above the lowest rocks. There are three main routes and a short problem. Diagram 1.

13   Left Hand Gully   30m   Very Difficult
Walk left along the heather terrace and look for two vegetation filled channels. These are the Left and Right Hand Gullies. Climb up through greenery, occasionally emerging on to rock at a number of chimney pitches.

14   Right Hand Gully   30m   Very Difficult
The first half is vegetated; higher up it steepens to give a chimney, topped by more greenery.

15   Hawthorn Rib   40m   Difficult
This route takes in the cleanest rock on the second band, and is the way followed by most parties climbing towards the top tier. It lies between Right Hand Gully and the finish of Rowan Rib. Follow a vague rib which has a wall to its right, and merges with the heather to the left.

16   Atom Slab   5m   Severe
Above Rowan Rib, and separated by heather from the main body of rock of the second band, is a minute crag. There are some problems, and in particular a polished topwall may be climbed on the way to the final tier.

Band Three — Diagram 1. This third and final tier of rock contains several fine routes, in addition to which the increase in height gives a superb view of the surrounding Trossachs. The lowest and fore-most part of the crag is taken by the classic Last 80. There are five routes to the left, beginning with the continuations of Left and Right Hand Gullies.

17   McLay's Chimney   30m   Very Difficult
The leftmost route on the tier. A jammed block may just be seen at about half-height. The chimney is now overgrown, but if cleaned would provide some climbing.

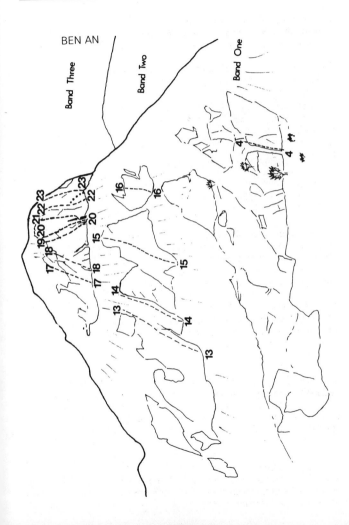

BEN AN

Band Three

Band Two

Band One

18 Right Hand Gully Continuation 27m Severe
About 10m right of McLay's Chimney and a route for the enthusiastic botanist.

19 The Spare Rib 24m Severe
A few metres left of the foremost rocks is a deep, slanting chimney. This route climbs the rib a few metres left of the chimney. Climb up and left to an edge, continue more directly. A few lines and an entertaining traverse may be found on the steep wall left of this route.

20 The Oblique Crack 21m Very Difficult   ★★
The deep-cut chimney just left of the foremost rocks. Follow the chimney, which slants leftwards until it runs out; continue on mixed ground to the top.

21 Coriander 24m Very Severe 4c   ★★
Starts 3m left of The Last 80. The wall bounding The Oblique Crack on the right is overhanging. On the lip of the overhang, about 3m up, will be seen a large quartz hold. Use the hold to gain the slab above, and climb grooves always to the left of The Last 80, to finish several metres left of the route. Protection is poor.

22 The Last 80 24m Severe   ★★★
This very enjoyable route climbs the front of the face, beginning at a small overhang where the south and east faces of the tier meet. Pull over the bulge on good holds and continue fairly directly on well marked rock. An easier variation starts a few metres right, in a corner, and traverses left to meet the original route at about half height.

23 The Rent 24m Very severe 4c   ★★★
Just right of the variation start to The Last 80 is a vertical, undercut crack; the right wall vertical and the left slabby. The start is usually overcome by jamming, after which excellent climbing leads to the top.

34 The Record Slab 8m Moderate
After finishing a route on the top tier, a short stroll leads to the summit. This is found to be the apex of an easy angled slab of good rock, timed ascents of which provide much hilarity. The rules are simple. The ascent should be made unaided, from a standing start, and with toes just touching the lowest point of the slab. Finish with both feet on the summit. Six seconds is a good time.

Map: Sheet 64, G.R. 527 797

CRAIGMORE

INTRODUCTION

Craigmore is a compact and justifiably popular outcrop just north of Glasgow. The crag varies in height from 10m to 15m at the higher left end, to smaller problems at the right. The rock is a macroporphyritic basalt, closer to gritstone in character than any other in the area. Holds and friction are generally excellent, cracks are rounded. Trees provide some belays for top-roping. The Crag faces NNE and is slow to dry, 2–6 days. Midges are rife later in the summer.

ACCESS

From Glasgow take the A809, Glasgow-Drymen road. Just past the Carbeth Inn (good beer) turn right and take the B821, Blanefield road for 1km. The crag will be visible amongst trees to the left. Poor parking for about a dozen cars on the verge at a stile. By public transport take the Drymen bus from Glasgow Buchanan St Bus Station and walk from Carbeth Inn. The local farmer is so far understanding; please respect his needs and stay off crops etc. Routes are described from left to right.

Chimney Area

The extreme left hand end of the crag is bounded by a slab with a useful descent to its left. The first route is on the left end of this slab.

1   Route 1   7m   4b
Start just left of the descent route at a vertical crack, up this on to slab, continue up crack to top.

2   Pullover   7m   4c   ★
Start 3m right of Route 1 at another crack. Pull onto slab and trend leftwards.

3   Block Chimney   8m   3a
Climb up chimney to top.

4   Honey   7m   4c
Climb wall right of chimney block without using left edge or tree.

5   Chimney Arête   8m   4c
The left arête of The Chimney is climbed throughout.

6   The Chimney   8m   4a   ★
Climb the prominent chimney, finishing leftwards.

7   Polo   8m   5b
The short crack right of the chimney, with a problematic start.

8   Silver Arête   8m   4a   ★
The arête right of Polo is climbed direct, then up slab and exit left.

9   Glug   8m   3b
The groove adjacent to Silver Arête, finishing up that route.

10   Grooved Arête   10m   4c   ★
The next arête. Aim for groove and follow this and arête to exit at tree.

11   Golf   10m   4b
Climb wide crack a few feet right of Grooved Arête to join that route.
Finish at the same point.

12   Kit Kat   10m   3b
The obvious curving groove right of the block is followed to a ledge,
then the continuation groove above.

13   Angel   10m   4c
From ledge on Kit Kat ascend diagonally rightwards across wall.

14   Wide Eyed   10m   6a   ★★
A good boulder problem type route. Start at thin crack 3m right of the
previous route. Up cracks to spike then easier up wall above.

15   Chimney Area Girdle   30m   4c   ★
A low level traverse of the above area. Start as for Route 1, go across to
Block Chimney, on to tree then on to Silver Arête via The Chimney and
Polo. Continue up to block on Kit Kat, hand traverse this to finish.

Main Area

This extends from the corner with the holly tree through a system of grooves to the obvious undercut boulder next to the path. The first route starts round the corner to the left of the holly tree.

16   Arrowhead Left Hand   11m   4b   ★★
Start at the left side of the pinnacle. Enter scoop, up crack then traverse left for about 3m then up.

17   Arrowhead Direct   11m   4a   ★★
As for previous route to scoop, then up outside of the pinnacle.

18   Arrowhead Right Hand   11m   3b   ★
Climb wide crack on right side of pinnacle and continue on same line to finish. The wide crack can also be reached by starting at left-hand crack and climbing diagonally rightwards at about 4c.

19   Cariad   13m   5b
Start just right of Arrowhead Right Hand. Up wall to gain groove, up this and pull into crack on right to finish, avoiding grass ledges.

20   Magic Crack   13m   5c   ★
The prominent crack 2m right of Cariad. Ascend crack to overlap, over this on right and up groove.

21   Holly Tree Corner   16m   4b   ★
Up corner to tree stump, step left on to wall then diagonally left until possible to traverse rightwards on slab above overlap.

22   Traverse Finish   16m   4c   ★★
A fine, airy finish, traversing horizontally right beneath overlap to finish up short arête.

23   The Beast   15m   5c   ★
Start below groove in arête of Holly Tree Corner. Pull directly into groove and follow this to slab, finishing up wall on left avoiding right arête.

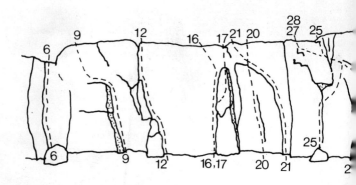

24   Jolly Green Dragon   15m   5c   ★★
Start 2m right of The Beast. Gain the shallow groove without using boulder and pull round right into short finger crack. Make a hard move up on to ledge and finish up short groove.

25   Craigmore Corner   13m   5b   ★★★
The classic of the crag, taking the big corner capped by an overhang. Up corner to overhang, trend right and up to ledge, finish up groove. Alternative finishes to the left of, and through, overhang.

26   Tom & Jerry Wall   13m   5a   ★★★
Another very fine route, with a problematic start. Start below arête. Move up and left to reach good pocket, easier up wall and arête, finish up short groove.

27   .Rampage   16m   4b   ★★
Start below curving groove right of arête. Up and left to cracks, up these and ramp above to large ledge overlooking Craigmore Corner. Traverse left to arête on skyline and up this.

28   Curving Groove   15m   5b   ★
Gain and climb the groove direct to join Rampage. Follow this and the groove above.

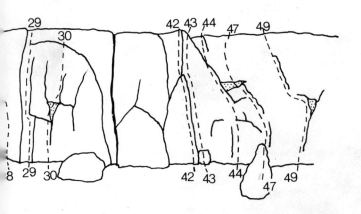

29   Daylight Robbery   12m   4c   ★
The next groove along is climbed all the way.

30   Basil Brush   12m   5b   ★
Start just right of the last route in overhung niche. Pull out of this
leftwards them back right into narrow groove and up this.

31   Alternative Finish   5b
A harder finish than the original. From the slim groove on the ordinary
route pull into and follow the slanting crack on the right to finish.

32   The Niche   10m   4c   ★★
Start 1m right of the last route below an obvious niche. Climb up into
niche, pull out right up cracks to ledge then up wall on right.

33   Variation Finish   5a
From the niche pull out left then up to join the sloping crack of the
alternative finish to Basil Brush and up this to finish.

34   Crib   10m   5a
Start below small overlap right of The Niche. Climb up to easy angled
arête then up this, avoiding crack on right.

35   Rampant   10m   4a   ★
Follow the ramp throughout.

36   Grotty Groove   10m   4a
Up Rampant for 3m then right onto ledge. Up dirty groove to top.

37   Sunday Wall   12m   5b   ★
Start 2m right of Rampant. Climb wall direct to horizontal crack, up wall
to rib then up rib.

38   Variation   12m   5b   ★
Traverse right from horizontal crack to arête and up this.

39   Hot Dawg   10m   5a   ★
Right of Sunday Wall is a block. From top of this up wall, left to arête and
finish up this.

40   Gregor's Groove   10m   4a   ★
Climb prominent groove to ledge, then sloping ramp on left.

41   Mirage   11m   4b
Start down and right of the last route. Climb crack on left side of short
wall to ledge, move left and finish up short ramp above overlap.

42   Solo   11m   4a
Up right arête of wall and arête above wall to finish.

43   Nap   10m   3b
The broken groove round the corner from the previous two routes is
climbed all the way.

44   Sancho   12m   4c
Right of the groove is a short overhanging wall above some boulders.
Up this crack into groove, then up grassy gully.

Layback Crack Area

This starts at the undercut boulder and extends rightwards to the
pinnacle split by the obvious handjamming crack. The first two routes
described are on the boulder.

45   Moss Slab   5m   3a
Climb the easy angled slab on the front of the boulder.

46   Terror   5m   5c   ★
Direct up the overhung arête of this boulder.

47   Bwana   13m   5b   ★
Climb crack on right side of boulder to ledge. Up overhanging crack
above to niche, cross overlap to slab and finish up overlaps on left.

48   White Hope   13m   5c   ★★★
Climb groove left of Layback Crack until it is possible to move right to
finish up the slanting crack of that route.

49   Layback Crack   13m   6a   ★★★
A popular classic. Climb easy but strenuous flake crack, then make a
hard move up and left for a jug. Finish up leftward slanting crack above,

50   True Finish   12m   6b   ★★
Follow the rightward slanting finger crack from where the normal route
escapes left.

51   Crag Mate   12m   5a
Start below crack, 6m right of Layback Crack. Up crack and leftward
slanting groove above.

52   Salamander   10m   5b
Start 1m right of Crag Mate. Up to scoop without using holds on
adjoining routes, step up left and ascend wall on right to a rib and up this
finish.

53   Samson   10m   5b
Start 2m right of Salamander below crack. Climb crack to inverted 'V'
then up into groove.

54   Right Hand Start   6a
Start at the left side of boulder below Sabre Crack. Climb diagonally
leftward to reach Samson.

55   Sabre Crack   8m   4c   ★★
Climb crack above boulder and finish up arête. The grade is lowered to
4b if the boulder is used.

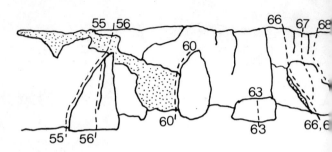

56   Stiletto Crack   8m   4c   ★★
The fine handjamming crack to the right of Sabre Crack.

57   Rapier Arête   8m   5b
The arête just right of Stiletto Crack is climbed direct, avoiding both adjacent cracks.

Blade Area

Right of Stiletto Crack is an area of more broken rock, then a large elliptical boulder known as the Blade. Right again is another boulder, then an area of higher rocks bounded on the right side by an arête.

58   Swiss Roll   8m   3b
Climb wall at back of bay to ledge and up right sloping ramp above.

59   Central Way Down   13m   2a
A useful descent route. From left end of blade scramble leftwards to ledge, along this and up corner.

60   Blade Left Hand   3m   4a
Up left side of blade, just below white streak.

61   Blade Right Hand   5m   2a
Up right side of blade just below white streak.

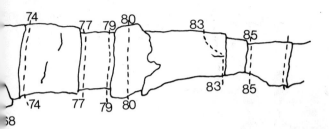

62 White Streak 5m 5b
From the top of blade climb the wall above, trending leftward. Climb the crack on the boulder below and right of the blade.

63 Tae a Moose 3m 4a
Climb the crack on the boulder below and right of blade.

64 Tic Tac 3m 5b
Climb wall right of previous route using right hand rib only.

65 Bugs Bunny 6m 3b
Climb the gully behind the last two routes.

66 Weasel 10m 5b   ★
Start in niche at left end of area of higher rocks. Pull up on to leftward sloping ramp. From its end move rightwards on to wall and up to ledge. Finish up wall above.

67 Stoat 10m 5b   ★
Start as for the previous route. From top of niche step right then straight up to ledge. Finish up rib.

68 Autobahn 10m 5a   ★★
Up groove in centre of wall to its top. Move left to another groove and up this.

69   All Hope   10m   5a   ★★
Start 2m right of Autobahn at a crack. Up this to ledge on right, step left and climb groove to ledge. Step right and up wall.

Burnt Rock Amphitheatre

The path now goes uphill and the height of the crag decreases to about 3m, when the path trends downhill again. At the highest point of the path is a useful descent route. The first route described takes the arête where the path starts to go uphill.

70   Hendo's Obsession   8m   5c   ★
Climb the arête then follow All Hope to the top.

71   Elf   6m   3b
Start 4m right of, and round the corner from All Hope, next to a short groove. Go left to arête then by short crack to top.

72   Elk   6m   3a   ★
Climb the groove to the top.

73   E11   6m   4a   ★
Crack and wall just right of previous route.

74   Tarantula   6m   5b   ★★
Just right of E11 is a short ramp. Up ramp and pull over overlap using flake. Up wall above.

75   Leech Direct   5m   6a   ★
Round and right is a short vertical wall. Climb the centre of this wall direct, avoiding holds on adjoining routes.

76   Leech   6m   5b   ★
Up corner and hand traverse back leftwards to its end. Finish direct from here.

77   Eel   5m   4c
Up corner to top. Hard finish.

78   Coal Face   5m   4b   ★
Cracked wall right of Eel.

79   Charcoal Chimney   5m   4a   ★★
The prominent chimney.

80   Black Beauty   5m   5a   ★★
Wall right of chimney, avoiding holds on that route.

81   Black Power   5m   4c
The arête right of the last route.

82   Mat Black   3m   4b
Wall immediately right of arête.

83   Cockroach   3m   3a
Start at crack of last route, but finish leftwards.

84   Pygmy Crack   3m   2a
Next crack rightwards.

85   West Way Down   2m   2a
Obvious descent route down the corner to the right.

86   Beetle Arête   3m   3a
Climb arête just right of descent route.

87   Beetle Wall   3m   3b
Wall right of arête.

88   Beetling   3m   3a
Up narrow wall right of previous route and over portruding block.

Little Buttress
The path goes downhill to the foot of a small buttress with two wide cracks, bounded on the right by a series of short grooves. The first route starts at the left side of the buttress half way up.

89   East Wall   3m   5a
Move rightwards on to buttress from ledge and up to top.

90   Pinnacle Wall   7m   4c   ★★
Below East Wall is another wall. Climb this keeping to the left of the cracks.

91   Donald Duck   5m   4a   ★
The left hand crack.

92   Mickey Mouse   5m   4b   ★
The right hand crack.

93   Piglet   5m   5a
Climb the wall just right of Mickey Mouse, avoiding all holds on that route.

94   Pigs Ear   6m   5a   ★
Start as for Piglet. After 1m move right to the arête and finish up this.

95   Silk Purse   6m   5b   ★
Climb the start of the arête to Pigs Ear and finish up slab.

96   West Wall   6m   5b   ★
Climb the wall right of the last route and finish up slab.

97   Hy Mac   6m   4c
Climb corner and groove just right of West Wall.

98   Mr Smith   5m   3b
Next groove rightwards.

99   Roadhog   5m   4b
The arête right of the groove.

100   Wren's Nest Groove   5m   4a
Up groove 2m right of Roadhog.

101   Black Plague   35m   5a   ★
A right-to-left girdle from Hy Mac to Bugs Bunny, following the obvious line all the way.

Extreme Right-Hand Slab

Continuing rightward round the crag, past the little buttress, the rocks become more broken up and eventually become a series of isolated boulders. The first route lies about 50m right of Little Buttress, where there is an obvious slab left of a pinnacle.

102   Tree Wall   5m   5a
Climb the short wall left of the slab, avoiding right arête and tree above.

103   Left Arête   9m   4a   ★
Start left of the obvious crack in the slab. Pull up to gain the left edge of the slab, follow edge and short wall above.

104   Cracked Slab   9m   3b   ★
Climb the obvious crack splitting the slab, taking the right-hand branch to finish up wall above to left.

105   The Slab   9m   4a   ★★
Just right of the obvious crack is a short undercut crack. Pull up from the left to gain this crack then climb slab direct, avoiding right edge and crack on left. Finish up wall above at its highest point.

106   Right Arête   6m   4a
Pull up to gain the right edge of the slab which is climbed direct.

107   Short Chimney   3m   3a
Start just right of the slab and climb the short chimney.

108   Cave Route   5m   3a
Start as for Short Chimney. Instead of following that route go into the cave, exiting through a hole above. More difficult for the stout.

109   Slab Traverse   12m   4a
Start as for Tree Wall. Climb wall for a few moves, gain arête on right, traverse right across slab to Right Arête and finish up this.

110   The Wizard   6m   6a
Climb up short chimney then stand on the huge jammed block. Gain arête on right (left edge of Tarot pinnacle), climb this to top.

Extreme Right-Hand Amphitheatre
This is the area immediately to the right of the slab.

111   Tarot   6m   3b
Just right of the slab is a flat-topped pinnacle. Gain the right edge of the pinnacle from the left, continue up the edge.

112   Strabo   3m   4a
The short wall behind Tarot has a sloping corner on its right (usually wet). Climb the blunt rib left of the corner, step left into a scoop and up the wall above.

113   Plonk   3m   3b
Start as for Strabo then climb the blunt rib directly.

114   Sluice Gate   3m   3b
Climb the obvious sloping corner.

115   Tartar   5m   3b
Just right of Sluice Gate is an obvious wide crack. Climb crack direct.

116   Suzy Q   6m   5b   ★
The arête right of Tartar. Step on to ledge from below, follow crack above.

117   Wheeler Dealer   5m   3b
To the right of Suzy Q is an obvious corner with boulders at its base. Climb corner.

118   Victory V   5m   4c
Start as for Wheeler Dealer. Pull out on to the capped block on the right (without using the back wall or standing on the block), go up and over the block above.

119   Wopitee   5m   4c
Start below the obvious roof to the right of Victory V. Climb up and gain the wall above the roof, continue directly to top.

120   Isomer   6m   5b
Start as for Wopitee under the roof. Climb up to below roof, traverse to right edge, go right and up crack to finish.

121   Expo   5m   5b
Start just right of Isomer. Climb edge then go up across Isomer to reach flat holds above. Finish up left edge, avoiding vertical cracks.

122   Two Tree Wall   8m   5a
Round the edge from Isomer is a wall with two trees above. Climb up to the ash (avoiding left arête and crack on right), go up using second tree to a ledge. Finish up wall above.

123   Toad   8m   4c
Climb crack to right of Two Tree Wall to reach a ledge (avoiding trees on left). Finish up wall above.

124   Rizla   3m   3a
Just right of the final wall of Toad is a groove. Climb it.

125   Amphitheatre Girdle   16m   5a   ★★
This is a girdle of the Extreme Right-Hand Amphitheatre. Start in the boulder-filled gully left of Strabo. Step up into the scoop of Strabo, traverse right to Tartar, step down and across to the ledge of Suzy Q. Go across right to Wheeler Dealer. Step down to a small sloping ledge and traverse right below the overhangs (crux). Go round the right edge and traverse below the two trees to step on to the grassy ledge on the right.

Pine Tree Boulders
Some 16m right of the Extreme Right-Hand Amphitheatre is a pile of scattered boulders below a Scots Pine. The last eight routes lie on the boulders.

126   East Slab   5m   3b
The first boulder met walking rightward, facing east toward the main crag. There are three routes: The Scoop 3a; The Central Crack 3b; The Right Arête 3b.

127   Three Tier Slab   5m   2a
The obvious slab below and to the right of East Slab.

128   Arty Farty   3m   3b
Directly above Three Tier Slab is an obvious wide crack with a jammed chockstone. Climb the crack.

129   Vanguard   3m   5a
Climb the narrow wall just left of Arty Farty (avoiding adjacent cracks).

130   Horseplay   3m   3b
The overhanging crack on the left of Vanguard.

131   The Bulge   3m   3a
Climb the edge to the left of Horseplay.

132   Sunshine Arête   3m   5a   ★
The arête right of Arty Farty. Climb it direct.

133   Sunburn   3m   3a
The pile of blocks right of Sunshine Arête. Climb on left-hand side.

Map: Sheet 64, G.R. 517 766

CRAIGTON

INTRODUCTION

A pleasantly situated outcrop of rough basalt similar to Craigmore. Facing north-east it takes a couple of days to dry after summer rain. Most of the climbs are short, but seem longer due to the steep bank below. Good belays are available at the top and many routes are top-roped.

ACCESS

The outcrop faces Hilton Park Golf Club, high on the west side of the A809 Glasgow to Drymen road. From the club car park the crag can be seen right of the wooded hillside and behind the pylons. It is closer than it looks.

x2 21/7/91 — 1 top rope/self
— 1 solo

1 Jughandle Corner 4m 3b
At the left end of the outcrop is a small buttress topped by a wind-swept tree. Climb the short corner crack left of the alcove.

x2 21/7/91 — 1 T/R self
— 1 solo

2 Elbow Crack 4m 4c
The crack in the alcove's left wall. Better in autumn !

3 Machiavelli's Crack 6m 5c ★
The steep crack in the left side of the next buttress.

4 Jam Crack 4m 4b
Takes the cracked corner on the right.

21/7/91 — Top rope/self

5 The Rasp 5m 4a
The painful wide crack on the left side of the next buttress.

6 Mantelshelf Wall 6m 5c *21/7/91 — Top rope/self*
The mantelshelf and slab. *not slab*

7 Hairy Mary 6m 5b ★
The lefthand groove topped by a chockstone.

21/7/91 — Top rope/self
— unsuccessful
used rope

8   Easy Lady   6m   3a
The righthand groove.

9   Two Hand Crack   4m   4b
Twin cracks up and further right.

10   Boa Constrictor   9m   4c
A tight off-width behind the flake.

11   Farewell Groove   9m   4c
Takes the narrow ramp behind the flake.

12   The Clam   12m   5b   ★
The chimney-crack through the overhang.

13   Octopus   11m   5c   ★
The right end of the overhung recess leads to a crack. Or traverse into
the crack from the right at 5b.

14   Chockstone Groove   4m   4a
A vee-groove, right.

15   Lone Tree Groove   3m   4a
The next crack.

16   Gremlin's Groove   9m   5b   ★
The overhanging groove further right. A bit nasty.

17   Lazy Layback   9m   3a
Some broken rock leads to the next buttress. This takes the broken
groove and wide layback crack.

18   Affront   9m   4c
Climb the rib and cracked arête further right.

19   Sidestep   9m   4c
Up crack on the left, step right and climb crack above.

20   The Groove   9m   4c
The big groove.

21   The Doddle   9m   5c   ★★
A bulging wall split by a sloping ledge. Climb the centre of the wall direct.

Two routes climb the broken rock rightwards: Isolated Buttress 4b, a thin groove and Deception 4c, a small wall.

22   Deceiver   4m   5b
This is the obvious deep groove in the large block separated by deep cracks.

23   Shield Right Edge   4m   5b
Climbs the right edge of the obvious shield-like flake.

The small walls and cracks rightwards are taken by: Route 1, 4b; Route 2, 2a; Twisted Crack, 4c; Black Crack, 5b; Ledge Wall, 4a; Small Wall, 4b and Small Wall Groove, 4c.

Map: Sheet 64, G.R. 541 795

PILLAR CRAG

INTRODUCTION

A small but enjoyable crag of columnar basalt offering a lot of well protected crack climbing. It faces North, but is lichen-free and dries quickly. A good alternative to crowded Craigmore. Most routes can be top-roped.

ACCESS

The crag lies in trees on the south side of the B821 about one kilometre east of Craigmore, before the winding descent into Blanefield. There is a small parking place for cars on the north side of the road on the edge of the wood. The crag is opposite and is reached by crossing a marshy field and scrambling through the trees.

1 In The Groove 4m 5a
The first groove at the left hand end.

2 Moss Crack 5m 2b
The broad crack.

3 Keystone Corner 4m 2a
The jammed boulder corner.

4 Serpent's Chimney 6m 4a
The obvious chimney, finishing left.

5 The Ride 6m 5a ★
The arête right of the chimney.

6 Twin Roots Chimney 6m 3b
The next chimney right, with a low chockstone.

7 Club Foot 11m 5c ★
The thin cracks right of Twin Roots Chimney.

8   Butterfingers   9m   5c   ★★
The fine thin crack.

9   The Slot   9m   5a   ★
Right again is a corner crack with a hard start.

10   Sidestep Wall   9m   5a
The next thin corner.

11   The Horror   11m   5b
Climb one of two jam cracks to a ledge and the groove above, left.

12   Melting Pot   12m   4c   ★★
An expanding jam crack, right, leads to a higher ledge and chimney.

13   Pinnacle Chimney Direct   11m   4b
A groove followed by a crack on the left.

14   Pinnacle Chimney   11m   3a
Climb the right side of the pinnacle and the groove above.

15   Damocles Groove   11m   4c   ★
Follows the groove below the single poised block. A good reference
point.

16   Pillar Groove   11m   5a   ★
The groove right of the poised block.

17   Candle Snuffer   11m   3b
The chimney formed by three large sections of column. An apt name.

18   Pillar Front   11m   5a
The front edge of the fallen column.

19   Chockstone Chimney Direct   11m   4b
The left of two cracks leads to a chimney right of the fallen column. The
right crack is 5a.

20   Mick   11m   3b
The wide pod-shaped crack.

21   Lurcher's Chimney   11m   4c
The nasty looking inverted-vee groove.

22   Manky Crack   11m   4b
A crack with a small tree.

The broken area, right, is taken by two routes; Grand Slam, 5a and Fingerlicker, 5c.

23   Avalanche Chimney   11m   4c
A wide crack right of the broken rock, with a tree at the top.

24   Cracker Crack   11m   4c   ★★
A cracking jam crack.

25   Hiroshima Groove   11m   5b   ★★
The smooth groove.

26   Twiggy's Crack   11m   3b
Up crack right of the tree and the cracked groove on the left.

Up and right are three dirty grooves: Woody Groove, 2a; Thunder Block Groove, 2b; Pinnacled Groove, 4a.

27   Right Hand Crack   4m   4b   ★★
A good short jamming crack.

28   Right Hand Wall   4m   4c
The wall right of the crack.

DUNGLAS

INTRODUCTION

This conical volcanic plug is situated 2km east of Blanefield in open countryside at the foot of the Campsie Fells. The rock is micro-prophyritic basalt with marked hexagonal columns on the North and East faces. Most of the climbing is on the West Face where the rock takes a sheet-like structure. Routes are between 18m and 30m high and take about two sunny days to dry.

ACCESS

From Glasgow take the A81 towards Blanefield, turning east on to the A891 at Strathblane. The crag is soon seen on the right side of the road. A farm track leading to it is private, but there is a layby 700m along on the right. Cross the field and a disused railway track to the foot.

West Face

A steep face about 60m in length. The obvious features are a left to right ramp, Curioser and Curioser, and a cross shaped crack in the centre, The Cross. At the left end there is a fence and the first route starts about 40m left of this.

1   The Gentle Touch   18m   Hard Very Severe   5b
Start at a rib about 8m left of the shallow corner of Pullover. Up shelves past a spike and surmount overhang, crux, to a belay. Traverse right to a break and climb the centre of the arête on large holds to an awkward exit.

2   Pullover   19m   Very Severe   4c
Start at the shallow corner about 5m left of the fence. Climb the corner past a peg runner, pull up and traverse a few feet left along a shelf. Continue up and right past blocks to exit up the groove above. The easiest of the longer routes and a good introduction.

3   Curioser and Curioser   40m   Very Severe   4c
This follows the slanting ramp, starting as for Pullover. Move up then across right to a small ledge. Cross the wall to a second ledge, then up right to basin hold. Traverse right past narrowing to the second cave. Step right surmounting the overhang and finish up crack.

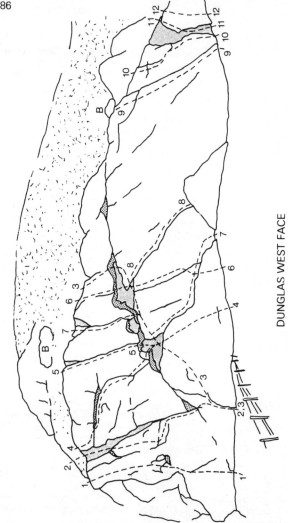

DUNGLAS WEST FACE

4   Skirmish   25m   Very Severe   5a   ★
The original route on the crag with some bold climbing. Climb the wall
about 5m right of the fence, trending slightly left to ledge and caves. Go
through the overhang left of The Cross and continue leftwards to a thin
crack and horizontal break. Traverse left, crux, to finish. A direct start
climbs the wall above the fence at the same grade.

5   The Cross   21m   E1   5b   ★★
Follow Skirmish to the cave. Move right and follow the crack through
the overhang to the top. The best climb on the face.

6   A Feet of Arms   18m   Hard Very Severe   5b
Below a slanting crack about 8m right of the fence. Climb wall to base of
the crack. Up this and the wall on the right to a ledge. Climb the
deceptive wall to finish. Some athletic moves in well protected
situations.

7   Downfall   37m   Hard Very Severe   5b
Follows the obvious leftwards traverse line about 10m right of the
fence. Climb up to the traverse and follow it to the cave. Traverse right
past narrowing and ledge and up overhang right of The Cross. Up wall
trending left to finish by vee-break and drooping spike.

8   The Ramp   13m   Moderate
The slanting break right of Downfall provides easy access to the upper
wall.

9   Wall of Horrors   13m   E2   5c   ★
Near the right-hand end of the face is an overhanging wall with a thin
crack. Climb up to small niche and jug. Continue past flake and through
'overhang.

10   Little Gripper   13m   Very Severe   5a   ★
Climbs the overhanging rib right of Wall of Horrors. Up bulging wall to
exit via jammed flake on the right. Traverse left, up wall to ledge then up
and left to finish at a break.

11   Moss Flop   8m   Difficult
Climb the shallow corner right of Little Gripper to finish trending right.

12   Last Grasp   8m   Severe
Start at the blunt rib right of the last route. Climb wall, step left to block
and finish up grass shelves.

13   A Dream of Brown Trousers   Very Severe   5b
A low level, left-to-right girdle with interesting moves in entertaining
positions. Climb to a height of 5m at the extreme left end. Follow a
line to The Ramp then past shelves to some difficulties by Little
Gripper and the crux beyond Moss Flop. Finish on grass.

East Face

A large but rather featureless face with a large corner in the centre.
The unsoundness of some hexagonal columns and the areas of steep
grass have restricted development. The first two routes are on an
easy angled rib of fair rock left of the corner.

14   Rubbish   30m   Difficult
Climbs the groove left of the rib to finish on easy ground.

15   Ribbish   31m   Severe
Start below the rib at a boulder. Climb the rib to a small overhang and
take this by a groove on the right, past a spike. Continue up the slabby
rib to a grass ledge. Step right and up slabby rock to a steeper exit.

16   Dunglas Corner   30m   Severe
A splendid climb, full of character, taking the central corner left of the
broad rib. Up corner trending right at the top, past small trees to finish
by the loose corner above.

17   North East Arête   24m   E2   5c
Takes the steep edge bordering Dunglas Corner. Start right of the
edge then climb it trending right beneath overhang and jug. Surmount
this, crux, then easier to join Dunglas Corner.

North Face

A rather menacing part of the crag with much unstable ground. A large
scree covered ledge splits the face into two tiers; impressive corners
above and overhangs below. Both routes take lines on the lower tier.

18   Joker's Groove   23m   Very Severe   4c
Climbs the corner right of the overhangs. Up rib and enter corner.
Trend left past flakes and finish up wall on left, crux. Loose rock.

19   The Nightmare   20m   E2   5c
This takes the hexagonal slabs right of the obvious and unclimbed
hanging crack. Start at the inset corner on the left of the slabs. Climb
this and a steeper corner, over slabs above, crux, to small ledge and
shattered blocks. Traverse left along shattered rock to edge. Up to
ledge and wall above. An apt name.

Map: Sheet 64, G.R. 719 771

AUCHINSTARRY QUARRY

INTRODUCTION

Glasgow's most popular quarry offers excellent climbing at all grades, including some hard modern classics. Recent landscaping by the district council has produced a good car park and a pleasant climbing atmosphere.

The rock is quartz-dolerite and the quarry's southerly aspect means it dries quickly after rain and allows climbing for most of the year. Some routes do collect grit after bad weather and like all quarries there is some loose and friable rock.

Belays are generally good, as is the protection, though sparse in the higher grades. Climbers should check that protection pegs mentioned in the text are in place.

ACCESS

By car, take the A80, Glasgow–Stirling road. Turn on to the B8048, west to Kirkintilloch, following the signs for the B802 to Kilsyth and passing through the village of Croy. The quarry is on the right before entering Kilsyth. Croy is the nearest rail station (2km) and Kilsyth is served by bus from Buchanan Street.

For the routes inaccessible from the quarry forecourt descend Knockdown (56), Peg Route (58), Accord (85) or Brash (96). Care should be taken on the descents and easy ground where blocks and broken glass wait to surprise the unwary.

Promontory

The left end of the quarry is made up of slabs and corners overlooking the car park.

1   Pod   5m   Hard Very Severe   5b   ★
The obvious pod on the far left. The short wall left is 5c.

2   Green Onion   7m   Hard Very Severe   5b
The groove and corner 4m right of Pod.

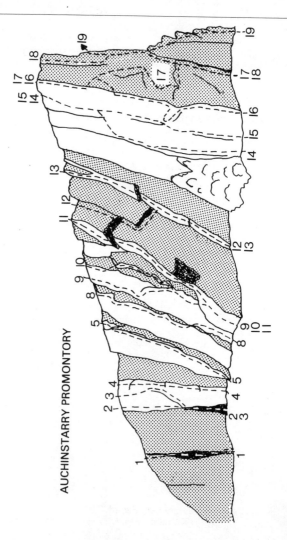

AUCHINSTARRY PROMONTORY

3 I–Spy 11m E1 5c   ★
This strenuous route follows the problematic corner to a bulge and the obvious curving flake crack. Use of ledges on the left reduces the grade.

4 Mr Men 13m Very Severe 4b   ★
A serious lead following the delightful short arête.

5 First Footer 16m E1 5c   ★★
Climbs the fine open groove direct. Finish up poor rock.

6 Positively 4th Street 16m Hard Very Severe 5a
A scrappy route climbing a short crack and bulge left of Rodeo.

7 Rodeo 9m Very Severe 4c
The groove behind the tree.

8 Access Route 12m Difficult   ★
The broken rib left of the slab overlooking the car park.

9 Scream 13m Hard Severe 4b   ★★
On the right of the slab is a curving crack, climb this. The slab has been climbed at 5c.

10 Anarchist 14m Very Difficult
The obvious line up the broken buttress right of Scream.

11 Tar 14m Severe
Gain and climb the cracks and grooves on the edge of the buttress right of Anarchist.

12 Knock Back 14m E1 5b   ★★
The slabby corner right of Tar is climbed to an overhang. Break left and follow the shallow groove and crack with interest. A bit loose at the crux.

13 Slinky Lizard 14m Hard Severe 4b
This steady route follows the slabby corner to the top.

14   Cat's Whiskers   17m   E3   5c
The next wall is dominated by the arête of Nijinski. Start at the left end
of the wall and follow a thin crack to exfoliating flakes, finishing up the
wall above, crux.

15   Death Is The Hunter   17m   E4   6b   ★
Start 2m left of the arête at a short shallow groove. Climb this and the
blunt arête above to gain the scoop on the right. Climb the crack above
and left, finishing up Cat's Whiskers or by moving right to the arête.

16   Nijinski   17m   E5   6a   ★★★
Climb the bold arête behind the tree, moving left into the scoop.
Arrange protection in the crack of Death Is The Hunter before moving
back to the arête. Climb the arête until forced on to Blade Runner near
the top.

17   Blade Runner   17m   E5   6a   ★★
This route climbs the wall right of Nijinski. Follow the crack of
Promontory Direct before hand traversing left and surmounting a small
overlap to a reasonable nest. Arrange poor, small runners before
climbing the wall up and right to a crack. Finish up the arête. A direct
start is possible at 6b.

18   Promontory Direct   17m   Hard Very Severe   5a   ★★
An excellent route with the crux in an exposed position. Climb the crack
on the left side of the shattered pinnacle, then up and left to finish up
the crack. An alternative start takes the thin crack right at 5c.

19   Spirogyra   19m   Very Severe   4c   ★★
Start up the pinnacle's jagged right edge. Climb the crack on the wall
above before moving right to gain a sloping ledge. Traverse this and
climb the corner at the end.

20   Carouselambra   17m   E5   6b   ★★
This route climbs the obvious cracks in the overhanging wall below and
right of Spirogyra. Climb the right crack, then the left one end finish up
spirogyra.

21   Fish Rising   17m   E2   5b
Start 8m right of Carouselambra just right of an open groove. Ascend
the left side of the blunt arête to the top.

22   Tit For Tat   17m   E2   5c
Climb the shallow groove capped by an overhang, round the arête from
Fish Rising.

Amphitheatre
Further right the crag goes into a series of walls and grooves shaded by
trees.

23   Flake Wall   12m   Severe
About 6m right of the brick building is a short overhanging corner. Climb
the right wall, step left to ledge, gain holds on wall and up flakes.

24   Foxtrot   13m   E2   5c
Climb the vague crack in the wall right of Flake Wall.

25   Valentine   13m   E2   5b
Climb the sharp arête right of Foxtrot.

26   Black Death   13m   Hard Very Severe   5a
The shallow, rightward slanting groove right of Valentine is climbed
direct.

27   Newcastle Brown   13m   Hard Very Severe   5a
A lot further right is a steep slabby wall split by two cracks. Climb the
left one and the shallow groove.

28   Roll Up   13m   Very Severe   4c
The right-hand layback crack.

Mascarade Buttress
This is the impressive steep buttress which rises straight from the pool.

29   Boulder Problem   18m   Very Severe   4c
Start at the left edge at a block with a bore hole. Climb the block, step
left into a groove and follow it before going right to another groove. Up
this past ledge to a scoop and the top.

30   Soft Machine   13m   E2   5c
Climb the shallow poorly protected groove right of Boulder Problem
through roof to join Maypole. A serious route.

MASCARADE BUTTRESS

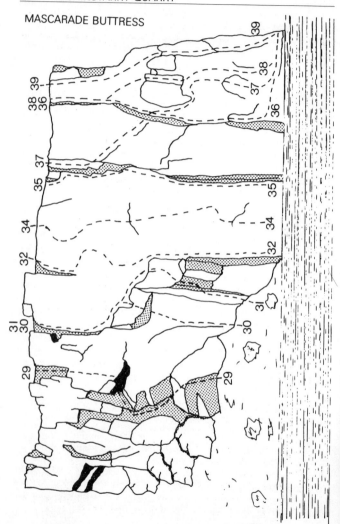

31   Maypole   24m   Very Severe   4c
Right again is a short vertical groove. Climb it to a ledge, over an awkward bulge to a small ledge. Move left to finish up the groove above.

32   Ekofisk   27m   E1   5a
Below Maypole and right is a slim groove rising from the pool. Gain this from the left and climb to a ledge on the right. Up the wall above moving right then left into the groove above.

33   High Dive   27m   E3   5b ★
Climb Ekofisk to the ledge. Step right and follow a line of holds. Make a very long reach up and right to better holds and finish directly.

The next six routes are best approached by a low level traverse from the right of the buttress.

34   Surface Tension   27m   E5   6b ★★★
This climbs the centre of the impressive wall. From the start of Mascarade step down and left to footholds below an overlap, 2m above the water. Make hard moves up, to holds leading to a peg. Climb past the peg with difficulty to a resting place and downward pointing borehole. Move up, small nuts, then back left into the centre of the wall. Continue past a hard move to obvious holds leftwards.

35   Mascarade   27m   E1   5c ★★
The long vertical groove in the centre of the buttress. Variations are possible on the right wall. Easier when clean!

36   Whiplash   27m   E1   5b
The smaller bottomless groove right of Mascarade. Climb to top of a pinnacle and the groove and shallow scoop above.

37   Red Lead   27m   Very Severe   5a ★★★
An enjoyable route with a finely placed crux. Climb the centre of the white slab to a horizontal break. Step down and left to a hidden layback crack. Follow the crack and traverse left across Whiplash to a thin diagonal crack. Climb this and the vertical crack above.

38   White Slab   27m   Hard Severe   4b   ★★
Traverse left a few feet above the water to the foot of the white slab, crux. Climb up to a hand-sized crack, continue to a ledge and finish up the shallow scoop of Whiplash on the left.

39   Demons and Dead Lizards   30m   Hard Very Severe   5a
Follow the thin crack right of White Slab to a ledge and climb the crack above to the top.

Little Amphitheatre Wall

The wall right of Mascarade Buttress has a number of pleasant short routes.

40   Layback Corner   9m   Hard Severe   4b
The first small wall ends in a corner with an obvious thin crack high up.

41   Blocky Pillar   9m   Difficult
About 12m right is a shattered pillar. Climb the left side.

42   Ready Mix   9m   Very Difficult
The right side of the pillar.

43   Calico   9m   Very Severe   4c
About 12m right is a small square-cut column, just left of an arête. Climb the corner crack and wall on its left.

44   Bunkum   9m   Severe
Climb the easy angled groove right of Calico to ledge. Finish right of corner.

Fourth Wave Area

Moving right an arête just out towards the pool, with an obvious open corner beside it.

45   Cracked Arête   16m   Very Severe   5a   ★★
Climb the bold arête and continue up the prominent crack.

46   Fourth Wave   16m   Very severe   5a   ★
Climb the obvious corner with a hard move near the top.

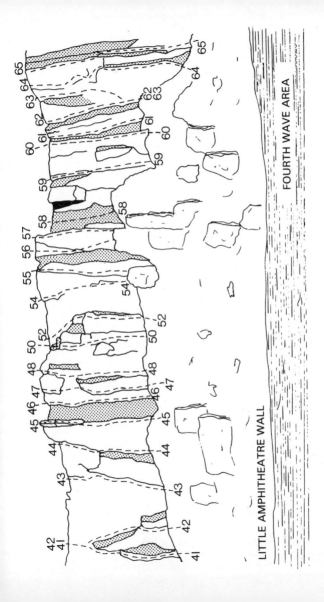

LITTLE AMPHITHEATRE WALL

FOURTH WAVE AREA

47   Maverick   16m   Very Severe   5a
Start as for Fourth Wave before gaining a slim groove on the right.
Climb the bulging crack to ledge and the crack above.

48   Discord   16m   Very Severe   4b
Start below a bottomless crack right of Maverick. Gain the crack and
follow it to a ledge, finishing up the crack on the right.

49   Caftan   16m   Very Severe   4b
There are three vertical bore holes in the wall right of Discord. Climb up
to the right side of a protruding block and up the wall and groove above
left.

50   Bazaar   16m   Very Severe   4c
Start a few feet right of Caftan and climb to the right of the protruding
block, followed by the groove above left.

51   Nostalgia   11m   Very Difficult
Start above and to the right of Bazaar. Traverse leftwards across the
wall to gain an open groove.

52   Ice Edge   11m   Very Severe   5a   ★
There are two prominent corners facing each other. This route climbs
the prominent overhanging arête of the left-hand one.

53   Mastalgia   11m   Very Severe   4c
This is the steep corner with a thin crack in the back.

54   Higher Beginning   11m   Very Difficult
Climbs the wall midway between the corners.

55   Cossack   11m   Hard Severe   4b
This is the right-hand, wide, stepped corner.

56   Knockdown   6m   Very Difficult
Climb the short wall left, into a groove.

57   Hooked On   6m   Very Difficult
Climb the rightward sloping rock, right of Knockdown.

58   Peg Route   6m   Difficult
Climbs from right to left up the short wall right of Hooked On. The most
popular descent route.

59   Faresaver   13m   Very Difficult
Down and to the right is a large slab. Climb the long groove on the left edge.

60   Lion Cub   13m   Severe
Climb the right edge of the slab.

61   Lion   13m   Very Severe   4b   ★★
The obvious vertical corner right of the slab is climbed by back and footing. A good route, but some loose blocks at the top.

62   Chevron   15m   E1   5b
The open groove 3m right of Lion. Climb the groove surmounting an overhang at half height and continue up the groove above.

63   Scrumpy   15m   Hard Very Severe   5a
Start as for Chevron, but break right up ledges to gain the corner crack and follow this.

64   Moonshine   17m   Hard Very Severe   5a   ★
Climb up to ledges below and right of Scrumpy and follow a crack in the left wall to the top.

Grooves Area
Right of Moonshine the cliffs get larger and from a distance the area displays a series of long grooves.

65   Thumblena   23m   Hard Very Severe   5a   ★★
Climb the streaked wall and move leftwards to gain a slim groove. Up this and the arête to finish. A bold start.

66   Kelvin Way   23m   Hard Very Severe   5a   ★
The hanging open groove. Climb the short wall to gain the groove and follow it with a detour on the left wall at 16m, or direct at E2.5c.

   The next five routes are reached by a scramble up and right to a terrace below a smaller face.

67   Mac's Wall   20m   Hard Very Severe   5a
Climb the wall right of Kelvin Way to gain a curving jam crack.

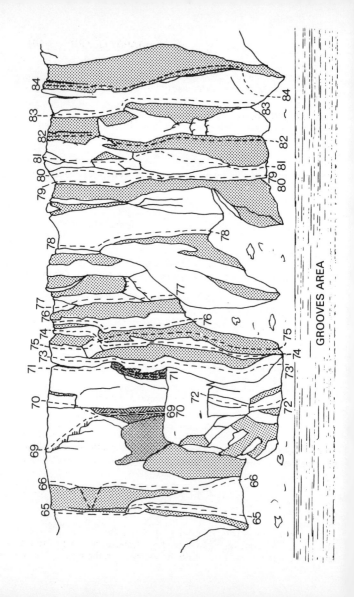

68   Boltzman's Approximation   16m   Hard Very Severe   5a
This is the slightly loose crackline, left of The Scythe.

69   The Scythe   13m   Severe
The wide curving shattered groove is followed for 6m, before finishing
left up flakes.

70   Short Reach   13m   E1   5b   ★
Start as for the Scythe, but follow the easy loose chimney over a bulge
to a ledge. Move up and right and climb the arête rightwards.

71   Pigeon Hole   13m   Very Severe   4c
About 9m right of Short Reach, climb blocks to a ledge and finish up the
corner above.

72   Exorcist   4m   Hard Very Severe   5b
Below the terrace a short overhanging crack faces the pool. Climb the
crack to an awkward mantel finish.

73   Separated Edge   24m   Hard Very Severe   5a
Further right a long groove runs the height of the face. This route climbs
the left arête. Climb the wall to reach a jug high on the right, then easier
to a bulge which is taken direct to a pinnacle. Climb it by a fine crack,
over a small roof and up the arête above.

74   Talisman   24m   Very Severe   4c
Climb the long groove to a roof, step right on to a rib and gain the wide
crack above right.

75   Knife Edge   24m   E2   5c   ★ ★
A good route with an athletic crux. Climb the right rib to the sharp arête
and follow this to a roof. Pull over at the right end and climb the arête
above.

Right of Knife Edge is a small bay with a slab sloping up rightwards to
grooves in the wall above.

76   Nickelodeon   21m   Hard Very Severe   5a
This takes the groove just right of the Knife Edge arête. Up the groove
and over bulge to overhang. Climb the V-groove on the right to finish.

77 Middle Groove 15m E1 5b
Climb the groove past a white scar to overhangs, moving left to arête.

78 September Groove 20m Hard Very Severe 5a
Further right is a grassy bay with a groove above. Climb this leftward curving groove to a ledge and finish up the corner crack above.

79 Christmas Corner 23m Hard Very Severe 5a
Right of the bay is a steep corner with a thin crack. A bit dirty.

80 Wild Fire 23m Hard Very Severe 5a   ★
Follow Christmas Corner before moving right to the thin crack and then the wider crack.

81 Balance Of Power 23m E4 6a   ★★
This climbs the steep slab between Christmas Corner and Fusion. Climb the slab to a small pocket where small nuts can be arranged. Move up and right to arête and layback it to a good jug. Continue up the arête to finish up the overhanging arête right of Wild Fire. A finger-tip ripper.

82 Fusion 23m Very Severe 4c   ★★★
Right of Balance Of Power are two obvious crack lines. This takes the left-hand one. Enjoyable jamming.

83 Sandman 23m Very Severe 4c   ★★
Climb the right-hand crack and the broken corner above.

84 The Dream Machine 23m E3 6a   ★★★
Climb crack line in the arête right of Sandman and continue up the arête and pillar above. An excellent route.

Shield Bay
Further right the cliffs get smaller and are reached by a 20m scramble.

86 Civic 5m Very Difficult
Climbs the shallow groove and detached block 2m right of Accord.

87 Model T 5m Very Severe 5a
The blunt arête left of a vertical bore hole.

88   Car Wash   5m   Very Difficult
The short corner right of Model T.

89   Sidekick   8m   Hard Very Severe   5a
Climbs the wide vertical crack some 3m right.

90   Sidekick   8m   Very Difficult
A crack and easy angled groove.

91   Sidewalk   9m   Very Severe   4c   ★
Climbs the obvious right-angled corner.

92   Walk Don't Run   11m   Very Severe   4c
Start 2m right of Jaywalker below an overhang. Surmount the overhang
and the vertical crack above left.

93   Road Runner   11m   Severe
Right again is a vertical groove. Climb up right of this to a bulge. Turn it
on the right to a ledge and finish up the wide crack above right.

94   Lilt   10m   Very Severe   4c
This takes a leftward slanting crack on the wall and left of the
Square-Cut Pinnacle.

95   Brogue   11m   Very Difficult
Start about 2m right of Lilt and climb a broken groove past a sapling.

96   Brash   11m   Very Difficult
The wide leftward trending crack directly above the Square-Cut
Pinnacle. A reasonable descent.

Square-Cut Pinnacle

This obvious feature juts out into the quarry pool. The pinnacle has
steep sides cut by cracks and becomes more broken higher up.

97   Think Of England   10m   E1   5c   ★
The obvious overhanging crack on the left of the pinnacle.

98   Quick Buck   10m   Very Severe   5a   ★★
This climbs the leftmost of the cracks in the pinnacle's right wall.

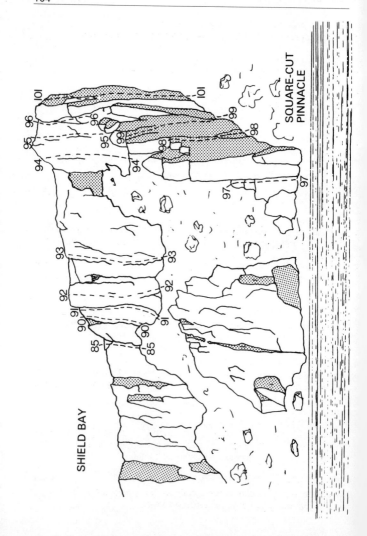

99   Half A Dollar   10m   Very Severe   4c
The thin cracks right of Quick Buck, starting from the right.

100   Dime A Time   12m   Severe
The rightmost wide diagonal crack on the pinnacle.

101   Black Friday   16m   Hard Very Severe   5a
Higher up the right wall is split by cracks. Follow the left edge of the wall moving right under a small overhang. Loose.

Trundle Slab Area
Rightwards a large slab, split on the left by a crack, rises from the pool.

102   Sunday Slab   13m   Very Difficult
The short slab left of the rock scar at the left end of the large slab.

103   Replicant   30m   E3   5c
Right of the rock scar are two flakes low on the wall. Start just left of 'Colin OK' and finish up the groove in the arête above the terrace.

104   Trundle   33m   Very Severe   ★★
The crack up the slab and the wide groove above the terrace. The slab left has been climbed at E1, 5b.

105   Walk On The Wild Side   30m   E1   5a   ★★★
Climb the faint crackline in the slab right of Trundle. Protectable with micro wires.

106   Midas Touch   30m   E2   5b   ★
Climb the groove on the right edge to flat edge. Move right and climb the arête above, finishing by a short overhanging groove. A serious route.

107   Southern Man   40m   E2   5b
A left to right girdle starting from the top of the pinnacle. Traverse into the flake on Trundle. Descend into scoop and follow holds to the arête. Step down into the corner and finish up that.

108   Gold Rush   30m   E1   5b   ★★★
This excellent route climbs the corner on the right of the slab, finishing up the overhanging corner above the terrace.

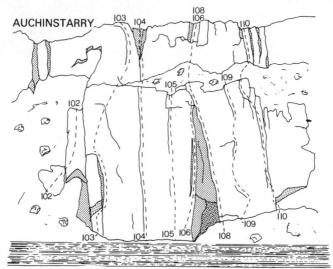

AUCHINSTARRY

TRUNDLE SLAB AREA

109   After The Gold Rush   30m   E2   5a   ★
This route climbs the impressive wall right of the corner via a
depression in the centre. Above the terrace finish up Gold Rush. Some
doubtful holds.

110   Fool's Gold   30m   Very Severe   5a
Start at a niche and crack to the right. Climb the crack to the start of an
easy angled groove. Avoid this by moving left on to the wall and climb
cracks and grooves. Above the terrace climb the slim groove up right.

Crazy Paving Buttress

To the right a steep sweep of cliff reaches from quarry floor to the top. A
wide corner crack is obvious in the lower half.

111   Deep Throat   33m   E3   5c   ★★
This bold route follows the left edge of the large buttress. Start left of
the corner and climb a shallow groove, moving right to a bore hole.
Climb up and left past a peg to a flat hold right of the arête. Follow easier
ground to large ledge and climb the short awkward wall above.

112 The Owl 33m Hard Severe 4b
Right is a wide corner-crack. Climb it to a ledge and continue up the wall
above, right, to a shallow corner.

113 Power Play 19m E1 5c   ★★
This takes the thin crack in the triangular recess right of The Owl, to
finish on the ledge. Finish up Foxy Woxy.

114 Foxy Woxy 19m E1 5b   ★★
From the ledge above Power Play step left into a slim groove. Follow it
to a ledge, then up wall on the right, hard, past a tree to the top. An
interesting route. The crack of The Owl provides alternative access to
the ledge.

115 Child's Play 20m Very Severe 4c
The vertical crack and niche right of Power Play.

116 Crazy Paving 35m Very Severe 4c   ★
This starts on the left side of the blocky slab a few metres to the right.
Traverse onto the slab and cross it to a groove. Up this and move right to
the arête. Climb flakes to the top. A direct start is possible at E1,5a.

117 The Idiot 35m Hard Very Severe 5a
Right of the broken slab is a small sloping ledge leading to a short
overhanging crack. Climb this and scoop and rib on the left to finish up
Crazy Paving.

118 Crazy Daisy 35m Hard Very Severe 5a
About 8m right of Crazy Paving are two short cracks above a wall. Climb
the grassy groove and move right to the cracks. Above, scramble up
and climb the left corner in the headwall.

119 Think Snow 26m Very Severe 5a
Just right at a small groove with a tree in it. Climb the groove and
layback corner above. Scramble up to a short wall and climb through the
headwall via a good crack. The arête left of the first groove is possible at
6a.

120 Evasive Action 16m Very Severe 4c
About 13m right is a wall with a corner-groove on its right. Climb this
exiting right.

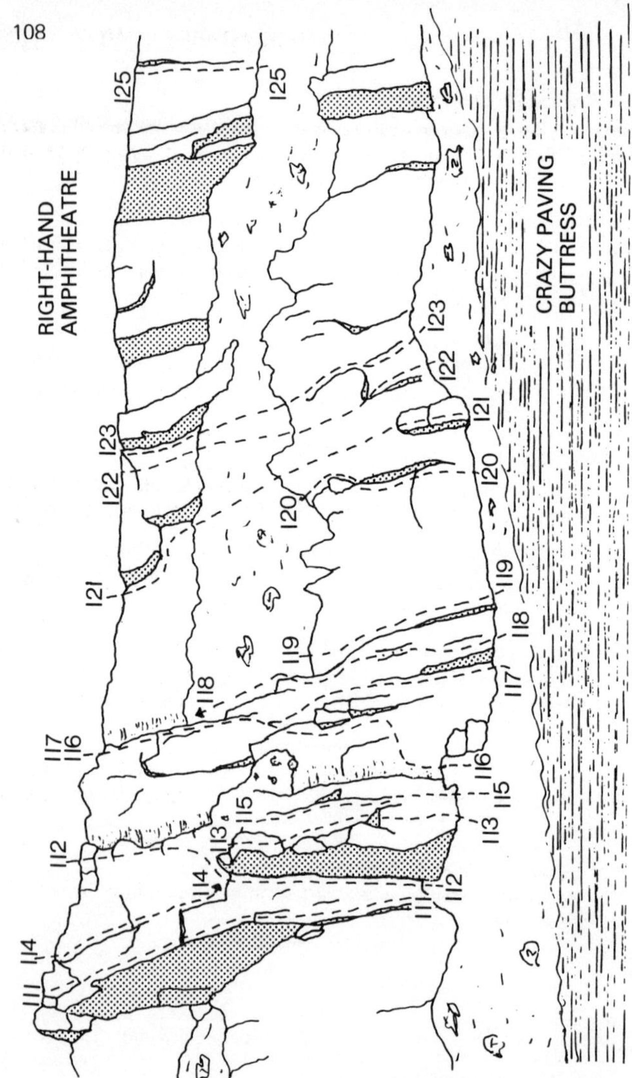

RIGHT-HAND AMPHITHEATRE

CRAZY PAVING BUTTRESS

Right Hand Amphitheatre

This area is in three distinctive sections – the lower cliff right of Evasive Action, identified by the 'ear' of Urea, the upper cliff above the terrace and the wall at the right end of the quarry.

121   B.C's Return   25m   E1   5b
Left of Urea there is a squat pinnacle. Climb the blunt arête to reach a horizontal break. Move right to groove above overlap and finish via overhang in headwall.

122   Cold Spell   26m   Very Severe   5a
Start a few metres left of Urea below a corner and overhang. Climb these and the easy angled slab to finish up the headwall just right of a bore hole.

123   Urea   26m   Very Severe   4c
Climb the diagonal crack on the right of the prominent 'ear', to a wide crack and easier ground. Climb slab and scramble to final corner.

124   Ladder Buttress   26m   Very Severe   4c
Right of Urea is a short rib. Climb it direct to easier ground, finishing up the bulging headwall on good holds.

125   Footloose   20m   Hard Very Severe   5a   ★
Start at the far right end of the upper tier. Climb the hand crack and the slanting crack to finish by obvious layback flakes in a good position.

126   Jam Rag   50m   Hard Very Severe   4c
The large cliff has a free-standing pillar on the left side. Climb the chimney between the pillar and the main face to belay in a groove. Up grooves and loose blocks and loose arête to top.

127   Daylight Movies   50m   Severe
The large cliff is split by a leftward slanting ramp. Climb this and the corner above.

Map: Sheet 64, G.R. 769 798

COWDEN HILL QUARRY

INTRODUCTION

Cowden Hill lies about 5km east of Kilsyth. The rock is quartz dolerite like Auchinstarry, but the quiet atmosphere provides a sharp contrast. The only routes are on the south face which dries quickly after rain. Since its development the quarry has been a bit neglected and the climbs deserve more traffic. There is scope for new routes. Fence posts at the top provide belays. Descent is possible down broken ground right of the routes.

ACCESS

As for Auchinstarry, but continue into Kilsyth. Follow the A803 east towards Bonnybridge. Take the third turning on the left after Kelvinhead, easily missed, and park on the right after an old railway bridge. Follow the track which leads up and left into the quarry.

South Face

This faces the entrance to the quarry.

1 Lorraine 35m Very Severe 4b
Start 10m left of the lowest part of the cliff. Climb the short wall to a ledge, then leftwards up a blunt rib. Follow grooves on the right past a pinnacle to the top.

2 Ostrich 35m Hard Very Severe 5a
At the lowest part of the face, climb the short broken wall to a ledge, then a shallow groove, just right of Lorraine, to a small ledge. Traverse left to a bore hole then up and left over short walls.

3 Kerrygold 35m Hard Very Severe 5b ★
Starts about 3m right of the lowest point of the face. Up the narrow diagonal slab and the parallel diagonal cracks above. Step right to a slab and finish up the short corner above the terrace.

4   Ground Control   35m   E1   5a
The next obvious feature is a short overhanging groove. Climb the shallow groove just left to a ledge, go up and left to make an awkward and poorly protected mantelshelf to the base of the groove. Follow the groove to the top.

5   D–Day   25m   Hard Very Severe   5b
Climb the overhanging groove then the shallow groove to a ledge above right. Climb the groove above or swing right round a loose block. Finish up the wall just left of a gorse bush.

6   Newton Blues   23m   E1   5c
About 7m right of D–Day is an obvious square-cut corner reached by a 7m scramble. Climb the corner and the groove above.

7   Ladybird   37m   E1   5b   ★★
Start below a small corner-crack about 10m right of Newton Blues. Up a short wall to a ledge, just right of the block crack. Continue to the top of the detached block, then right and up corner to another ledge. Make a diversion on the left wall until the corner can be re-entered. Walk right for 10m and climb the wall right of corner.

8   Klingon   37m   E2   5b
Start just right of Ladybird. Climb grooves to a ledge halfway up the wall. Continue up the wall with an awkward move rightwards below a small overhang near the top. Finish up the corner above.

9   Hole in the Wall   17m   E1   5b
Start 4m right of Klingon. Gain the obvious scoop in the blank wall from the right. Finish more easily.

10   Narita   10m   E3   5c
Start as for Hole in the Wall, but take a faint right trending line to the top.

Map: Sheet 64, G.R. 722 761

JACKDAW AND LOWER GIRNEL QUARRIES

INTRODUCTION

These two quartz dolerite quarries are on opposite sides of the B802 on the outskirts of Croy, one kilometre south of Auchinstarry. Jackdaw is a less than desirable hole in the ground on the north side, and has one excellent route. Lower Girnel is on the south side, has two good routes and a belaying problem at the top. Both are worth a visit and there is much scope for new routes.

ACCESS

As for Auchinstarry. Park on the north side of the road, 'Ancient Monument Croy Hill' signpost, just before the right turn downhill to Auchinstarry.

Jackdaw Quarry

Follow the ancient monument signpost for a few metres and the quarry is on the left.

1 The Dispossessed   20m   E2   5c   ★★
At the back of the quarry is a steep slabby wall split by two cracks. Climb the left one, exiting left at the top. An abseil may be necessary to the start if the water level of the pool prevents a traverse.

Lower Girnel

On the opposite side of the road this quarry hides among the trees.

1 Pillar Power   18m   E2   5b
This takes the lefthand side of an obvious pillar in the centre of the quarry. Climb the thin groove and finger crack to finish. Strenuous and well protected.

2 Obelisk   18m   E2   5b
Start right of the pillar. Climb the wall with difficulty and step left into the crack, finishing leftwards. Good, but unprotected at the start.

Map: Sheet 64, G.R. 429 613

JOHNSTONE QUARRY

INTRODUCTION

The only recorded climb is on a compact buttress of quartz dolerite overlooking the forecourt. Some of the quarry is being worked and discretion should be used.

ACCESS

Leave the M8 at junction 10 and follow the A740, A761 and A737 to Johnstone. The quarry is the higher of two off Craigbog Road opposite the public park. It is called 'High Craig' in the Geographia street atlas of Glasgow. Park beyond the quarry entrance and scramble through the trees on the right for about 200m.

1   Tom's Crack   20m   E3   6a   ★★
The left side of the buttress is split by a fine bulging finger crack. Climb it and the off-width above.

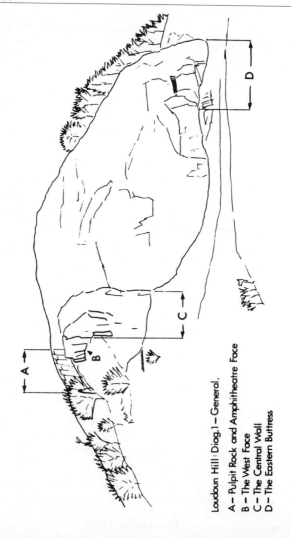

Loudoun Hill : Diag. 1 – General.

A – Pulpit Rock and Amphitheatre Face
B – The West Face
C – The Central Wall
D – The Eastern Buttress

Map: Sheet 71 G.R. 609 379

LOUDOUN HILL

INTRODUCTION

The rocks lie on the south flank of Loudoun Hill (316m), some 4km east of Darvel, just north of the A71. Loudoun Hill, like Dumbarton Rock, is the remnant of a volcanic plug, though in this instance the rock is a beautifully rough trachyte. The walls, cracks and chimneys will provide much pleasure over a wide range of difficulty and in a superb rural setting. The rocks divide naturally into four areas (Diag.1).

ACCESS

The best approach from Glasgow is probably via East Kilbride and Strathaven. By public transport, take a Strathaven bus from Buchanan St Bus Station, Glasgow, changing to a Kilmarnock bus at Strathaven. Alight at a secondary road branching north from the A71, some 4km east of Darvel and 1km east of the Loudoun Inn. Take this road, by car or on foot as far as a gate opposite the crag, next to an expanding gravel quarry. Routes are described from left to right. The large, isolated pinnacle on the extreme left of the face is the Pulpit Rock, while the wall of rock curving gently right from the Pulpit is known as The Amphitheatre.

1 Pulpit Chimney 20m Moderate
Immediately left of Pulpit Rock climb cracks easily to a ledge. Move slightly left and continue to top.

2 Slings 12m E1 5b   **
Climb wall on left face of Pulpit Rock, up cracks past old peg to finish up groove.

3 Lunge 16m E2 5c   ***
On the left face of the Rock and right of Slings is an undercut nose of rock. Climb this on finger holds, up cracks, over bulge and finish up steep wall.

4 Pulpit Crack 20m Very Severe 4c   **
The deep crack on the left wall of the Rock. Climb this to a ledge then finish up the arête.

116

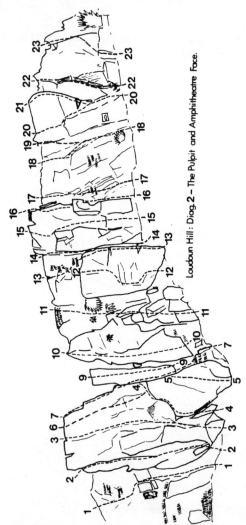

Loudoun Hill : Diag. 2 – The Pulpit and Amphitheatre Face.

5   The Mirror   5m   E2   5c   ★
A direct start to the arête. Climb the wall immediately left of the arête,
and right of Pulpit Crack, using small flake holds.

6   Reflections   16m   E1   5b
The Mirror with a more direct finish. Follow that route to the ledge then
finish up cracked bulge to top.

7   Pulpit Arête   20m   Very Difficult   ★★★
The obvious arête, starting behind a large tree. Step on to the arête
from a ledge on the right and continue pleasantly to top. The arête can
be started more directly at V.S.

8   Senile Slab   8m   E4   5c   ★★
The steep slab on the west face of Pulpit Rock. Commonly top roped as
there is no protection.

9   Sandwich Rib   12m   Severe
Climb the rib lying in the gully on the right side of the Rock.

10   Amphitheatre Arête   16m   Very Difficult
The first obvious clean arête on the right of the Pulpit Rock.

11   Gorse Route   10m   Difficult
Climb mixed ground, painfully, just right of an overhanging nose of rock.

12   Mantelshelf Wall   10m   Severe
A small, rectangular buttress stands out from the rest of the
amphitheatre. Climb left edge to a ledge, move right and up.

13   Cling   10m   E1   5b   ★
Climb right edge of the above buttress.

14   Shattered Corner   10m   Severe
Climb shallow V-groove bounding small buttress on right.

15   Frustration Wall   10m   Hard Severe
Just right of Shattered Corner wall. Climb twin cracks to a niche,
continue up groove, step left and finish.

16   Frustration Eliminate   10m   Very Severe   4c

Climb right wall of small arête right of Frustration Wall, finish directly up thin crack above.

17   Conclusion Wall   10m   Severe   ★
Just right of Frustration Wall is an inset groove left of a mossy wall. Follow the groove.

18   Easy Groove   10m   Moderate
Start just right of the mossy wall at a small bush and climb the easy angled groove.

19   Tombstone Traverse   10m   Severe
Start as for Easy Groove and climb directly up a mossy groove, trending right at the top.

20   Epitaph   10m   Very Severe   4c
The clean wall here has a chipped niche. Start below triangular overhang, climb up to overhang then go left.

21   Epitaph Variation   10m   E1   5b   ★★
Climb to triangular overhang as before then follow good crack on right hand for grade.

22   Coffin Chimney   7m   Very Severe   4b
On the wall right of the Epitaph wall is a repulsive, green slot which overhangs. Climb it.

23   Frustration Chimney   10m   Severe
Climb the groove right of the overhanging green slot.

The West Face — Diagram 3

A short descent from the right end of The Amphitheatre leads to the West Face. Prominent at the left end of this face is a small crag; bounded on the right by a groove and on the left by a flake crack.

24   Trench Groove   11m   Difficult
Climb the gorse-filled grooves, immediately left of the flake crack.

25   Trench Direct   12m   Very Severe   4c
Round the edge from Trench Groove is the flake crack, which gives a few jamming moves leading to the ordinary route.

26   Contortion Groove   10m   Very Severe   4a
This is the recessed V-groove bounding the small crag on the right; there is a mossy patch on the right wall. Climb the groove, to join Trench Groove above.

27   Sadist's Groove   10m   Hard Very Severe   5a   ★
The most obvious line of this face. Start immediately right of a V-groove, gain a recess, go up and left to a prominent spike, then back right to a grass tuft and up.

28   Tottering Layback   8m   Severe   ★
The shallow corner at the right of the green wall, with a small niche at its foot. Climb the corner to a flake, layback round it and continue to finish.

29   Chalkster   12m   E2   5c   ★★
On the left side of the next buttress along will be seen a series of flakes. After a difficult start, climb flakes and cracks until a step right is possible at 7m. Up thin crack to large ledge, then more easily to top.

30   Dee's Crack   10m   Very Severe   4c   ★★
Named after a certain Professor of Physics whose classes were not being attended. Climb the very obvious tapering crack.

31   Automation   8m   E1   5b
Immediately right of Dee's Crack is a rusty crack. Climb it.

32   John's Last   10m   Hard Very Severe   5a
Climb the groove 2m right of Dee's Crack.

33   Dee's Doom   11m   Very Severe   4c
Start as for John's Last, traverse left above a small niche and finish up Dee's Crack.

34   The Belk   10m   E1   5b   ★★
This climbs the centre of the wall right of John's Last. Start at an arrow, climb straight up passing a thin crack, gain a ledge and trend right to top. Poorly protected.

35   Ring   10m   Very Severe   5a
Start immediately right of The Belk at a shallow, mossy groove. Climb this to ledge and continue up and right.

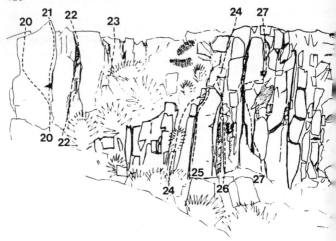

LOUDOUN HILL: DIAG. 3 — THE WEST FACE

36 Strife 10m Severe
At the foot of the wall on the right is a large perched block. On the wall behind the block is a gorse bush. Climb past this to a ledge and continue above in a shallow groove.

37 Knee Grinder 10m Severe
Climb up to same ledge as Strife, continue up and left to ledge, then up and right to top.

38 Rocking Stone Groove 13m Moderate
Start as for Strife, behind large blocks, continue up and right over blocks. A useful descent route following a route near The Arête, once the route has been correctly identified.

39 Evening Groove 11m Severe   ★

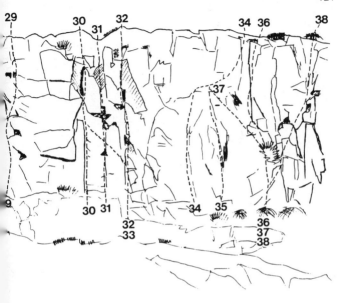

Climb wall right of perched blocks.

40   Slab and Groove   13m   Severe
Climb first half of Evening Groove then follow an obvious slabby groove
up and right.

41   Cave Crack   11m   Very Severe   4c   ★★
The West Face curves downwards on the right, ending in a wall with a
prominent crack. Climb the crack direct by jamming, leading to a recess
capped by a large block.

42   The Hobbit   45m   E2   5b
The girdle traverse of the right section of The Amphitheatre. Climb
halfway up Cave Crack, then follow the line of least resistance
leftwards to finish up Dee's Crack.

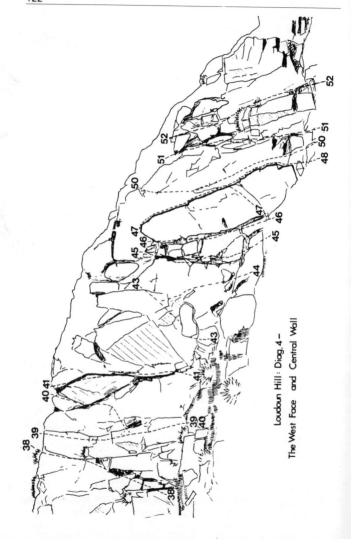

Loudoun Hill : Diag. 4 –
The West Face and Central Wall

The Central Wall — Diagrams 4 and 5

This wall is dominated by a huge, sharp-edged flake leaning against the wall. The arête of the flake gives a classic route. To its left is a clean buttress, the left wall of which is taken by Cave Crack. The next four routes ascend the front of the buttress left of the arête.

43 Young's Stairway   16m   Difficult
Start just right of Cave Crack, and follow the obvious traverse line up and right across the face to above the arête. Finish by the easiest line above.

44 Stairway Direct   20m   Very Difficult
At the left end of the wall, climb past green streaks to a block at the start of the normal route. Continue as for normal route.

Almost directly beneath the prominent arête, an old dry stane dyke crosses the path to adjoin the crag below a belt of overhanging rock. The next two routes begin at some broom at the right end of the overhang.

45 Original Route   45m   Difficult
Start behind the broom, step right on to a clean rib and continue to the foot of the wall left of the arête. Climb a shattered fault up and right to above and behind the arête. Finish by a variety of routes.

46 The Left Crack   45m   Very Difficult   ★★
First pitch as for Original Route to the foot of the wall left of the arête. Then climb the left side chimney-crack formed by the arête and the main wall.

47 The Edge   45m   Very Severe   4b   ★★★
A magnificent classic route. Start directly below the arête, a few metres right of the dry stane dyke and just right of a mossy wall. Climb walls and ribs to gain the foot of The Left Crack. Traverse right across the left of the arête, swing on to the exposed edge, and continue directly up the arête. Finish by a variety of routes.

48 The Edge Direct   45m   Very Severe   4c
A harder though poorer variation. Start as for The Edge and climb to the foot of the arête. Climb directly up the front of the arête.

49 Foxglove Chimney   45m   Severe   ★★★
The right-hand chimney-crack formed by the arête and the main wall.
Start as for The Edge, climb pleasantly up and right of the arête to the
foot of the crack. Climb directly up the crack to gain the top of the arête.
Continue to the top.

50   The Splits   44m   E1   5b   ★★★
Some 10m right of the old dyke, a clean rib and groove lie just left of a
large block, which is about 10m up the face. Climb the rib and groove,
passing just left of the block to belay at the foot of the Foxglove
chimney. Climb thin crack on wall above to small ledge, bypassing old
peg, then move right and up to top.

51   Jackdaw Chimney   37m   Very Difficult   ★
First pitch as for The Splits to belay at the foot of the corner across the
wall from Foxglove. Follow the corner up and right to the top.

52   Mij   37m   Severe
Start as for The Splits and climb directly up to belay below the smaller of
two roofs. Climb the crack splitting the roofs.

53   The Ramparts   37m   Very Difficult   ★★★
A red groove leads up past the right side of the large block. Climb this
past the block then past a nose of rock to belay at the foot of the corner
right of the belt of overhangs. Follow the corner with a move over a
bulge on good holds. Finish more easily by a choice of routes.

54   Short Term Effect   37m   E1   5b   ★
Climb as for The Ramparts to the foot of the corner then climb the thin
crack on the left wall of the corner.

55   Staircase Crack   40m   Very Difficult
About 30m right of the dry stane dyke, defining the Central Wall, is a
clean rib. Climb the left side of the rib, continue up short wall above, go
left and climb corners, grooves and short walls of good rock about 10m
right of The Ramparts.

Loudoun Hill: Diag. 5 –
The Central Wall

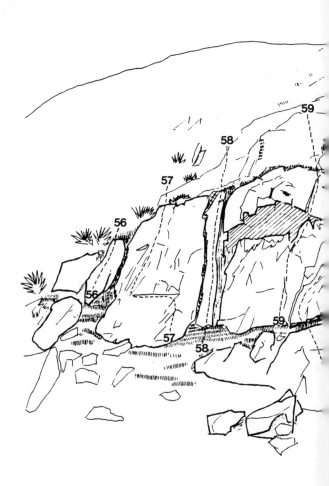

LOUDOUN HILL: DIAG. 6 — THE EASTERN BUTTRESS

The Eastern Buttress (The Strathaven Face) — Diagram 6

The path continues down and around the south side of the hill, leading to the Eastern Buttress. The main feature is a large roof near the left end of the face. A few metres down and left of the roof is an overhanging wall with a prominent, horizontal crack. Above this wall is a blunt rib. The next rib left is taken by the following route.

56   Broom Arête   10m   Severe
Climb the arête left of the blunt rib, difficult low down.

57   The Hand Traverse   12m   Very Severe   4c
Climbs the horizontal crack in the overhanging wall. Step off a flake at the right end of the wall, hand traverse left to a ledge, climb the shallow scoop above, just right of Broom Arête, or climb the blunt rib directly above the overhanging wall.

58   Nose Rib   16m   Severe
Climb the rib which bounds the left side of the large roof.

59   Suicide   18m   Very Difficult
Climb the rib which bounds the right side of the large roof, to gain a flake. Climb the wall above, trend left then up.

60   Dusk Route   26m   Difficult
Just right of the roof, a small wall descends to the foot of the crag. Climb this to a ledge, go up the left side of a nose of rock trending right, then back left above the roof to finish up Suicide.

61   Spitfire   38m   Severe   ★
The prominent corner about 15m right of the large roof. Gain the foot of the corner by grassy ledges, climb the corner or the right wall to a ledge, make an awkward step up and continue more easily.

62   Wall and Groove   40m   Severe
A groove can be seen a few metres right of Spitfire, starting just above a horizontal fault. Gain and follow the groove, trending right at first then up.

63   The Blitz   40m   Very Severe   4b
Above the left end of a large grass ledge is a prominent crack. Climb directly up the wall immediately left of the crack.

64   SCC Wall   40m   Severe
Climb the wall just right of the prominent crack, directly above the grass ledge.

65   Breakfast Route   35m   Very Difficult
Climb the mixed ground right of the main face.

66   East Face Girdle   80m   Severe
Start as for Broom Arête, traverse right above the overhanging wall, make a difficult move down a groove to gain the left end of the large roof (crux), traverse under roof to flake belay at right end. Continue rightwards to the corner of Spitfire, just above is a horizontal fault which cuts across the whole face. Gain this fault and follow it to the end of the face.

67   Central Wall Girdle   70m   Very Severe   4c   ★
Start as for Staircase Crack and climb until level with the bulge of The Ramparts. Traverse into the corner just above the bulge and climb left across the wall to gain the rib between The Ramparts and Mij. Follow the rib for a few metres until it is possible to traverse left to the wall taken by The Splits. Reverse top crack of The Splits then move left to the top of the arête. Step left on to wall and climb into a small undercut groove (crux). Finish by a choice of routes.

Map: Sheet 63, G.R. 220 605

THE QUADROCKS

INTRODUCTION

The rocks lie at a height of about 230m, just over 1km NE of Largs town centre. They are visible on the hill behind the town. There are three crags: Low; Main; and High. The rock is a sound, rough basalt. The crag is named on the map as the 'Cauld Rocks', which may be misleading, as the rocks will catch any sun in the afternoon and evening. The outlook is superb.

ACCESS

By public transport train from Glasgow Central to Largs. By car from Glasgow follow the A78, coast road. Just north of Largs town centre gain access to Burnside Road by any one of several routes (follow signs for the Inverclyde Centre). This leads in under 1km to a large car park outside the Centre. Gain the hillside behind the Centre and reach the crags in 10 minutes, avoiding a shooting range on the south side of the Centre.

Low Crag — Diagram 1

1 Far Groove   6m   Very Difficult
Climb the open groove directly.

2 Far Wall   7m   Very Difficult
Climb a cracked wall to below an overhang, turn this on the left by a slabby shelf, or better, climb the overhang directly.

3 Boulder Rib   7m   Very Difficult
Go directly up the rib on good holds and gain a sloping shelf at the top. Pass large boulder on the right.

4 Dank Chimney   7m   Difficult
Climb the messy chimney immediately right of Boulder Rib.

5 Boulder Problem   7m   Very Difficult   ★
Easy climbing up to the boulder then an awkward move to gain its top. A short, steep wall remains. The stability of the boulder is in some doubt.

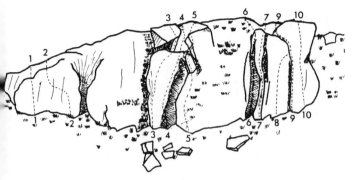

Diag. 1 :   The Quadrocks – Low Crag.

6   Choc–Chimney   7m   Severe   ★
A deep chimney-crack containing a swinging chockstone. Strenuous.

7   Sentry–Box Crack   6m   Severe   ★
Climb easily to the sentry-box from which a hard move is made to gain
the ledge above. Finish up a short wall.

8   Fingers Wall   6m   Very Severe   4b
This brutal little wall problem joins Curving Crack at two-thirds height.

9   Curving Crack   6m   Very Difficult   ★★
A good route. Climb the crack direct.

10   Curving Crack Wall   6m   Very Difficult   ★★
Go straight up the attractive wall on good holds.

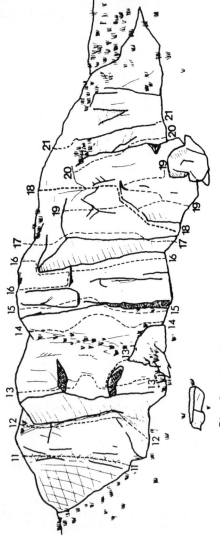

Diag. 2: The Quadrocks – Main Crag.

Main Crag — Diagram 2

11   Easy Face Groove   7m   Very Severe   4a
Climb the right edge of the easy face. The shallow groove is climbed direct and is awkward.

12   Green Corner   10m   Very Difficult
The obvious large corner at the left end of the main face. Climb the corner, exiting directly or by easier shelf on left.

13   Overhang Route   10m   Very Severe   4b   ★
Step left from convenient boulder then right to below small roof. Climb roof by slot high up for right hand, strenuous. The first overhang can also be climbed direct, raising the grade.

14   Flake Wall   10m   Hard Very Severe   5a
This steep route climbs the tall, narrow wall. Gain foothold in the middle of the wall then make some hard moves up and left to better holds.

15   Vee Groove   12m   Very Severe   4b
Climb green groove, step right then left into V-groove which is climbed directly. The finish is hard. A variation finish is to step left to another groove on upper wall and finish up that.

16   Big Corner   12m   Severe   ★★
The very obvious corner running almost the full height of the crag. Climb the corner direct for the best sport or move left near the top and finish up open groove.

17   The Arête   12m   E2   5b   ★★
The right bounding edge of Big Corner. Start in the corner and as soon as possible make a hard move right on to the face. Continue up the arête. No protection.

18   The Traverse   12m   Very Severe   4c   ★★★
Probably the best route on the crag. Make a rising traverse across the steep face to a flake. Gain top of flake and enter a bay above. Exit left or right.

19   Traverse Face Direct   10m   Very Severe   4b   ★★
A number of variation starts to the traverse exist, and these are indicated on the diagram, but there is only one direct finish. From about

the middle of the traverse climb straight up very steep rock to a small niche. Finish more easily.

20   The Nose   9m   Very Severe   4a
Follows the right hand end of the traverse face. Start round corner, move up left to the edge and follow this to top.

21   Slab and Corner   9m   Severe
Climb slab in corner to right of The Nose until rock becomes vertical then reach for holds high on left.

22   Sunburst Red   9m   E3   5c   ★★
Climbs short wall at right end of crag, starting at prominent hole in the rock.

High Crag

This is the outcrop well up and right of Low and Main Crags. The main line is quite long and follows a direct line from the lowest rocks. It is very pleasant and about difficult in standard. Other short problems can be found. Finally, the Main Crag has been girdled from left to right, finishing up The Traverse.

Map: Sheet 63, G.R. 240 773

CRAIGMUSCHAT QUARRY

INTRODUCTION

This is the obvious large quarry on Tower Hill in Gourock. The rock is trachyte, mostly shattered apart from that rock flanking the entrance. Most of the climbing is out of sight of the entrance and routes dry quickly after rain. Tree belays on top. Protection pegs may be in place on some routes, though most of the routes were first led without pegs. Climbs are described from left to right. Routes without an adjectival grade have not been led.

ACCESS

The entrance is on the north side of the quarry and is located behind the scrapyard in Broomberry Drive. Climbing is not permitted in the quarry, and routes in this section are described for future reference, should circumstances change.

West Face

This is the face to the west of the quarry entrance. The rectangular hanging slab above the graffiti 'JADA' is a fairly obvious feature and is crossed by Jihad, Dune Messiah and Mu'ad D'ib. Bright Lights takes the corner above the tree about 6m left of this.

1   Blasted Wall   30m   6a
About 10m left of Bright Lights is a large wall. This route climbs the vague, wide 'pillar' on the right of the wall. Climb up 10m to gain the left side of a small steep slab. Move right and up a few feet to the niche below the overhang. Gain the steep parallel cracks on the wall above the overhang by difficult moves, then follow the cracks to the top.

2   Bright Lights   30m   Hard Very Severe   ★★
Climb the obvious corner above the small tree to a small ledge on top of the flake. Climb the diagonal crack on the left to the top.

3   Push the Button   25m   E2   5c   ★
Start 4m right of Bright Lights in a corner capped by an overhang of doubtful looking blocks. Climb the left wall to the bulge then up and

right over the blocks to gain the slab. Step left on to the rib then follow the steep crack above to the top.

To the right of Push the Button, three short ribs lead to a short, steep slab. The following three routes cross this slab.

4   Jihad   25m   E1   5b   ★
Climb the short rib to the right of Push the Button to gain the slab. Up this to the V-groove above which is followed until it is possible to step left on to the steep arête which leads to the top.

5   Dune Messiah   25m   E1   5b
Start a few metres right of Jihad. Climb the short rib to the right of 'JADA' graffitti to slab. Up this to thin crack. Follow crack to easier ground.

6   Mu'ad D'ib   25m   Very Severe   5b
Climb just right of Dune Messiah to smooth slab. Make thin moves across this past a peg runner to big ledge. Scramble to top.

7   Grooves Route   25m   Severe   ★
Start a few metres right of Mu'ad D'ib. Climb grooves to top.

8   Overhung Arête   25m   Severe   ★
Climb directly up overhung arête just right of the previous route.

9   Beak Arête   25m   Hard Very Severe   4c
About 15m around the corner to the right of Overhung Arête is an obvious arête with a beak shaped projection at about 7m. Follow arête to whin bushes at top.

10   Whin Route   25m   Hard Very Severe   5a
The line just right of Beak Arête.

11   Stairway Grooves   25m   E1   5a
Left of the old wooden steps is a groove. Follow this to the top.

The following two routes can be seen from the road.

12   Cutlass   15m   Hard Very Severe   ★
There is a red brick building quite near the quarry gate. 8m left of this is an arête. Climb the crack to the right of the arête.

13   Gatehouse Corner   10m   5c
To the right of Cutlass is an ominous corner above a girder jutting out from the wall of the brick hut. Climb the corner direct.

East Face

14   Concrete Arête   10m   Very Difficult
Climb the left hand arête behind the concrete structure. This route is visible from the entrance.

15   Pocket Wall   10m   6b
To the right of concrete Arête is a wall with a couple of crystal pockets in the middle. Climb wall direct to groove at top.

16   Borehole   10m   Very Severe
5m to the right of Pocket Wall is a 3m long diagonal slanting borehole. Climb this to its top, then:−
(a) Left Hand Finish − Carry straight on up to a leftward trending groove which leads to a sloping ledge. Traverse this to the top.
(b) Right Hand Finish − Traverse right along the ledge to an obvious good hold below the sloping grass ledge. Gain the ledge and continue with a rightward trend to a groove leading to the top.

17   Hangover Groove   10m   E1   5b   ★
Climb the corner to the right of Borehole to the overhang. Climb the overhang direct and continue up the vertical wall above to finish by the same groove as Borehole Right Hand Finish.

18   Bulger Wall   10m   Hard Very Severe   5a
The wall to the right of Hangover Groove has a series of small ledges. Climb these and continue rightwards to top.

19   Bulging Buttress   15m   Very Severe   4c
About 25m right of Bulger Wall is a flying buttress. Gain this by an awkward move then more easily to the finish up the final loose wall.

COURT KNOWE

INTRODUCTION

This compact crag nestles into the wooded flank of historic Court Knowe, reputedly the hill from which Mary Queen of Scots watched the Battle of Langside. An old quarry of sound dolerite, it faces an entrance to Linn Park, and is itself within the public park system. Climbing is therefore subject to official scrutiny and climbers should behave accordingly. The maximum height of the crag is 6m, with the climbing mainly on steep walls and cracks.

ACCESS

By train from Glasgow to Cathcart. Then take Merrylee Road to follow the north bank of the River Cart until Old Castle Road is gained. This leads up the hill to Court Knowe on the left, opposite Linn Park. Numerous bus services also go to the area. Climbs are described from left to right. The climbing is effectively confined to the rock right of the earthy amphitheatre, with the most prominent feature being the square-cut South Buttress. This has a left wall overlooking the amphitheatre and the main face looking over the road to Linn Park. Finally the Right Wall lies slightly back and right of the main face. As the crag is in the shade the rock has a coating of lichen, very slick when wet. The first three routes lie on the left wall. Routes are described from left to right.

1 Squirm 3a
The short chimney at the left end of the overhanging left wall.

2 Grotty Groove 4a
The earthy, loose chimney right of Squirm.

3 Chockstone Crack 4c ★
The nearest to an off-width crack, with a grassy finish.

The next seven routes are to be found on the main face of South Buttress, facing the climber entering Court Knowe.

4 Blue Tit's Nest Crack 5a ★★
Climb the cracked arête at the left end of the main face.

5 Wullie's Crack 5a ★★
A metre or so right of the left edge. Make a hard balance move on to a hold and continue.

6 Layback Crack 4c ★
Climb the crack left of the central crack.

7 Coleptera Crack 3b
The obvious central crack, some vegetation.

8 Thin Finger's Crack 5c ★
Climb the crack right of the central crack.

9 Mountain Climber Route 4c ★
Start below Thin Finger's Crack and climb the wall, trending up and right.

10 Last Route 4a
Start up the right edge of the main face, left of large tree. At top move left across wall to finish.

The following eight routes are found on the wall right of the main face, with the first on the small face inset from the right edge of the main face.

11 Andrew's Wall 4c
Climb the small wall just right of the edge.

12 Everest Corner 3b
The corner behind the large tree, at the left end of the right wall.

13 Right Wall 3b
The small wall just right of the corner.

14 Easy Arête 3a ★
The obvious arête right of Everest Corner.

15 Flake 2a
The obvious flake springing out right from half-way up Easy Arête.

16   The Long Reach   4a   ★
The wall and slab left of the prominent muddy crack.

17   Mudcrack   4b
The obvious muddy crack near the right end of the right wall. Follow crack, moving left below top on to slab.

18   Consolation   3a
The right edge of the blank wall.

19   Girdle Traverse   5b   ★
The girdle of the crag, starting from Blue Tit's Nest Crack and finishing at Consolation. Crux is crossing the blank wall left of Consolation.

Map: Sheet 64, G.R. 474 558

NEILSTON QUARRY

INTRODUCTION

This small quartz dolerite quarry is popular with beginners and its western aspect and lack of midges make it ideal for summer evenings. There are two main buttresses; broken wall and slabs on the left and steep grooves and cracks on the right.

ACCESS

On the left hand side of the back road to Dunlop, about half a kilometre south west of Neilston Village. Parking is possible close by. There is a regular rail service from Glasgow Central.

Left Buttress

Descriptions for this broken and rather confused buttress are not definitive and climbers should follow lines of least – or most – resistance. There are three small hawthorns at the base.

1   Right Angled Corner   11m   Difficult
Climb the front of a small square buttress left of the first tree. Finish up grassy slabs.

2   Corner and Groove   11m   Difficult
Take the corner on the right and grassy slabs above.

3   Flake Route   11m   Very Difficult
The indefinite flake line between the first and second tree. Finish up walls and grooves.

4   Pinkerton's Corner   11m   Severe
Climb the wall just right of the second tree, past a break. Continue above from the recess.

5   Corner Arête   11m   Severe
The broad arête, right, is climbed followed by a leftward line.

6   Kristeen's Crack   9m   Very Difficult   ★
Climb cracks in the left wall of the deep Y-shaped recess 7m right of the second tree.

7   Polish Direct   4m   Hard Severe
The short, steep wall just left of third tree.

Right Buttress
This part of the quarry starts with the Strawberry Tower, an obvious large block above a curving crack.

8   Juggy Crack   11m   Very Difficult
Climb the short crack on the left side of the tower.

9   Strawberry Crack   9m   Severe   ★★
The fine curving crack below the tower.

10   Spiney Boulder   12m   Very Difficult
The indefinite crack in the wall of Strawberry Crack. Finish straight up.

11   Easy Gully   12m   Difficult
The grassy trough, right, finishing right or left.

12   B.N.I.   12m   Severe
A small black-streaked wall left of the arête.

13   Broken Arête   12m   Very Difficult
Obvious !

14   Y-Crack   12m   Very Difficult
The short loose looking crack.

15   Stephen Slab   12m   Hard Severe   ★
This is the short reddish wall.

16   Crack Corner   12m   Very Difficult   ★
Start about 8m right of Strawberry Crack where the main face begins.
This route climbs a rightward slanting corner-groove, left of a stepped
overhang.

17   Polish Hangover   12m   Very Severe   4c   ★
Climb the steep arête and overhang to finish up Crack Corner.

18   Intrusion Line   12m   Very Difficult
This takes the leftward curving groove and crack right of Polish
Hangover.

19   Punk Rock   14m   E1   5b   ★
Follow Intrusion Line until it is possible to move right to a crack with an
old jammed nut in it. Climb the wall above.

20   Curving Crack   14m   Hard Very Severe   5a   ★
Climb the long leftward curving crack, finishing up the wall just right of
Punk Rock.

21   Willie's Route   14m   Severe   ★★
Start at the broken crack line, below and right of the tree stump. Finish
right.

22   Fornication   14m   Very Severe   4c
Round the corner from Willie's Route there is a white speckled wall.
Climb cracks in the left side.

23   Grassy Crack   12m   Severe
Start 2m right of Fornication. Climb the mossy crack to an overhang,
move left and climb the broken crack in the speckled wall.

24   Jig-saw Jive   12m   Very Difficult
The mossy crack-line passing the overhang of Grassy Crack on the
right.

25 Grot Gully 12m Moderate
Yuck.

26 Peg Leg 2m Hard Very Severe 5b
The short crack in the quarry's right wall was once pegged.

THE KELVINBRIDGE AND FINNIESTON WALLS

This section of the guide would be incomplete without at least a mention of two areas of man-made training walls in Glasgow. The Kelvinbridge area lies under the west end of the Kelvin bridge at Great Western Road, opposite to the Kelvinbridge Subway Station. From Great Western Road steps at the southwest corner of the bridge lead down to the Kelvin Walkway and the walls. The left section of wall is sandstone, easier than the short section of wall on the bridge itself, which is of granite. Both walls are harder than the Finnieston Railway Wall, described below. Routes and traverse are obvious; good arm and finger training ground, though in the public gaze.

The Finnieston Railway Wall lies on the north side of the Clyde Express Way. There is neither parking nor a pavement in front of the wall and approach must be made on foot along the verge. The safest way starts from the covered pedestrian approach leading from Finnieston Station to the Strathclyde Exhibition Centre (signposted). Leave Argyll Street and go south on Finnieston Road. Turn right and go west alongside the Express Way. The climbing area begins about 100m east of the pedestrian bridge over the Express Way and consists of a very long length of sandstone wall, just off the vertical and with beautifully-designed holds. The traverse is rarely more than 4m off the ground. On a sunny day the heat can build up rapidly, while traffic noise is considerable (portable cassette-player recommended). Do not climb over the wall. Good strength and stamina training.

CRAIG MINNAN   Map: Sheet 63, G.R. 641 322

A steep little outcrop in a fabulous setting. Approach from Muirshiel Country Park, 3km north-west of Lochwinnoch. Follow the signs to Windy Hill from where the crag can be seen. Routes are not described.

The Stirling Outcrops

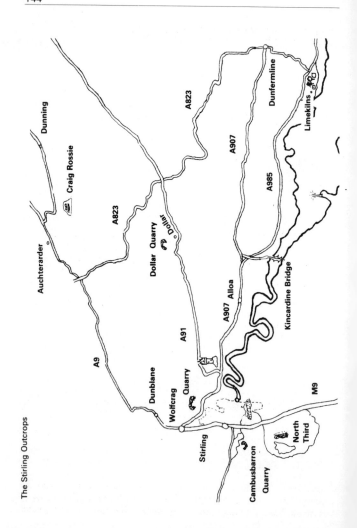

THE CENTRAL OUTCROPS

INTRODUCTION

The central outcrops are a small but diverse group of cliffs roughly centred around Stirling. Despite the fact that most of the cliffs described here are virtually unknown to the climbing population at large they provide a very interesting and worthwhile addition to this guide and will probably gain much popularity in years to come.

The cliffs underneath The Wallace Monument in Stirling provide some very good climbing; however, as little information is available and as a strictly enforced ban on climbing is in operation, no attempt has been made to describe the routes here.

HISTORY

Though the rambling cliffs of the Ochils have been scrambled upon in the dim and distant past, the first real climbing in the area took place in the mid-seventies when Bob Conway and friends from the naval base at Rosyth climbed a series of routes on The Wallace Monument cliffs. During one cleaning session however, a large block ended up on the road below the cliff with the result that climbing was banned. The ban continues to this day, a sad loss as many of the original lines were good.

In the late 1970's Ian Duckworth, Allan Pettit and Pete Billsborough adopted Wolfcrag Quarry as their local training ground. The walls of this small quarry were very steep and sheltered, and therefore it made a fine bouldering area; unfortunately, the rock was also very smooth, and so to increase the amount of climbing available they chipped lines of holds all over the wall. Ian Duckworth led Leonardo and Ian's Wa', then Tony Kay took over as the main activist with ascents of Up On The Catwalk, Experiments in Incest and (after some jiggery pokery) Tribal Look. More recently Craig Macadam soloed Waterfront and The Outsider (one of the quarries few all natural routes) and Ron Cowels led Lock-it and Thirty Frames a Second.

In the early 1980's more cliffs were discovered. Ron Cowels in particular deserves credit for the discovery of North Third, Limekilns and Cambusbarron Quarry, the three best cliffs in the area.

At North Third Cowels was responsible for cleaning and climbing most of the routes to give a fine series of crack climbs. The real prize, however, was the superb diagonal crack of Red Shift. This particular climb repulsed numerous attempts from a variety of climbers until it was eventually led free by Gary Latter in 1984. The direct start was added by Kenny Spence on an earlier, abortive attempt.

The Limekilns was a unique find — two limestone blocks hidden in the woods beside the Firth of Forth. The first route here was Humbug by Martin Bennett in 1981. Then Tony Kay, Neil Morrison and Neil Paxton swooped in to exploit the potential. Morrison led Cruel Summer, New Gold Dream, Colours Fly and The Struggler whilst Tony Kay added most of the eliminate lines on the Humbug face and the fine arête of Methods of Dance. Cowels eventually got in on the act with Marley's Ghost but by now all eyes had turned to the two superb cracks splitting the overhanging north face of the Sentinel. These held out until early 1984 when Kenny Spence led Velvet Glove and John McKenzie led Iron Fist. The most recent routes here are Tony Kay's alternative finish to Methods of Dance and Allan Pettit's Elgin's Wall, the first route on the Gellet Block.

Cambusbarron Quarry received its first route in 1983 when Tony Kay and Ron Cowels climbed Big Country Dreams, with one rest point. This very fine climb soon attracted other climbers to the quarry. In early 1984 Murray Hamilton free-climbed Big Country Dreams and went on to add Formica Crack, Murray's Route and Murray's Corner, while Rab Anderson added Fuel for Thought. An intense May Day weekend's activity led to Oink Oink, Quantum Grunt (since made harder by the unnatural disappearance of a small tree which the first ascentionists used to start the climb) and the intriguing Both Ends Burning being created by Duncan McCallum, Graham Pedley and Kenny Spence. Craig Macadam led Visions of Monaco and Purr-Blind Doomster, the latter being straightened out by McCallum before being led without the in-situ protection by Spence. The last big climb of the summer was Gary Latter's route Power of Endurance. As well as these full length climbs Graham Livingstone added a number of worthwhile boulder problems, of which Spanking the Monkey is particularly bold and impressive.

Of the less important cliffs Dollar Quarry is perhaps the best. It was developed by Jamie Main in 1981 and though of limited potential it did give some very worthwhile climbs, particularly Applause from The Gallery and Energy Transfer.

1985 — This year's poor weather limited further development of the Central Outcrops. By far the greatest activity was at the Gellet Block at Limekilns, which now boasts over 20 routes, many being the work of D.Baker, A.Borthwick, A.McCord, D.Moffat and M.Russell. Of the harder routes the generally acknowledged classic would seem to be

Duncan McCallum's Ivy League, Murray Hamilton being responsible for The Charleston to the left.

At Cambusbarron McCallum was again busy, sticking his neck out on The Crowd, while Rab Anderson also helped to fill in the remaining lines with Economy Drive.

NORTH THIRD

Map: Sheet 57, G.R. 760 892

INTRODUCTION

This natural dolerite outcrop lies 10km to the south-west of Stirling, set picturesquely above North Third reservoir on the edge of the Campsie Fells. The climbing is characterised by long straight cracks which give some fine problems in jamming.

After short periods of wet weather the cliff dries quickly. After longer periods of rain and during much of the winter the crag can take a long time to dry out.

ACCESS

Approaching Stirling from the south leave the M80 at exit 9, follow the A872 southward towards Denny leaving it at the first turning on the right, leading back under the motorway. Follow this, turning left after a caravan and camping site, turn left again after Milnholm farm and follow the road for 2km to take the right fork. Follow this road and the crag comes into sight on the right, above the reservoir. Limited parking above the dam. The climbs are described from left to right.

Birds and Bees Buttress

This buttress lies directly above the dam, and is easily recognised by the prominent groove and huge nose to its right.

1 Faulty Tower 12m Very Severe 4b
This route lies on the small buttress to the left of the Birds and Bees Buttress, starting from a cave on the right.
Swing left out of the cave into a crack which is followed to the top.

2 Beeline 14m Hard Very Severe 5b
Takes the prominent groove in the centre of the buttress.
Climb the groove with a hard start and an exciting finish over the bulge.

3   Cuckoo Crack   14m   Very Severe   5a
The crack lies just below and left of the huge nose.
   Climb the crack to a glacis under a roof, traverse right into a groove to finish direct.

The Red Tower

This area lies above and several hundred metres to the right of the dam, the most obvious feature being a striking red tower set in a bay. The climbs are situated around this. The best descent is down the slope to the left.

4   The Flying Dragon   20m   E2   5c
The crack in the left wall of the bay.

5   Jezebel   20m   E1   5b
The crack to the right of Flying Dragon is marginally easier but more sustained.
   Follow the crack, through a strenuous bulge. The groove above is followed until forced out left to finish. Good thread belay.

6   Jim's Chimney   22m   Very Severe   4b
The chimney to the right of Jezebel is followed to finish on its left wall. Rather friable.

7   Red Shift   23m   E5   6a
This route climbs the fine diagonal crackline crossing the red tower. Start at the foot of the tower.
   Gain the crack via hard moves up a groove. Follow the crack, with particularly trying moves round the arête, to finish straight up.
Variation: Climb the bulging crack to the right of the initial groove (6b).

8   Beemer   15m   E3   5C
This route climbs the bulging chimney crack 15m to the right.

The next route lies 150m to the right of the bay.

9   Sma Gell   12m   E2   5c
The obvious crack splitting a bulging nose. The climb gets increasingly harder and more difficult to protect as the crack gets wider.

Map: Sheet 57, G.R. 772 923

CAMBUSBARRON QUARRY

INTRODUCTION

This fine abandoned quarry bowl offers a good selection of high standard single pitch routes, mostly following prominent cracks or grooves. The routes are generally well protected and are all situated on the left-hand face at the back of the quarry. The quarry is very sheltered and the face catches the evening sun in the summer, though the routes are seldom dry in winter.

ACCESS

From the south leave the M90 at Junction 9 and head towards Cambusbarron. Follow the main street through the town, turning left at Quarry Road. The entrance to the quarry is found where the road turns rightwards. The climbs are described from left to right.

1 Power of Endurance   25m   E4   6b   ★
The wall near the left-hand end of the face is split by a vague hanging crack-line. Start below this.
   Follow obvious line of holds leading to thin blind crack. Up this making a hard move to become established on the upper wall. Take a leftward-trending line to gain ledge, from where an awkward move rightwards leads to the top.

2 Quantum Grunt   25m   E4   6a   ★★
A strenuous and technical groove which has made a monkey out of many! Start below the groove system a few metres right of the previous route.
   Make difficult initial moves to gain groove proper. Mantle into niche and continue up groove above. A thin fingery crux leads to good holds. Either step left via undercuts or pull rightwards to finish (easier but not so good).

3 Visions of Monaco   25m   E3   5c
Ascends the obvious groove and cracked arête. Protection is sparse in the lower section. Start at a prominent break.
   Climb up and right passing good resting ledge to gain foot of crack. Up this with a hard move near the top.

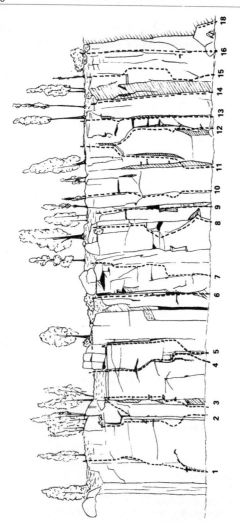

CAMBUSBARRON QUARRY

4 Big Country Dreams 25m E3 6a   ★★★
An excellent route tackling the striking S-shaped crack-line. Start just right of the main crack-line.
   Climb on to jutting block and pull leftwards to follow thin crack leading to a good resting position below final crack. Finish up this with a hard move near the top.

5 Grace Under Pressure 25m E2 5b
The shallow flared chimney line just right of Big Country Dreams, starting just right of that route.
   Gain chimney line and follow it past a good undercut hold to an easier finish.

6 Formica Crack 25m E3 6a   ★
The shallow pod with the hand crack in the back. Start below this. From ledge below crack make a few awkward moves to gain better jams. Continue more easily in the same general line to the top.

7 The Purr-Blind Doomster 27m E4 6a   ★★
An enjoyable well protected crack contrasting with a bold upper section on the upper arête. Start just right of Formica Crack.
   Ascend thin crack to an obvious vertical slot at its top. Make a delicate traverse rightwards and up to gain obvious jutting spike. Move up and right round the arête to finish.

8 Quasi Pulls Through 27m E3 6a   ★
Start 5m right of The Purr-Blind Doomster, below a steep reddish groove capped by a bulging roof on its right.
   Up groove to block. From here make a long reach leftwards to gain a good hidden hold (crux) and resting spot. Step right under small roof to finish up a groove.

9 Oink Oink 27m E2 5c   ★
Just right of the last route are twin parallel groove-lines. Start below these.
   Make a hard pull to gain the foot of the right-hand groove and follow this, occasionally using the left-hand groove for holds and protection. Finish up the wall above.

10 Both Ends Burning 27m E5 6b   ★★★
2m right of the last route is a fine finger-crack splitting a featureless

wall. This provides a sustained technical pitch with a surprising middle section.

Up crack to gain good flat hold on left wall for rest (crux). Regain crack with difficulty and follow it strenuously to easier ground.

11   Fuel for Thought   27m   E3   5c
Climbs the slender groove in the arête to the right of Both Ends Burning, gained from the corner on its left.

Climb the corner to a flake. Move up and across right to gain the groove. Climb this and go up right over the top of a huge block to finish.

12   The Crowd   27m   E5   6a/b
Takes a line between Fuel for Thought and Running on Methane. Climb the hanging groove past 3 poor pr to reach a ledge (crux). Continue boldly up the groove, with a hard move to finish (poor RP's).

13   Running on Methane   27m   E4   6a   ★★
A sustained pitch up the groove and hanging crack 6m right of the previous route. Start below this on the right wall of the short arête. Climb the arête to gain good holds and runners at the foot of the groove. Follow this past a bulge with difficulty to a stopping place. Step left, then move up right to the top.

14   Murray's Groove   27m   E1   5c
The obvious corner at the right end of the face, finishing on the left.

15   Adulterer's Repentance   27m   E3   5c
The bold arête and wall left of Economy Drive. Climb the arête to a spike, step right on to the wall and climb scoop to larger holds. Move left on to block, finishing on good holds.

16   Economy Drive   27m   E3   6a
Climb the thin crack up the wall just left of the large corner to the right of Adulterer's Repentance.

The following two problems are located on the slabby face of the fallen block on the far right of the quarry.

17   L.D.V.   3m   HVS   5c
The slabby right arête of the boulder.

18   Spanking the Monkey   4m   E5   6a   ★★
The very bold left arête provides an intimidating friction problem with an appalling landing.

The quarry to the right and behind the main crag contains one route at present.

19   Easy Contract   28m   E2   5b
The finger-crack towards the back of the quarry on the left-hand wall. Climb crack to where it splits; follow right-hand crack to finish.

Map: Sheet 57, G.R. 789 981

WOLFCRAG QUARRY

INTRODUCTION
This small greenstone quarry is a good all-year round training ground. It is a natural suntrap and lies in a very sheltered position, and even during heavy rain the steepness of the walls makes climbing on dry rock possible.
    As well as the eleven routes described here there are numerous boulder problems and traverses, mostly with very safe landings.

ACCESS
Approaching from the south leave the M9 at its end at junction 11 and follow the A9 back southwards to Bridge of Allan. After crossing the bridge take the first left and follow the road up two hills, turning right at the top of the second. There are a few parking places here. The quarry lies opposite, partly hidden by a grassy mound. The climbs are described from left to right. The best descent is to follow the rim of the quarry back down towards the road.

1   The Arête   12m   E1   5b
On entering the quarry the first obvious feature is a slabby arête. This is climbed to a very loose and scary finish.

2   In Trance as Mission   15m   Very Severe   4c
A poorly protected route through the roofs, starting 30m right of the

arête. Start just left of an obvious short crack at a 'Giants Staircase'. Follow this to the roof and traverse rightwards along ledges to a tree. Finish up this.

3   The Outsider   12m   E2   5c
A bold route up the arête just right of the last route.
Start up the short crack to a ledge; a precarious mantle on to the arête leads to an easier but bold finish leftwards.

4   Up on The Catwalk   12m   E2   6a
A variation on the previous route; protection, once found, is good.
From the precarious mantle swing right on to the overhanging wall, climb this to a precarious finish.

5   Leonardo   10m   E2   5c
Start 5m right of The Outsider, just to the left of a thin crack.
Follow a line of holds up the wall, a peg protecting the final long reach.

6   Tribal Look   12m   E3   5c
A good sustained route starting up the thin crack-line just to the right of Leonardo.
Climb the thin crack, past a horizontal niche, to a good break. Follow this right to a flake, up this and boldly through the overlap to gain a line of hidden jugs leading right to the top.

7   Lock-it   10m   E3   6a
A direct start to Tribal Look. Start 3 metres to the right at a thin crack. Climb the thin crack past a peg to gain the flake of Tribal Look.

8   Experiments in Incest   20m   E1   5c
Climb the groove to the right of Lock-it then traverse the break leftwards to the big ledge of The Outsider; finish here or up the arête.

9   Ian's Wa'   10m   E1   5c
The smooth vertical wall 18m right of the last route. Climb the wall just right of a shallow chimney to gain two good holds below an overlap, over this via a long reach to finish straight up.

10   Waterfront   10m   E2   6a
Gain a standing position on the low break to the right of Ian's Wa'

without using the arête, move through the overlap via a precarious layback, a long reach left leading to bigger holds. Finish up Ian's Wa'.

11   Thirty Frames A Second   14m   E2   5c
10m right of the last route is a groove line, this route takes the wall to the right. Start at a rib 3m to the right of the groove.
   Climb the rib to a ledge on the left, leave this by a thin crack then a flake on the right, at the roofs swing right across the wall to gain ledges on the arête. Bolt belay.

Map: Sheet 58, G.R. 963 991

DOLLAR QUARRY

INTRODUCTION
This small dolerite quarry is set on the southern slopes of the Ochils, above Dollar. Facing south to south west, the quarry dries quickly except during the winter, when seepage keeps much of the rock damp. The quarry is split into two tiers. The lower is rather broken and vegetated and all the climbing takes place on the upper tier.

ACCESS
Approaching Dollar on the A91 from Stirling, leave the main road by turning left at the bridge in the town centre. Follow the National Trust signs for Castle Campbell. After leaving Dollar take the third track on the right which leads to a car park below the upper tier. The climbs are described from right to left. The best descent for all routes is the earthy gully which lies between God Nose and Modern Dance.
   The first route is level with the parking area, directly ahead as you drive in.

1   God Nose   15m   Very Difficult
Start just left at an undercut wall, beside a tree.
   Climb directly to a second tree from where a rising traverse can be made, first rightwards then back left to finish.

2   Modern Dance   12m   Very Severe   4c
15 metres to the left of God Nose lies a V-gully; this route climbs the slabby left wall.
   Follow a short groove, until a move up right via a mantleshelf leads to an easy finishing flake.
Variation: A direct start has been made at 6a/b.

3   Double Indemnity   18m   Very Severe   4c
Starts as for Modern Dance but finishes leftwards up a groove line. Climb the groove to a ledge on the left, traverse this leftwards round a rib to gain a slabby groove which is followed to the top.

4   D.A. Groove   15m   Severe   4a
The slabby groove 12m to the left is followed to an exciting finish.

   The remaining routes lie on the walls of the corner-like feature at the left end of the quarry.

5   Everyone Loves Strawberries   6m   E2   5c
A diabolical little problem with an alarming landing. Start from a pile of boulders 25 metres left of D.A. Groove.
   Climb straight off the boulder pile until better holds lead right to an easier exit.

6   Applause from The Gallery   13m   Hard Very Severe   5b
One of the best routes in the quarry. Start beside a tree below an obvious block and overhanging groove.
   Up short overhanging arête until below a roof; either move left and over the roof or follow a crack up and back left to the lip. From the large ledge move up and right via a flake and delicate scooped wall.

7   Energy Transfer   15m   E3   5c
A bold problem up the fine overhanging groove.
   As for Applause from The Gallery to the ledge. Make some hard moves up the groove to gain a loose ramp leading back righ to the top.

8   Who Dares Wins   20m   E3   5c
Another bold route awaiting an even bolder direct start.
   Follow Energy Transfer to the jug at the top of the groove. Move left into a scoop and exit this leftwards to gain a horizontal crack. Follow this to a ledge and climb straight up with a huge reach past a peg to finishing jugs.

Numerous variations climb the slabby left wall at the corner, the best of these seem to be:-

9   Tent Roof   15m   Very Severe   4b
Start in the centre of the slabby left wall.
   Move up to a ledge, traverse leftwards to the cracked arête, follow this to an exit rightwards.

10   Electric Edge   15m   E1   5a
This route climbs the left edge of the wall.
   Make a tricky mantleshelf on to the arête, which rapidly eases with height.

CRAIG ROSSIE

INTRODUCTION

The Ochils contain a large quantity of rock most of which is much too broken or loose to be worth climbing. So far Craig Rossie is the only cliff which has been found to provide reasonably sound rock and good climbing. It stands proudly overlooking the A9 between Gleneagles and Perth.

Facing N.E. and at an elevation of 450m it takes a couple of summer days to dry, but the steep approach is amply rewarded by a roadside mountain crag surrounded by succulent bilberries.

ACCESS

From Stirling go 20km N.E. along the A9, turn off for Dunning and then turn up the forest track directly beneath the crag. 1km up this track there is limited parking at a Z-bend. Strike up the hill on foot from here.

The three existing routes lie on the highest of the two tiers visible from below and are described as approached. Routes 1 and 2 need a belay line from the summit fence.

1   Bristler   30m   E1   5b
The big chimney/groove with the alarmingly loose flakes at its top.

2   Blazer   30m   E2   5c
100m further up the hill is an open corner with a pale bulge guarding its base. Climb over the bulge and up the corner, swinging blindly out onto the face at the top. Finish up a mixture of tombstones and oatmeal.

3   Fizzler   10m   E1   5c
On the last short buttress is a series of vertical cracks; climb these.

LIMEKILNS

INTRODUCTION

These remarkable blocks of limestone lie hidden away on a wooded ridge behind the village of Charleston on The Firth of Forth. They provide superb climbing and deserve to become popular. The first block, 'The Sentinel', is a 15m high cube with over a dozen routes – a sort of limestone Higgar Tor. 'The Gellet Block' lies 200m away, far larger than its neightbour. It is unfortunately rather loose, but extensive cleaning has provided many good climbs.

The rock here dries very quickly and even during the winter it is usually possible to do some climbing.

ACCESS

Approaching from Kincardine, the A985 is followed east to the first turn off to Charleston, just after The Waulkmill snack bar. Entering the village a Post Office and store are passed on the left. Park here and follow the path behind the wall on to the ridge. The Sentinel is on the left after several hundred metres. The Gellet Block is a similar distance beyond. At the time of writing, climbing is not permitted. Routes are described in the hope that this situation will improve.

The climbs on the Sentinel are described first. Descent is by abseil from the numerous trees on its summit.

1 Pickwick 12m Very Severe 4b
The fine left arête of the slabby south face is followed delicately and with no protection.

2 Hunter and The Hunted 12m E1 5b
A fragile and bold eliminate to Pickwick's right. Start 3m to the right at a bulge.
Climb straight up with minimal holds and no protection.

3 Humbug 12m Very Severe 4c
The obvious finger-crack in the centre of the face is followed past some old nails to a tricky finish.

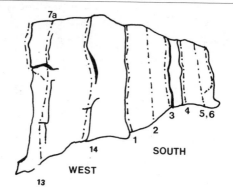

4 Kiln Dance with Me 12m E1 5a
Another eliminate which climbs the vague crack-line just right of Humbug.

5 Empires and Dance 11m Hard Very Severe 5a
Start 2m left of the right arête and climb straight up, passing a curious thread.

6 Dingley Dell 10m Severe 4b
Start as for Empires and Dance but move right at the thread to climb the arête on large but loose holds.

7 The Struggler 13m E3 6a   ★
Start just left of Cruel Summer.
   Boulder up the wall until forced into Cruel Summer. Move back left via an undercling to a peg runner and climb the steep cracks to finish as for Cruel Summer.

8 Cruel Summer 13m E2 5c   ★★
The obvious hanging corner gives a good, well protected climb. Make some hard moves into the corner and follow it to exit left.

9 Colours Fly 15m E1 5c
The wall to the right of Cruel Summer. Start just right at Cruel Summer, move up to a small ledge, then right to a tree. Gain the ramp beyond. Follow this left, passing another tree, to finish straight up.

NO.1 BLOCK   THE SENTINEL

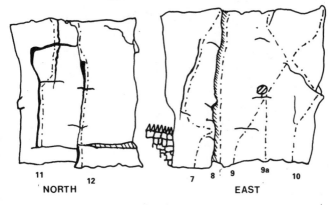

11 **12**
NORTH

7 **8** **9** **9a** **10**
EAST

10   Marley's Ghost   13m   E2   5c   ★

The right arête is climbed boldly to the ledge; move left up the ramp then back right to finish up the arête.

The North Face

11   Velvet Glove   13m   E4   6a   ★★★

The north face is split by two obvious weaknesses. This route takes the left-hand one.

Gain the hanging corner/crack and follow it over a bulge to below the roof. Step right and follow a crack to the top.

12   The Iron Fist   13m   E4   6a   ★★★

The central crack.

The West Face

13   Methods of Dance   13m   E3   6a   ★★★

The fine left arête provides an excellent climb.

Gain the slim groove just right of the edge and climb it past a pr, to gain a hanging block. Move left to the arête and climb it on good but widely-spaced holds.

Variation: Finish up the right-hand side of the arête   (E3 6a).

14   New Gold Dream   13m   E1   5b

The groove line to the right.

Climb the groove to a ledge. Move past a pr into a short hanging corner which is followed to the top.

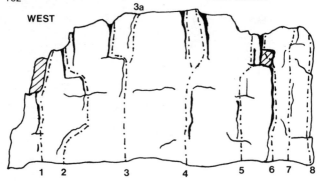

THE GELLET BLOCK OR NO. 2 BLOCK

Descent achieved by the stone staircase down the north face.

West Face

1   Slots   12m   HVS   5b
Climb the thin crack at the left-hand end of the wall via finger slots to a
ledge and finish up the slim corner.

2   Sunsetter   14m   HVS   5a
Gain and climb crack just right of slots to step left and finish up either of
two short cracks.

3   Forbidden Colours   15m   HVS   5a   ★★
Climb directly up the wall right of Sunsetter, move left and finish up
wide crack. A direct finish goes straight up the thin crack where the
ordinary steps up left (E1 5c).

4   DT's   15m   VS   4c   ★★
Climbs the short crack in the centre of the face to finish up the obvious
twin cracks.

5   D-Day   14m   HVS   5a   ★★
Climb the thin crack and wall 1½m left of White Ensign to pull up crack
just left of that route's niche.

6   White Ensign   14m   VS   4c   ★★
Takes the obvious wide crack.

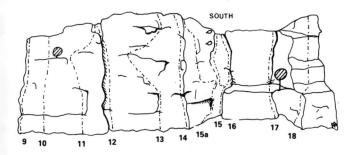

SOUTH

9 10 11 12 13 14 15a 15 16 17 18

7 VE Day 14m E1 5b
Follows thin cracks up the wall right of White Ensign.

8 Neutral Gear 14m VS 4c ★
Climb the right arête, staying on the left-hand side.

South Face

9 Lion Rampant 14m VS 4b ★
Climb the left arête, staying on the right-hand side.

10 Wall Straight 14m E1 5b ★
Climbs straight up the wall in between Lion Rampant and Protectless.

11 Protectless 14m E1 5a
Climb the shallow groove and wall left of Red Flag to step up right and finish as for that route.

12 Red Flag 14m VS 4c
The obvious corner-crack, stepping out left at the top.

13 Grasp the Nettle 15m E2 5b
Climb the thin crack in the wall right of Red Flag to reach a PR, step up left and move up to next PR. Step up right and continue to top.

14 Edge of Fear 15m E2 5b/c
A route which would benefit from a good cleaning. It takes the arête right of Graps the Nettle. On the first ascent the arête was apparently gained by a traverse at quarter height from Red Flag.

15a   Through the Motions   15m   E3   6a   ★★
Slightly eliminate but surprisingly good climbing up cracks left of Dead
Ringer. Start just left of Dead Ringer. Step up to pull over the right-
hand end of the roof and climb the crack to a break. Make a move up to a good
hold and runner where Dead Ringer traverses in then move left and
climb the crack directly, passing a loose block, to just below the top
where a move left enables a finish to be made on the arête.

15   Dead Ringer   15m   E1   5b   ★
Takes the left-hand corner of the amphitheatre to a ledge, steps left and
follows the thin crack past two iron rings.

16   Two Ringer   15m   VS   4c
The left-hand corner is followed all the way to the top.

17   One Ringer   15m   VS   4c
The right-hand corner, passing a tree.

18   Link Rib   15m   S
The stepped rib started on the left.

A few short problems exist either side of the arête to gain the first
ledge of the rib, the best being up the wall left of the arête without using
the arête. (HVS 5c).

East Face

19   The Charleston   15m   E4   6b   ★★
Climbs thin cracks up the wall right of the arête. Start at the foot of a thin
crack. Move up to this, step left and up to gain the break. Step up and
move across to gain flanges on the right then climb the thin crack to the
break. Move up the wall above to gain the arête and climb the right side
of this to the top.

20   The Ivy League   17m   E3/4   6a   ★★★
Takes the obvious groove/crack right of The Charleston to gain the top
break. Move left to pull over the small roof by flake holds and continue
to the top.

21   Yuppie   18m   E4   6a
A serious route with poor protection and some suspect holds. Climb
the wall just right of The Ivy League and move up slightly left past a thin

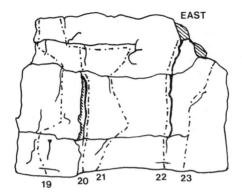

EAST

19 20 21 22 23

crack to gain ledges. Go up to a block and hand traverse the break to finish as for The Ivy League.

22 Elgin's Crack 14m E2 5c ★★★
The obvious crack is followed in its entirety.

23 The Sting 12m E2 5b
Climb up to a ledge right of Elgin's Crack and follow the thin crack to a steep ramp trending right to the top.

24 Rock Around the Block 76m E3 5a, 5c, 5c
A girdle traverse from left to right starting across the West Face.

1. 90 feet. Belay on the left edge on a platform. Move up and right until a step down enables the ledge system to be gained and followed across the face to the arête. Move around this and across to belay in the crack of Red Flag.

2. 80 feet. Move up and across to clip the top peg on Grasp the Nettle. Climb back down until the lower peg can be clipped and make hard moves up and right onto the arête. Step down to the block and traverse over to Dead Ringer, move up this to clip the lower ring and move into the corner which is descended to a ledge and belay. Great care should be taken in extending runners and protecting the second on this pitch.

3. 80 feet. Move up and across to gain the arête. A high runner can be placed in the top break. Step back down and follow the obvious foot ledge across the face. A good pitch.

OTHER CRAGS

WALLACE QUARRY   Map: Sheet 57, G.R. 816 951

This is the old quarry behind the waterworks office at the far south end of The Wallace Monument Hill. There are only two routes so far; Zeig Heil (E2 5c) climbs the obvious arête at the back of the quarry and Sandinista (E3 5b) climbs the totally unprotected wall 20m to the right.

WHITE CRAIGS   Map: Sheet 58, G.R. 184 034

KINNESTON   Map: Sheet 58, G.R. 195 024

These are the best sections of the extensive outcrop that rings the eastern edge of the West Lomond/Bishop Hill plateau overlooking Loch Leven. There are lots of extended boulder problems in the 5c-6b category on Kinneston, and White Craigs has a short but sharp route, Higher Art (E2 6a) which climbs a thin peg-scarred crack on the highest section of rock.

THE EASTERN OUTCROPS

INTRODUCTION

This section of the guide covers the outcrops in the Eastern Central belt of Scotland. This area stretches from Benarty Hill in the north to Fastcastle Head in the east, covered by maps 58, 65, 66 and 67 in the new OS. series. The countryside in between contains an interesting and very varied selection of crags which should cater for most tastes and abilities.

The climate here is much drier than in the other areas in this guide; in fact the area has one of the lowest annual rates of rainfall in Scotland. This, in combination with the low altitude and sunny aspect of many of the crags makes climbing possible throughout the year.

All the cliffs are easily accessible from Edinburgh. For those without their own transport the whole area is well covered by public transport and only Fastcastle Head and Benarty Hill are difficult to reach in this way.

HISTORY

Outcrop climbing in Scotland has, until very recently, been considered as something of a secondary activity. Whereas the history of the mountain cliffs is well known and well documented no-one seems to have taken much notice of what was being achieved on the outcrops. Consequently the history of these crags has been quite difficult to piece together and apologies are made for any omissions or inaccuracies.

Most of the early activity in the Edinburgh area centred around the cliffs of Holyrood Park. Indeed until the late 1940's this area was the scene of a series of developments which marked it as one of the main forcing grounds in Scotland.

Harold Raeburn was the first to explore the possibilities. The 1896 SMCJ includes an article and map by him detailing some 20 climbs on the Salisbury Crags. Around 1900 he made ascents of Fallen Column climb and the vicious central crack on the Dassies, while on Salisbury Crags he found a fine route up the buttress to the right of the Cat Nick. W. Inglis Clark, in the SMCJ of 1900, used photodiagrams for perhaps the first time for a Scottish outcrop, and included a photograph of an early ascent of Raeburn's Cracked Slabs Route. These routes, together with Collier's Climb up the left-hand buttress of the Cat Nick, paved the way for the epic ascent of Great Buttress (originally 'Eastern Buttress of

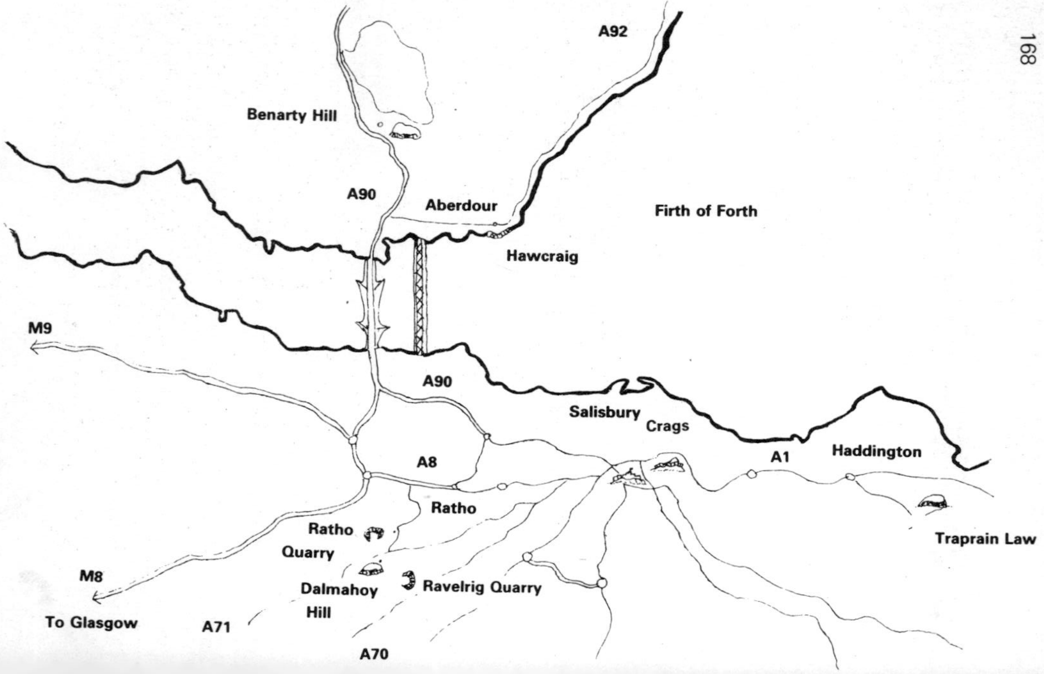
A92
Benarty Hill
A90
Aberdour
Firth of Forth
Hawcraig
M9
A90
Salisbury Crags
A8
A1
Haddington
Ratho
Ratho Quarry
Traprain Law
M8
Dalmahoy Hill
Ravelrig Quarry
To Glasgow
A71
A70

Salisbury Crag, W. A. Morrison & F. S. Goggs; c. 1905. Photo: A. E. Robertson Collection.

Opposite: Dave Cuthbertson on the first free ascent of *Requiem*,
Dumbarton Rock. Photo: Gary Latter.

Above: *The Edge*, Loudoun Hill. Climber: Ian Sykes. Photo: Ken
Crocket.

Above: *Both Ends Burning*, Cambusbarron Quarry. Climber: Duncan McCallum. Photo: McCallum Collection.

Opposite: *The Power of Endurance*, Cambusbarron Quarry. Climber: Murray Hamilton. Photo: Rab Anderson.

Sahara, Ratho Quarry. Climber: Duncan McCallum. Photo: Calum Fraser.

Opposite: *Naked Fun*, Burrow Head. Climber: Craig Macadam. Photo: George Macadam.

Newbridge Viaduct,
Climber: Kenny Spence.
Photo: Duncan McCallum.

the Great Quarry') in 1902. Climbed by Morrison, Newbigging and the Swiss guide Briquet, this route caused quite a stir at the time, not so much for the difficulty of the climbing as for the steep, exposed and loose nature of the rock.

The 1914-18 war left a long shadow over Scottish climbing and it was not until the 1930's that activity began to pick up again. Around this time Jimmy Hewit, Alan Horne and Archie Hendry added a series of routes to the area around the South Quarry on Salisbury Crags. Hewit's Groove, Horne's Slab and Archie's Slab all gave climbing at VS/HVS standard at a time when few cliffs in Scotland could offer any routes harder than severe. Apart from the usual problems of dubious rock and no protection these climbers now had to contend with a ban on climbing which had come into operation after the Great War, and which has undoubtedly contributed to the general lack of awareness of the historical significance of the climbing here. In 1939 Hewit wrote a guide to the Crags, unfortunately never published, but which formed the basis of the comprehensive guide of the late 40's by J.G. Parish, C.G.M. Slesser and D.H. Haworth, and also of a selective E.U.M.C. guide of around 1950.

As the 1940's approached a strong group of climbers from Edinburgh University appeared on the scene. The main activist was D.H. Haworth. Despite being a relatively obscure character nowadays he made an important contribution to Scottish climbing, with a string of classic routes throughout the mountain areas. He made many first ascents in Holyrood Park the finest of which was undoubtedly Steeplejack's Staircase, the original route in The Great Quarry at Salisbury Crags. As with many other hard routes of the day it was top-roped prior to its ascent; nevertheless it was probably the hardest route in the country at the time, and went unrepeated for nearly 15 years before Jimmy Marshall and Robin Smith made the second and third ascents. Both found the route very near their limit at the time.

In the early 50's G.F. Dutton discovered the pleasant crags on the southern flank of Traprain Law and with the Edinburgh J.M.C.S. climbed a few of the easier lines. In 1955 Robin Smith, The Marshall brothers and the 'Currie Boys' began to take an interest and soon the cliff was covered with a network of pleasant routes on good rock. Smith led Burp and Chute and Jimmy Marshall led Wobble, and Piglet by its left-hand variation. As well as these harder routes many of the classic easier routes such as Great Corner, Left Edge and M.S. Route were first climbed during this period.

The same group also explored the cliffs of Dalmahoy Hill, but unlike

Traprain the routes here were rather loose and vegetated and the cliff was quickly forgotten.

After this brief period of activity things remained quiet until new faces began to emerge in the early 60's. Dave Bathgate, Bugs McKeith, Brian Robertson and Ian Maceacheran formed the nucleus of a group of climbers that later became The Squirrels. In 1962 they discovered and developed The Hawcraig, a steep sea-cliff on the Fife coast. Maceacheran climbed Gaucho, Cranium Crack and The Beast, while Bathgate made ascents of Squirrel Slab, Diptera and, with McKeith, the High Girdle. Neil Macniven climbed Pain Pillar, still the classic route of the cliff, and Jim Brumfitt climbed Guano, which was probably the hardest of those earlier routes.

During the mid 60's climbers began to explore the more extensive sea-cliffs of the Fastcastle area. Ian Campbell had described some scrambling traverses by the Fastcastle in 1935, but the first real development was a series of routes on Fastcastle Head itself, climbed by a group of Newcastle climbers led by Gordon Davidson. That same year (1965) Dave Bathgate climbed the impressive sea stack called The Souter, by its landward face, and a year later returned with the rest of the Squirrels to climb some interesting routes in the very secluded bay to the east of the Brander. John Cleare visited the area while researching for his book 'Sea-Cliff Climbing in Britain' and added a route up the seaward face of The Souter.

Despite all this activity the climbing on this stretch of coast did not become popular with the majority of local climbers, and the area was not included in Graham Tiso's guide to 'Creag Dubh and the Eastern Outcrops', published in 1967.

After the publication of this guide only a few minor routes were added to the traditional crags, though 'Lord' John McKenzie's free ascent of Beatle Crack at Traprain was a fair achievement. It soon became obvious that Traprain and Hawcraig had little more to offer as far as new routes were concerned and development remained at a standstill, until attention turned to the many dolerite quarries dotted around the region.

In 1972 local climbers from Rosyth began to develop Rosyth Quarry, a small dusty crag just over the Forth road bridge.

Ravelrig Quarry was a better find. This was developed during 1973 by members of the MESL Mountaineering Club, with Chris Masterton in particular being responsible for many of the routes. Routes such as Headline, Beeline and Demo route were found to give good climbing on solid rock, and the cliff quickly became popular. Pete Myles and Alistair

Borthwick climbed Plumbline using a few nuts for aid, and Masterton later made a free ascent to establish one of the best routes in the area. Unfortunately in 1979 the local landowner blew up the Plumbline wall, totally destroying Plumbline and its neighbouring routes.

Around the same time members of The Jacobite M.C. began to add routes at Rosyth Quarry. Willie Jeffrey was the main activist with routes such as Waullie, Iconoclast and Inspiration, which all gave quite hard climbing.

The Jacobites also made the first inroads into Ratho Quarry – perhaps the biggest and most imposing of the local quarries. Willie Jeffrey again made some good ascents including Shear Fear, unfortunately top-roped prior to being led. This and Murray Hamilton's free ascent of Rained In at Ravelrig at about the same time were the first routes in the area to improve on the standard set by Haworth in 1946.

In 1975 members of the Edinburgh J.M.C.S. re-discovered the cliff on Dalmahoy Hill. After an extended gardening session they completed around 20 routes, most of which gave good climbing on rough rock. The only evidence of the passing of the Currie Boys some 20 years previously was a couple of rusty pitons on what is now called Resurrection.

Despite all this activity the quarries had so far only yielded rather scrappy and uninteresting routes (apart from the better climbs at Ravelrig). Climbers lost interest and once again development stood still. During the next five years, while the rest of Scotland was being shaken by an explosion of new routes and rising standards, the Edinburgh cliffs remained quiet. Combinations of Rab Anderson, Dave Brown and Murray Hamilton climbed Grinding, Wheelchair Route and Snowflake Crack at Ravelrig, and Murray Hamilton and Dave Cuthbertson added a few eliminate lines at Hawcraig, but otherwise little was achieved.

In 1980 the quiet was rudely shattered when Pete Hunter made a superb series of ascents at Ratho. Doomed Oasis covered some impressive ground but Diverticulitis and Pettifer's Wall were really fine routes, giving the hardest and best climbing in the area at the time. The following year he returned to add Sahara, Ouroborus Eliminate and Pete's Wall. In March and April 1981, unknown to local climbers, a group of Northumberland based climbers added a fine series of routes to the Brander area of Fastcastle. Kevin Howett, in particular, made some fine ascents with routes such as Blue Moves, Sea Sprite and the suicidally loose Lucky Day.

Though these events passed more or less unnoticed, local climbers began to re-assess the area and soon came to realise that there was plenty of scope for good new routes.

In March 1982 the short walls surrounding the Souter saw a sudden burst of activity. Kenny Spence was the first to spot the potential, but it was John (Spider) McKenzie who grabbed the best routes with his ascents of Fast Bleeder and Walnut. Rab Anderson, Bob Duncan, Jim Melrose, Jerry Handren and Alan Taylor got involved and in the space of a few weekends about 20 routes had been climbed. Though many of these routes are quite short they give good steep climbing in an unusual setting, and perhaps deserve to become more popular.

That summer Gordon Bisset climbed the excellent Golden Brown at Ravelrig and on the same crag Pete Hunter freed the old bolt route to give The Prowler.

At Ratho Rab Anderson led Slow Strain and in the East Bay Kenny Spence climbed a very fine and unusual route which he later named Gruel Brittania.

By now it was obvious that there really was a great deal to be done and a Gold Rush mentality began to develop. In August Spence, Hamilton, Anderson and Handren added another batch of routes to the Souter Area. The best of these was Souterrain by Spence, though Hamilton climbed a serious route up the wall to the right of Walnut to give The Porker's Wall – the first E4 in the area.

A point worth mentioning is that the routes at Fastcastle and Ratho required mammoth gardening sessions to reveal solid rock before ascents were possible. The lessons learned in the process were put to good use in the development of other areas in the future.

Spence scoured the countryside for new rock and came up with Benarty Hill. That September he climbed Cubism to give the crag its first route and at the same time cleaned off several other lines.

During the winter months Salisbury Crags are often to be found bone dry and basking in the sun. That winter the temptation of so much rock so close at hand proved too much, and after a series of night-time gardening sessions Jerry Handren added three routes to the area around Steeplejack's Staircase. This effort proved worthwhile and, despite the attentions of the Park Police, these routes have since become very popular.

1983 was a bumper year for the Edinburgh outcrops. Again it was Kenny Spence who led the field. In early April he led Wally 1 at Ratho and with Rab Anderson began to snatch up the remaining lines. Anderson led Welcome to the Cruise, Ane Ledge and Rebel without

Claws, but it was Spence who took the best lines with his ascents of Wallies 2 and 3, Artho and the superb 'This Septic Heil' – the hardest route in the quarry. The only climbers to intrude on this monopoly were Jim Melrose with Time's Last Gift, Jerry Handren with the Lone Groover and Gerry Rooney with Beanpud. Pete Hunter's routes at last got the popularity they deserved and almost all the new routes saw several repeat ascents. Thus in the space of a few months Ratho had become one of the best and most popular crags in the area.

Spence returned to Benarty Hill to climb the lines which he had cleaned the previous year. Dolly Parton followed a horrific wide crack, not dissimilar in appearance to the great lady's cleavage. The two other routes-Ram and A Fist Job — were both led by John McKenzie.

That summer, Spence tackled the tremendous north side of The Souter, a line which had been looked at by several other notables. The resulting route — Squid Vicious — turned out to be one of the best in the area, giving a very strenuous and serious climb.

Towards the end of the summer the pace of development began to slow down a little. During work for the guide Bruce Kerr led two old top-rope problems at Ravelrig to give Men at Work and Overkill. Jerry Handren climbed Prime Cut to give Queensferry Quarry its first route and in October added three more routes at Salisbury Crags to give Transatlantic Trip, Blackdance and After the Axe.

During the autumn yet another new crag was developed. This time it was Rab Anderson and Duncan McCallum who cleaned and climbed the first routes at Lennie Quarry. Though only six miles from the centre of Edinburgh, an evil pool at the base of the main wall had discouraged many would-be explorers; nevertheless routes such as Dive in Movie, Think Sink and Dunker's Delight gave good climbing in an exciting position.

By 1984 activity seemed to have slowed down as climbers began to explore other areas, particularly the newly developing Stirling outcrops. Perhaps the most notable event was the draining of Lennie Quarry, which immediately became very popular. New routes soon followed with Duncan McCallum leading Staying Alive and Chris Dale The Creature from the Black Lagoon. Later in the year Rab Anderson led White Tide and Murray Hamilton led Hard Contract, a very fine climb which had stopped several strong attempts and been the scene of at least one spectacular failure. In early 1985 Lennie received another batch of new routes, but the most important event was undoubtedly John McKenzie's superb lead of Staying Alive without using the two bolts that McCallum had placed for protection.

1985 – this was a very poor summer and few routes were added. At Lennie Quarry Murray Hamilton added Tar McCallum, a hard layback problem, while at Ratho Quarry the wall left of Godzilla finally received an ascent by Duncan McCallum. resulting in The Blob.

The bouldering areas saw a large proportion of the climbing activity in the east in 1985, the indefatigable Ken Spence being responsible for yet another significant addition with the cleaning of the Lennie bouldering wall.

BENARTY HILL   Map: Sheet 58, G.R. 155 980

INTRODUCTION

Benarty Hill lies on the south side of Loch Leven in Fife. There are several crags, all of which lie along the north rim of the hill. The routes listed are on the largest cliff, which lies just beneath the summit.

The cliff is composed of dolerite and lies at an altitude of 300m. It can be rather cold and slow to dry, but when in condition it gives some fine crack and groove climbing.

ACCESS

The most convenient approach is from the B9097 which runs along the north side of Benarty Hill. Follow this road until opposite the crag, where it is possible to park on the verge. From here walk along the edge of fields and up the hillside to the rocks. The climbs are described from left to right.

1   A Fist Job   18m   E1   5c   ★★
Near the centre of the cliff there is a bay with a chimney on the right and an obvious crack on the left.

Enter the crack from the right and climb it to a roof. Pull over the roof and layback to the top.

2   Dolly Parton   15m   E3   6a   ★
To the right of the bay containing A Fist Job there is a rock pillar with a wide crack on either side.

Climb the left-hand crack. To descend, abseil from the top of the pillar.

3   Cubism   18m   E3   5c   ★
To the right of Dolly Parton is a long narrow, square-cut buttress. This is the line of the route, which provides good but slightly contrived climbing. Start 4m up, on the left-hand side of the buttress.

Climb a crack to a ledge on the right side of the buttress. Step left and go up to a horizontal break. Climb up and right to a ledge then follow a crack until it is possible to step left on to the centre of the buttress. Climb up the right-hand side of the buttress (crux) to the top.

4   Ram   12m   E4   6a   ★
Towards the right hand side of the crag is a short steep wall. Climb up rough ground to the foot of the wall. Climb a crack on the right for 6m to reach an undercut flake. Traverse left to a thin crack which is climbed until it is possible to step right and climb to the top of the wall. Sustained.

THE HAWCRAIG

INTRODUCTION

The Hawcraig is a steep, south-facing sea-cliff on the north coast of the Firth of Forth. It provides a good selection of middle grade climbs in a warm and sunny situation, and as a result the cliff is quite popular.

The rock is a form of quartz dolerite. At the base of the cliff it is very sound and provides tremendous friction, but towards the top it becomes looser, especially between routes 19 and 22.

At high tide it becomes a true sea-cliff which, while presenting problems of access, definitely adds to the character of many of the climbs. At the top of the cliff there are several in situ bolts which provide belays and abseil points.

ACCESS

By car go over The Forth Road Bridge and follow the A92 to Aberdour. Once in Aberdour take a turn off signposted to Silver Sands; this is opposite the Drift Inn. This road leads to a large carpark after 400m. Several paths lead from here to the cliff top.

A fast and regular train service runs between Edinburgh and Aberdour.

At low tide there are three ways of reaching the base of the cliff. The best is probably to go to the east end of the cliff (left facing out) where a short scramble leads down into the eastern recess. Secondly it is possible to descend moderate rock which lies above the boundary between the high water mark and the hotel grounds. Thirdly, a path may be followed for several hundred yards westwards, along the cliff top, eventually leading down to the coast. The coast is then followed back to the rocks.

At high tide routes can be gained by abseiling from the nearest bolt. An exciting alternative is to traverse in to the chosen route — not for those of a nervous disposition!. The climbs are described from left to right facing the cliff. The obvious corner which lies within the hotel grounds is Cut Glass Corner (severe). The arête just to its left is Crystal Arête (E2 5b) and further left again are Porcelain (E1 5a) and Crockery (MVS 4c). Doo'Cot Wall (V. Diff) climbs the smooth wall a few m.right of Cut Glass Corner. All these routes are worthwhile, but are perhaps best avoided as the hotel owners take a rather dim view of climbing.

The next routes lie in an obvious recess at the western end of the cliff: the rocks above the recess are cut by a vague terrace.

1   Fish Head Arête   20m   Very Difficult
This route climbs the left arête of the slab to the left of the recess.
   Follow the arête to a tree stump belay at 8m, then continue up the obvious crack behind, trending right at the top.

2   Fish Head Wall   8m   Very Difficult
Start 2m right of the previous route. Climb the wall trending up and left to join the arête. Finish on the terrace at 8m.

3   Ugh!   8m   Hard Severe
Climb straight up the obvious crack 2m right of Fish Head Wall.

4   Eech!   8m   Very Severe   4c
At the back of the recess there is a corner with a quartz-filled crack. Climb this corner until forced to traverse left under the overhangs, joining Ugh! to finish.

5   Sacrilege   8m   Very Severe   5a
This is an eliminate up the bulge between Ugh and Eech to finish up the corner right of Eech!.

6   Squirrel Slab   12m   Very Severe   5a   ★
This route starts on the terrace, it provides a useful continuation to Sacrilege and is a very good route in its own right. Start just right of the tree stump belay of Fish Head Arête, below a slab with 'Ken' scratched on it.
   Climb the slab and surmount the bulge direct to gain easier ground.

7   Weasel Wall   8m   E1   5b
Just right of Squirrel Slab there is a blunt rib, right again is a smooth wall. Gain this wall from the right and follow it direct.
   NOTE: no repeat ascents are known of and at least one party has apparently failed to find a line here at this grade.

8   Cranium Crack   20m   Very Severe   4c   ★
This route starts just right Eech and climbs the obvious parallel fault at the back of the recess. Climb a crack to gain the fault which is followed to the terrace. Continue up a crack and corner, with a white left wall, to the top.

9   Conquistador Crack   7m   Very Severe   5a   ★
The overhanging crack in the right wall of the recess. Short and sharp.

10   The Groper   7m   Very Severe   5a
The vertical arête defining the right wall of the recess. It is climbed
without using the crack on the right. A harder finish is to overcome the
capstone on the left without using the holds common to Stomach-
Ache.

11   Stomach-Ache   7m   Severe
Climb the right-hand side of the arête left to join the last 2m of The
Groper.

12   The Beast   7m   Hard Severe   4c   ★
The obvious crack just right of Stomach-Ache gives a short but
awkward struggle.

13   Gismo   20m   Very Severe   4c
Start just right of The Beast below an obvious chimney topped by a
crack. Climb the chimney and move right to avoid the crack, then up to
the right-hand end of the terrace. Finish up an obvious groove just right
of the final groove of Cranium Crack.
Variation: The crack above the chimney may be climbed direct (HVS
5a).

14   Pain Pillar   20m   Very Severe   4c   ★★★
A local classic, giving exposed and interesting climbing throughout.
Start just right of Gismo and climb directly up the obvious pillar.

15   Gaucho   20m   Hard Very Severe   5a   ★★
A good climb up the deep groove to the right of Pain Pillar. Climb the
groove to a ledge on the right. The groove above contains a large block.
Continue up a small corner to the right of the main groove (pr) then
move back left to gain the main groove above the block. Finish straight
up the crack and bulge above.
Variation: From the ledge it is possible to move left into the main
groove. Continue up the groove pulling directly over the block to join the
original route (HVS 5a).

16   Rebel's Groove   20m   Very Severe   4c
Start 4m right of Gaucho. Climb an obvious twisting groove to a ledge,
Step left and continue up the steep cracked wall above.

17   Saki   20m   Very Severe   4c   ★
Start 3m right of Rebel's Groove. Climb the square-cut groove to a
ledge at 10m (poor protection). Continue up the black wall above and
finish by laybacking a flake on the left.

  To the right of Saki there is large, flat-topped flake at the base of the
cliff. At high tide this provides a useful starting point for all the routes on
this part of the cliff.

18   Slack Alice   20m   Severe
This is the obvious groove starting from the left side of the flake.

19   Brutus   20m   Hard Severe
From the top of the flake, climb a rib and the steep wall above.

20   Torment   20m   Severe
From the right-hand end of the top of the flake, climb by loose ribs to a
wall which is climbed straight to the top.

21   The Dwarf   20m   Hard Very Severe   5a
2m right of Torment are two obvious square-cut corners which are
climbed past an obvious small nose to the top.

22   Guano   20m   Hard very Severe   5a   ★★
An excellent sustained route. Start 5m left of the chimney at an obvious
overhung curving groove.
    Climb the groove to a pr. at 10m. Move right, then up and continue up
the corner to a bush. Straight up the wall above to finish.
Variation: From just under the peg, step left and continue boldly up the
wall above (E2 5b).

23   Ganja   20m   Mild Severe
Follow the vague groove midway between Guano and the chimney, to
join the latter two thirds of the way up.

24   The Chimney   20m   Very Difficult
Climb the obvious deep cleft in the centre of the cliff.

25   The Chimney Arête   20m   Very Difficult
The right-hand edge of the chimney is climbed on poor rock.

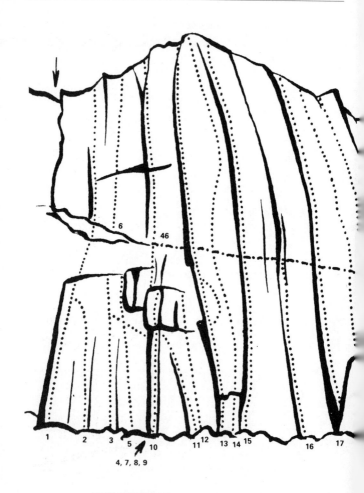

THE HAWCRAIG

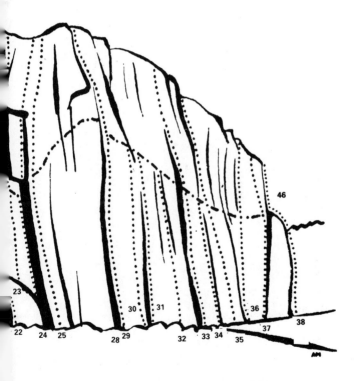

26   Sublimation   20m   Hard Very Severe   5a   ★
Low in the grade but a worthwhile exposed route.
   After a difficult start, follow the crack-line just right of Chimney Arête
to a groove splitting the obvious nose of rock. Either climb this groove
directly or finish more easily on the right.

27   The Arête   20m   E1   5b
This is the obvious arête right of Sublimation, and overlooking the Lilly.
It is climbed by a series of shallow grooves and eventually joins the
easier finish of Asinine.

28   The Lilly   18m   Severe   ★★
An interesting and unusual climb. Climb the obvious right-facing groove
6m right of the chimney. At the overhang move right and finish up an
easier groove.

29   Gunga Din   18m   Severe
Climb a groove 5m right of the Lilly, eventually joining that climb near
the top.

30   Crusader   18m   Hard Severe
Follow the rib between Gunga Din and Saracen, finishing as for The
Lilly.

31   Saracen   18m   Very Severe   4c
The obvious rusty groove is climbed steeply to finish as far the last
three routes.

32   Toerag's Wall   15m   Severe   ★
Left of the deep overhung recess is an obvious wall which is gained
from the right. Start below the recess.
   Climb the recess for a few m. Then step left on to the wall. Go
straight up to a balcony and finish easily on the left.
Variation: A direct start is possible (VS 4c).

33   Diptera   15m   Very Severe   4c
Climb the crack in the right corner of the deep overhung recess, pulling
over the overhang directly to gain a balcony. Finish up a small loose
groove above.

34   Escalator   15m   Very Difficult

Climb the arête forming the right wall of the recess up to the right end of the balcony and finish on the right up a small loose groove.

35 Tink 15m · Very Difficult
Follow the obvious left-slanting line to the right of Escalator, with an awkward mantleshelf at 8m. Finish on scrappy rock.

36 Halleluja Wall 15m Hard Severe   ★
Climb a wall and crack 4m right of Tink to move boldly right into a further groove finishing by gorse ledges. Some poor rock but worthwhile.

37 The Whang 12m Very Difficult   ★
A pleasant route. Climb an obvious crack on the left of a large obvious flake, moving left to finish.

38 Flake and Wall 12m Severe   ★
Climb up the face of the obvious flake on good holds and continue up the crack in the wall above.

To the right of Flake and Wall the cliff goes back into the eastern recess — a small cove at the eastern end of the cliff.

39 Shadow Corner 12m Severe
The obvious three-step corner to the right of the flake.

40 Destiny Groove 12m Hard Severe   ★
Follow the left-slanting groove to finish at the top of Shadow Corner.

41 Urmi 12m Mild Very Severe 4c   ★
Between Destiny Groove and Maureen is a crack starting halfway up a wall. Gain the crack directly and follow it to the top.

42 Maureen 12m Severe
Climb directly up the groove 5m right of Shadow Corner.

43 Welly Wall 12m Very Difficult
Follow large sloping shelves and a corner. Awkward to start.

44 Eureka 10m Very Severe 5a   ★
Strenuous but well protected. 3m from the end of the cliff is a right-facing corner. Climb the corner to an overhang. Surmount this strenuously and continue to the top.

45   Termination   10m   Very Severe   4c
A rather pointless climb. Climb the crack at the extreme right-hand end of the cliff without using the recess on the right. The top is loose.

46   The High Girdle   80m   Very Severe   ★
Start on the vague terrace at the left-hand end of the cliff, ie. above Fish Head Wall etc.

1.   4b   10m   Traverse round Pain Pillar to a small ledge on Gaucho.

2.   4b   20m   Follow the ledge system down and right belaying just before the chimney.

3.   5a   20m   Move across the chimney and into Asinine. Follow this then make an exposed step out right (crux) moving across to join The Lilly. Continue to a belay on the balcony.

4.   4b   30m   Continue at half height moving slightly down to the top of the flake on Flake and Wall. Up this to finish.
   A low level girdle also gives interesting sport-especially at high tide.

Map: Sheet 65, G.R. 134 804

NORTH QUEENSFERRY QUARRY 1

INTRODUCTION

This is the large water-filled bowl on the north coast of the Firth of Forth, almost directly underneath the Forth Rail Bridge. The quarry only contains one route at present and though access can be rather awkward scope exists for good new routes at all grades.

ACCESS

The Quarry is obvious from North Queensferry Village. The following route is best approached by abseil, from a telegraph pole just above the finish. To reach the telegraph pole it is best to walk along the perimeter wall of the coastguard station above the crag.

1   Prime Cut   22m   E3   5c   ★
A good route with some fine jamming and laybacking.
   Climb the overhanging corner crack in the south east corner of the quarry.

NORTH QUEENSFERRY QUARRY 2

LOCATION
East of Forth Rail Bridge & south of Carlingnose Housing Estate.

ACCESS
Park in the vicinity of the Roxburgh Hotel, walk uphill turning right onto an unmetalled road, continue under Forth Rail Bridge rising to a level area with a brick built shelter on left. Turn left just past this shelter and follow a track into the quarry. The quarry is overgrown and access is probably best starting at right hand side where an ill-defined path follows the quarry wall. The first area of good rock encountered contains The Boat, situated in a tree shaded bay, the walls and corners to its left being ripe for development. Following the quarry wall leftwards another tree shaded area is reached, this contains the magnificent corner of Scharnhorst as its centre piece. No further climbs are recorded to date. Stakes are in place above the two routes.

The Boat   12m   E1   5b
This is the first climb encountered, on the extreme right of the quarry. Climb the shallow, impending, left-facing corner crack with ledge at three quarters height. Strenuous.

Scharnhorst   21m   E1   5b
About 50 yards left of The Boat, shrouded by trees, stands a mighty corner. Follow the corner throughout.

Map: Sheet 65, G.R. 168 741

LENNIE QUARRY

INTRODUCTION

This fine quarry contains a worthwhile selection of routes in the upper grades. It is warm, sheltered and very quick to dry. When the climbing here was first developed the bottom 4 metres of the cliff were submerged by water. Since then, however, the pool has been drained, making access to the climbs much easier. It is hoped that this situation will continue.

ACCESS

The quarry lies in the grounds of Lennie golf course, not far from Turnhouse Airport. Follow the A8 out of Edinburgh as far as the Maybury roundabout. Take the road signposted to R.A.F. Turnhouse and follow it until the golf course clubhouse appears on the right. This is 15 minutes walk from the roundabout. Just beyond the clubhouse a dirt track appears on the right. This leads into the quarry after a 5 minute stroll. Several buses run from the city centre to The Maybury roundabout. As the quarry bowl is entered a long steep wall appears on the left. So far, all but one of the routes lie on this wall. They are described from left to right.

At the extreme left end of the wall there is a short vertical crack, just to the right of a dirty corner.

1   White Tide   18m   E2   5c   ★
Climb the wall to gain the crack. Up this to the top.

2   Tar McCallum   18m   E4   6b   ★★
Start 5m right of White Tide below a thin flake crack in an arête. Climb up a vague crack to gain the flake crack, and follow this to its end. Move left and finish more easily.

To the right of Tar McCallum is an obvious rectangular wall, below and slightly to the right of a sign on the perimeter fence.

3   Dive-in Movie   18m   E2   5b   ★★
A bold and open climb. Start by scrambling up to a ledge below the centre of the wall.

Climb a short crack moving leftwards. At its top move up and right to a small ledge then straight up to a large ledge above. Finish up the groove on the left.

4   Suspense Account   24m   E3   6a
Climbs the groove just left of Splashist.
   Move up to the groove and climb it over a bulge onto a hanging slab (pr). Move across left and continue up to ledges. Traverse left and climb the corner to the top.

5   Splashist   25m   Hard Very Severe   5a
This route climbs the right-slanting crack well to the right of Dive-in Movie. Start in the niche at the base of this crack.
   Climb the crack above the niche, step right and follow the crack to the top of a pinnacle. Step right and finish up a groove.

6   Aquaplay   25m   E3   6a   ★
The open groove to the right of Splashist.
Climb the groove (pr) to a small overhang, pull over this and continue up the groove to a large ledge on the left. Finish up a steep groove on the right.

   To the right of the previous route is a steep wall split by a band of overhangs just below half height. The next route climbs the impressive left arête of this wall.

7   Staying Alive   25m   E6   6a   ★ ★
A very bold and serious route.
Climb the arête for 4m, then up to overhangs to reach a poor pr. Move up and left to a large hold, get established on this and continue up a line of holds to the top.

8   The Creature from The Black Lagoon   25m   E4   5c
A rather loose and dangerous climb.
Follow Upside Drown up the thin crack until it is possible to move left round the arête on big holds. Climb the groove above past 2 pr to a ledge below the final groove. Climb this (crux) to the top.

   Almost in the centre of the cliff is a large open corner with a sapling at its base.

LENNIE QUARRY

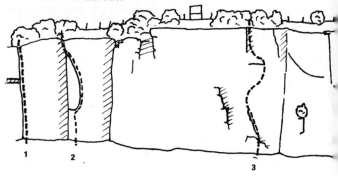

9 Upside Drown 24m E3 5c
This route climbs the wall to the left of the sapling, finishing up an open groove.

From the sapling move left on to a large flake and climb the crack above until a line of holds lead up and right into the open groove. Finish up the groove.

10 Dunker's Delight 22m E4 6a   ★★
A strenuous and sustained pitch up the wall to the right of the sapling. Step right onto the wall and climb to 2 pr. Gain the flake on the left and follow it to just below its top where moves up and right lead to better holds. Climb straight up to a large thread, then step right into an easier groove which is climbed to finish.

Well to the right of Dunker's Delight is a narrow groove with a very smooth wall to its right.

11 Rampo 24m E3 6a
Climb the thin crack in the wall left of Phase One. It is advisable to leave a rope in-situ for the loose upper part of the route which has not been cleaned.

12 Phase 1 25m E3 6a
Climb the narrow groove with difficulty until a ledge appears on the

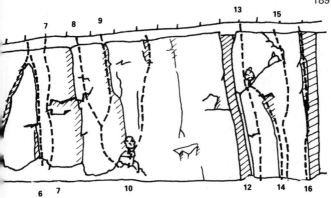

right. The upper half of the groove is easier, but rather loose. The second pitch of Hard Contract is a better alternative.

13 Hard Contract 25m E5 6b 5b   ★★★
The smooth wall to the right of Phase 1 is split by a hairline crack.

1. 15m Climb the crack directly, belaying beside a small tree. A superb pitch, very sustained and strenuous.

2. 10m Move left and climb the obvious cleaned crack.

14 Sunk and Disorderly 25m E3 6a   ★
To the right of Hard Contract is an open groove.
Climb the groove direct into the base of the pod, and climb this to gain a line of holds leading left to a small tree. Finish up Hard Contract.

15 Saturation Point 25m E4 6a
Climbs the wall between Think Sink and Sunk and Disorderly.
   Gain and climb the slim groove just right of Sunk and Disorderly. Make a few moves up a thin crack, and then move right (runner in middle of wall) to reach some holds. Move up and follow easy ground leftwards to finish.
   The original line of Sunk and Disorderly followed the thin groove of Saturation Point, to step left into the base of the pod (E2 5b, runners in Sunk and Disorderly). The direct line became possible after the water level was lowered.

16 Think Sink   25m   E3   6a   ★★
To the right of Sunk and Disorderly there is an obvious cracked arête.
This provides an excellent sustained climb.
  Climb the crack to gain the obvious niche. Climb out of the niche and
continue up the crack until it is possible to pull left on to a ledge on the
arête. Climb the left-hand side of the arête then move back round to
finish on the right.

  The wall opposite that on which all the above routes lie has only one
route on it at the time of writing.

17 First Affair   12m   E2   5b
Climbs the crack in the obvious corner at the right-hand side of the wall.
The finish is dirty and loose.

  Just to the right of the above route a long and very good bouldering
wall has been cleaned. It catches the evening sun.

RATHO QUARRY

INTRODUCTION

This large, abandoned quarry bowl faces south across the Forth and Clyde canal. The sunny, sheltered location and the quick drying nature of the rock make it possible to climb all year round. The rock is dolerite, fairly sound on most of the routes though some of the finishes require care.

Recent development has left Ratho with one of the largest concentrations of hard climbs in the South of Scotland – some of which rank with the best described in this guide.

ACCESS

Ratho Quarry lies on the north bank of the Forth and Clyde canal, about 1¼ km west of Ratho Bridge, Ratho village can be approached from either the A71 or A8. Cars are best left at the large carpark beside the Bridge Inn. From here cross the bridge and follow the wet path on the north bank; after 1¼ km on a small path leads off rightwards into the trees. Follow this path which soon leads into the quarry bowl.

There is a regular bus service between Ratho and St.Andrews Square bus station in Edinburgh. The routes are described from left to right.

The West Wall

This is the long steep wall which appears on the left as the quarry is entered. Towards the left-hand side is a huge open corner, the line of Godzilla. To the right of Godzilla the wall becomes more broken, until, towards the centre, it rears up into a series of steep grooves and arêtes before finishing in a very impressive smooth wall on the right.

1 Terminal Street 11m Very Severe 4c
The stepped groove at the left-hand side of the west wall.

2 Terminal Case 13m HVS 5a
Start 4m right of Terminal Street below a shallow groove.
Climb the shallow groove then traverse up and left to finish as far Terminal Street.

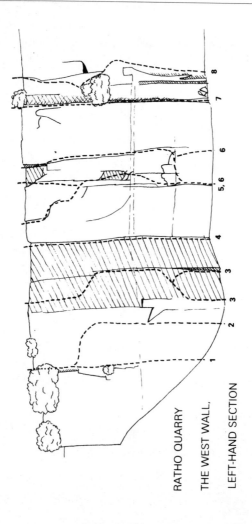

RATHO QUARRY

THE WEST WALL.

LEFT-HAND SECTION

3   The Blob   20m   E4   6a   ★
Climb the wall left of Godzilla, some suspect rock.
   The original route started up the left arête, to gain the groove. It is
also possible to reach this direct. Move up the groove into the middle of
the wall (good protection here). Make hard moves up and left until it is
possible to mantleshelf on to the top.

4   Godzilla   16m   E2   5b   ★
Climb the big open corner to a dirty finish.

5   Sahara   18m   E3   6a   ★★
After a rather nasty start this route gives some fine steep climbing.
Start 3m right of Godzilla below an obvious loose flake.
   Climb a thin crack, past the loose flake (pr) until it is possible to pull up
and right into a niche. Pull out of the niche (pr) and finish up the wall
above.

6   Doomed Oasis   18m   E2   5c   ★
This route starts as far Sahara but finishes up the right-hand crack in the
upper wall.
   As for Sahara to a standing position as the loose flake. Pull up and
right to the base of the crack. Up this to finish (2 pr).
   A direct start has apparently been climbed, going straight up to the
base of the crack (no grade available).

7   Scotty Arête   18m   Severe
The chossy arête to the right of Doomed Oasis.

8   Spiny Norman   18m   Severe
The even chossier wall right of Scotty Arête, moving left at the top to
finish as for that route.

9   Alan's Groove   18m   HVS   5a
To right of Spiny Norman is a long twisting groove which starts from a
tree at 5m.
   Gain the tree and finish up the twisting groove.

   To the right of Alan's Groove the wall continues as a series of loose
grooves and arêtes. Further along, almost in the centre of the west
wall, there is a large open groove starting from a platform 6m above the
quarry floor.

RATHO QUARRY

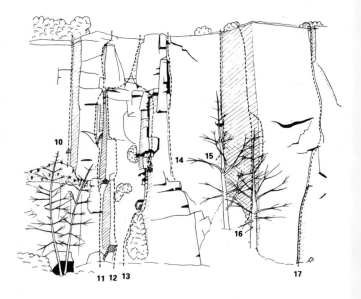

THE WEST WALL,   RIGHT-HAND SECTION

10   Diverticulitis   16m   E3   6a   ★★★
The open groove gives a superb sustained climb.
The groove is climbed direct except for a few moves on the left wall
after the ledge at 12m (pr at 7m).
   A variation has been climbed at E3/4 6b, climbing Diverticulitis to the
peg and traversing right to finish up the following route.

11   Welcome to the Cruise   25m   E2   5b   ★
Start down and right of Diverticulitis below a long series of grooves.
   Climb the grooves direct, moving left into the final steep corner
which provides the crux.

12   Ane Ledge   25m   E3   5c   ★
Start just right of the previous route below a sharp arête ending 16m up
the cliff. Climb the arête and a thin crack on its right to a small ledge.
Step left and layback boldly up the arête to a larger ledge. From here it is
possible to move left and finish up Welcome to the Cruise. An easier
but looser alternative is to move right and finish up Shoskred.

13   Shoskred   21m   HVS   5a
The long groove just right of Ane Ledge.

   To the right of Shoskred the West Wall goes back into a deep
vegetated corner before terminating in a very impressive wall. The next
two routes are reached by scrambling up the trees and blocks at the
back of the corner.

14   Once Upon a Flake Crack   14m   HVS   5a
The wide crack to the left of the corner, gained direct.

15   Quick Pull   12m   HVS   5a
The deep corner is climbed direct.

16   Slow Strain   22m   E2   6a
This route follows a line of thin cracks in the arête right of Quick Pull.
Start 4m upon the left hand side of the arête at a ledge.
   Climb the arête then move left into a thin crack. Up this (crux) to a
ledge. Climb the final wall trending slightly leftwards.
Variation: It is possible to avoid the crux by moving round the arête and
climbing a thin crack to gain the ledge. Easier and better than the
original way (E2 5b).

17   Pettifer's Wall   25m   E4   6a   ★★
A fine serious route up the impressive wall right of Slow Strain.
    Climb the black flake/groove to a small overhang (pr), move
rightwards over this and continue up a shallow groove to the top.

    Pettifer's Wall is the last route on the west wall, to its right is an area
of short loose walls and grass ledges, right again is a steep buttress
with an impressive left arête.

18   Sedge Warbler   22m   E2   5b   ★
Scramble up the left-hand side of the arête until it is possible to pull
round the right to gain a ramp, up this and the cracks above to a large
ledge. Up the cracked wall above to finish.

19   Time's Last Gift   25m   E2   5c   ★
Start below an obvious groove to the right of Sedge Warbler.
    Climb the groove, exiting right on to a ledge. Move on to a higher
ledge and continue up the groove on the left to a ledge. Finish up the
steep crack in the final wall.

The Back Wall

This is the long, rather featureless wall at the back of the quarry. The
left-hand side consists of a steep wall, split by two long flake cracks and
ending in a sharp arête. To the right of the arête is a short smooth corner
beyond which the wall continues as a series of short buttress and
corners lying just below the quarry rim.
    At the left-hand end of the back wall there is a short grey wall with a
smooth corner on the right.

20   Up the Creek   9m   E1   5b
The wide broken crack in the left-hand side of the wall.

21   Pete's Wall   9m   E1   5b
Climb to the foot of the smooth corner on the right-hand side of the
wall. Step left and make an awkward move on to a foothold. Climb the
small corner and wall above to the top.

22   Artho   10m   E4   6a   ★
This route climbs the smooth corner above the start of Pete's wall,
giving a short but action-packed climb.
    Follow Pete's Wall to an obvious cracked block. Traverse right into
the corner and layback up this to finish.

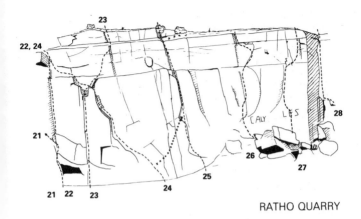

RATHO QUARRY

The Back Wall. Left-hand section

23   Ouroborus Eliminate   21m   E3   5c
Start a few m right of Artho.

Climb a line of thin cracks to a small ledge. [From here it is possible to finish easily up Ouroborus on the left, making the overall grade E2 5c]. Continue up a short ramp on the right (pr) and climb the wall above, trending rightwards to the arête. Finish up a groove on the right. Very necky in the upper section.

24   Ouroborus   30m   HVS   5a   *
The left-hand flake crack. Start 9m right of Artho.

Follow the flake to its end and continue to the top over grass and loose edges.

25   Shear Fear   21m   E2   5c   **
The right-hand flake crack.

Variation: The previous two routes can be connected by climbing the first 3m of Outoborus then moving right and up the wall to join Shear Fear [5b, xxx on diagram].

The following two routes lie on the wall between Shear Fear and the sharp arête on the right. Both give strenuous and sustained climbing protected mainly by numerous small wires.

26   Wally 3   16m   E3   6a   ★
Start 5m left of the arête below a shallow groove.
   Climb some loose flakes to reach the groove which is climbed exiting right at the top. Traverse left to a small corner. Up this to finish.

27   Wally 2   16m   E3   5c   ★
Not quite as fearsome as its neighbour but still a serious lead. Start just left of the arête.
   Climb the wall moving left to a shallow groove. Up this to a large hold then move right to finish up the wall just left of the arête.

28   Cornered   9m   E1   5c
The smooth, short corner in the centre of the back wall. Pr at 2m.

   Well to the right of Cornered there is an obvious pod-shaped groove. The following two routes take lines up the wall left of this.

29   Fairy Feat   12m   Very Severe   4c
Start 6m left of the pod-shaped groove. Follow a line of left-slanting flakes to the top.

30   Mon   12m   Very Severe   4c
Start just right of Fairy Feat and climb straight up the wall on good holds.

31   Beanpud   12m   E1   5b   ★★
The pod-shaped groove.

32   Rock-a-Boogie   12m   Very Severe   4b
Start just right of Beanpud. Climb the groove passing the block on the left.

33   Rebel Without Claws   12m   E2   5c   ★
A good short route which climbs the ramp just right of Rock-a-Boogie. Gain the ramp and climb it using its right edge.

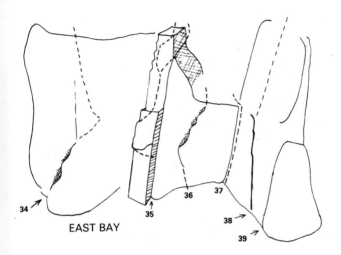

EAST BAY

The East Bay

This is the small tree-filled in the east corner of the quarry. All the routes give interesting climbing an excellent rock.

34 This Septic Heil 22m E5 6b ★★★
The overhanging wall on the left-hand side of the bay. A stunning problem. Gain a series of steps which are followed up and right to a resting place (2 pr). Hand traverse right, move up, then continue up the wall to a ledge (pr on ledge). Continue up loose rock on the right to the top.

35 Gruel Brittania 20m E3 6a ★★
This route takes a line up the sharp arête to the right of This Septic Heil. Climb a thin crack just right of the arête until it is possible to move left on to a ledge. Step up, then move right to regain the crack and follow this to a flat hold. From here it is possible to continue up the crack or the arête on the left.

36   Jumping Jack Splat   10m   E3   6a
Gain the stepped groove in the wall right of Gruel Brittania (pr) and
follow it to a large ledge. Move left to finish as for Gruel Brittania.

37   The Lone Groover   10m   E3   6a   ★
This route climbs the clean-cut groove at the back of the bay. It gives a
very sustained and technical climb.

38   Wally 1   20m   E3   6a   ★★
Low in the grade but with some fine technical climbing. Start 2m right
of the Lone Groover.
    Climb a thin flake to a small ledge then continue up the cracked wall
above.

39   Blue Rinse   20m   E1   5b   ★
Climb the broken groove just right of Wally and continue up the steep
flake crack to the top.

RATHO — NO 2 QUARRY

This small quarry lies about 100 yards to the north of Ratho Quarry in
amongst the gorse bushes just before some woods. A small pond lies
at its foot but ledges allow access to the routes. The quarry catches the
evening sun. There is a good rock platform at the top of the routes.

40   Right Under   10m   E3   6a
Climbs the obvious thin cleaned crack. Belay on a ledge immediately
before that from which the route starts. A little gem.

41   Left Over   10m   E3   6a
Climbs the cleaned corner left of Right Under, belay at the foot of that
route.

Map: Sheet 65, G.R. 136 671

DALMAHOY HILL

INTRODUCTION

The north side of Dalmahoy Hill contains quite a lot of rock, most of which is rather broken and vegetated. The following routes are on the largest and most continuous of these outcrops which lies towards the east end of the hillside.

The rock is columnar in nature, giving rise to a uniform series of grooves and ribs which can make identification of particular routes quite difficult. The cliff faces north and can be rather green and greasy during periods of wet weather, but in dry conditions it provides some pleasant slabby climbing on very rough dolerite.

ACCESS

Take the A71 past Dalmahoy Country Club until you reach a left turn signposted to Balerno. Take this to a T-junction, turn right and go over a railway bridge to a parking place beside a field next to Dalmahoy hill. Buses run along the A71, to and from Edinburgh. The climbs are described from left to right.

1 The Arête 7m Difficult
The short arête at the extreme left-hand end of the crag.

2 Professor Groove 7m Mild Severe
The groove in the slab right of the Arête.

3 The Corner 8m Severe
The corner right of Professor Groove.

4 Ivy Tower 12m Severe
The rib right of The Corner.

5 Lightning Groove 15m Very Severe 4a   ★
The first long groove on the left-hand side of the crag.
   Climb the groove through an overlap, finishing up the final groove on the arête on its right.

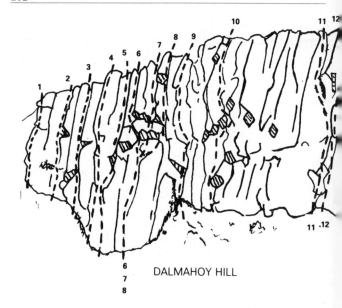

DALMAHOY HILL

6 Munich Climb 15m Severe ★
The obvious corner right of Lightning Groove.
　Go up a broken groove to below diamond-shaped overlaps, move left and climb a corner to the top.

7 Grass Widows 15m Hard Very Severe 5a ★★
A short technical problem which climbs the groove splitting the double overlaps to the right of Munich Climb.
　Follow Munich Climb to the overlap then gain the slabby groove above. Up this to finish.

8 Curving Groove 15m Very Severe 4c
Follow Munich Climb to the overlaps, but move right round the bulges. Finish up the rib on the left.

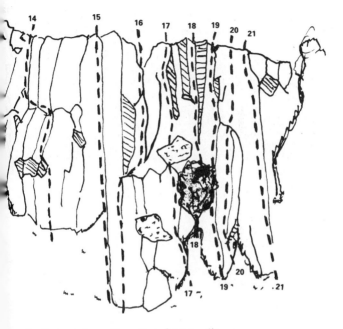

9 Resurrection 15m Very Severe 4b
Start at the next groove to the right of Munich Climb.
   Up the dirty groove to a wall. Climb this into an upper slabby groove,
then move left to small ledges. Finish up the groove above.

   To the right of Resurrection the cliff becomes shorter and steeper. So
far this section of cliff is ungardened and there is a smaller
concentration of routes here than at either end of the cliff.

10 Frustration 17m Very Severe 4c   ★★
Start 10m right of Resurrection, where some slabby ribs are capped by
a steep overlap.
   Climb ribs diagonally leftwards to reach a corner. Up this until forced
out right on to a large ledge. Climb the cracked groove on the left to the
top.

Some way right of Frustration a small Rowan can be seen on the upper face. The next route takes a line just left of the tree.

11 Triad 15m Very severe 4c
Start in an overhung niche just left of the obvious rib of Roots. .
Climb the overhang to a slab and surmount a further wall to a small ledge. Continue in the groove to the top.

12 Roots 25m Very Difficult
This route starts at a rib in the centre of the crag, where the upper slabs are at their steepest.
Climb the rib and the broken wall above up a twisting groove to finish up a short slab.

13 Insertion 25m Very Severe 4b
Just right of Roots are a series of slabs leading to a wall with a downward pointed flake.
Climb slabs to the base of the wall. Climb the wall to footholds on the flake. Move diagonally left to join Roots just above the Rowan tree.

14 Pop-it 15m Hard Very Severe 5a
This route climbs through the overlap to the left of Jack of Hearts. Scramble up slabby grooves to a steep wall. Gain the upper groove with difficulty, and so to the top.

15 Jack of Hearts 25m Very Severe 4c ★
This route climbs the prominent long central groove in the lower slabs. Climb the groove to double walls. Surmount these walls directly, then continue up the slab above.
Variation: Slant left after the first wall and climb diagonally right to the upper slab.

16 Fine Escape 23m Severe ★
The groove immediately right of Jack of Hearts.
Climb to an overhang and walk right to a break in the wall above. Climb up a twisting groove to slabs which lead leftwards to the top.

17 Draconian 16m Very Difficult
The groove right of Fine Escape.

18   Father's Day   16m   Very Difficult
Start at a tree below the overhang right of Draconian.
   Go up through a wall to a groove which is followed to the top.

19   Rearguard   16m   Severe
4m right of Father's Day is a rib. This is climbed to a mantleshelf move
left at 7m. An open-sided groove above is followed to the top.

20   Cake Walk   15m   Severe   ★★
This route takes the square-cut groove below the double-tiered rib, near
the coping slab to a second wall. Climb the wall above and follow a rib to
the top.

21   Birthday Party   15m   Very Severe   ★
This route climbs the obvious groove, and right-facing corner on the
upper slab, at the right end of the crag.
   Climb the long groove over a steepening and mantleshelf on to a
broad ledge below the final corner. Up the corner to finish.

Ravelrig Quarry — Right-hand Section

Map: Sheet 65, G.R. 146 670

RAVELRIG QUARRY

INTRODUCTION

This north-facing quarry offers a pleasant selection of one pitch routes on dolerite. The solid, slabby rock and the open situation make this one of the most amenable of the local quarries — especially on a summer's evening when the eastern half of the cliff basks in the sun. During the summer the rocks dry quickly after short periods of rain, but after longer spells of wet weather and during the winter much of the crag is kept wet by seepage.

ACCESS

The quarry is only 13km from the centre of Edinburgh. It lies 1½km NW of Balerno, beside the A70, 1½km west of the Balerno turn off. Just beyond a riding school there is a layby on the left (south) next to some woods. Cross a stile on the N. side of the road and walk along the edge of a field past a firwood. The quarry lies 50m. beyond the wood. (Danger Keep Out sign).

By public transport the best approach is to get a Balerno bus as far as the Balerno turn-off and then walk along the A70.

Since the routes here were first climbed the fine wall containing Plumbline has been reduced to the large pile of rubble which now occupies the right-hand side of the quarry. The routes are described from right to left.

Just left of the blast area is a shattered pillar (previously climbed by Trade Route). About 5m left of this is an obvious black crack.

1   Taurus   15m   Severe
Climb the steep crack for 10m then move diagonally left on large angular ledges leading to the top.

Left of Taurus the cliff is broken by grassy ledges.

2   Snowflake Crack   9m   Hard Very Severe   5b
Below the grassy ledges there is a black recess with a short overhang and corner. Climb the corner and exit rightwards after the overhang.

3   Flakedown   14m   Severe
Left of a grassy divide is a large projecting flake at 9m.
   Climb up and into a groove below and right of the flake. Just below
the flake move on to the left rib. Climb the flake and finish on the left.

4   Holy Moses   14m   Very Severe   4c
Directly below the flake is a crack. Climb this to just below the flake,
move right and up the outside edge of the flake to its top. Finish up and
left.

   Just left of Holy Moses there is a corner with a black slab on its left.

5   Men at Work   14m   E1   5a
The obvious corner.

6   Demo Route   14m   Hard Very Severe   5a   ★
Start at the bottom left-hand corner of the black slab.
   Climb a thin crack for 5m then move right and climb the wall to the
base of a groove. Up this to finish.

   The next two routes lie in the small bay to the left of Demo Route.

7   Overkill   14m   E1   5b
This route climbs an obvious groove in the right wall of the bay.
The groove is rather easy and grassy at first but it soon steepens, and a
few tricky moves lead past a flake to some good holds at the top of the
groove. Finish up the wall on the right.

8   A-Line   14m   Severe
Climb the short black corner 4m left of Overkill. Move up the right wall
to finish.

   The next routes lie 16m to the left on the large buttress in the centre
of the wall. This buttress is easily recognized by the big square-cut
overhang in its upper section. Below and right of the overhang is a large
black recess; the next route starts below this.

9   Golden Brown   16m   E2   5b   ★★
A fine route on good rock.
   Climb the right wall of the recess to a niche (pr). Pull out of the niche
and climb the wall above trending leftwards to gain a horizontal crack.
   Continue up and trend right to the top.

10   Rained In   18m   E2   5b
Below the overhang is a faint rampline, follow this for 5m then move left and go up to the left-hand end of the overhang. Traverse horizontally right under the overhang to join Golden Brown. Finish up this.

11   The Prowler   14m   E2   5b   ★
The highlight of this route is a bold move on to the obvious hanging arête above the overhang.
    Follow Rained In to below the overhang. Turn the overhang on the left and move back right on to the arête (old bolt runners). Up this to finish.

12   Beeline   12m   Very Severe   4b   ★
The deep corner to the left is climbed direct. It is possible to avoid the difficulties by moving on to the right wall.

13   Crack-Up   11m   Very Severe   4c
Start 12m left of Bee-Line.
Climb a steep crack to good holds in a niche. Finish up the wall above.

14   Punch-Up   11m   Very Severe   4c
Start 3m left of Crack-Up.
Follow a right-slanting crack to a detached pinnacle. Traverse left to a faint groove, up this and the slab above to the top.

    Left of Punch-Up there is a small wall with a broken crack leading to a break in an overhang:—

15   Headline   13m   E1   5b   ★
Climb the broken crack to the overhang. Move up and right through the break and pull left to a good ledge. Finish straight up.

16   Cream Cookie   13m   Very Severe   4c
Climb the line of loose cracks just left of Headline.

17   Currant Bun   13m   Very Severe   4c
Left of the previous route and right of a split boulder is a short corner with a good crack in the right wall. Climb the right wall of the corner to gain a broken crack. Up this to a recess. Finish up the clean corner on the left.

Ravelrig Quarry — Left-hand Section

18   Wheelchair Route   13m   E1   5b
Start just left of the split boulder.
   Layback up a groove. At the bulge move leftwards, then up to gain a good ledge. Finish more easily.

NOTE: There have been reports of rockfall having altered routes 13, 14 and 18, especially the latter. Great care should therefore be exercised if attempting these routes.

19   X-Ray   11m   Severe
Start 6m left of the split boulder at a clean right-sloping corner.
   Climb the right arête of the corner until it is possible to move back left into the corner, which is followed to the top.

HOLYROOD PARK

INTRODUCTION

Situated in the centre of Edinburgh, the cliffs in and around Holyrood Park have long been popular with local climbers. There is a large quantity of rock, most of which is south-facing and quick drying, BUT at present climbing on any cliff in the park is strictly illegal and anyone caught doing so is likely to be prosecuted. The route descriptions in this section of the guide are reproduced purely for their historical interest and no right to climb is to be inferred from their inclusion here.

The climbing is on various forms of basalt, varying from rough and solid to treacherously loose and frictionless. The most important cliff is Salisbury Crag, but there are other more secluded cliffs elsewhere in the Park.

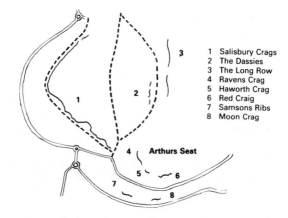

1 Salisbury Crags
2 The Dassies
3 The Long Row
4 Ravens Crag
5 Haworth Crag
6 Red Craig
7 Samsons Ribs
8 Moon Crag

ACCESS

To find Holyrood Park just look for Arthur's Seat which is a prominent landmark for miles around. Cars are best left at the large carpark beside the Royal Commonwealth Pool from where a short walk leads into the park itself.

All the cliffs are easy to reach, and by using the layout map their whereabouts should be obvious.

NOTE: Information has recently come to light which reveals that there are a considerable number of older climbs of which the author was unaware when this section was written. Their omission is regretted, and it is to be hoped that they will be included in any future edition of the guide.

Salisbury Crags

This is the long, impressive line of cliffs dominating the south western side of the park. The chief attraction for most is the excellent bouldering in the area around the south quarry. For the more adventurous, some of the longer routes give very good climbing in a superbly exposed position. The routes are described from right to left.

Pinnacle Quarry

The deep bay near the southern end of the cliff. On the left and rear walls are many short routes; the pinnacle is the obvious buttress on the right.

1 Falseface 12m Severe
Start at the left-hand side of the pinnacle at an arrow. Move on to a ledge then go up and right for 2m until it is possible to pull over a slight bulge to a ledge on the left. Climb the slab above, moving right to finish up a steep groove.

2 Pinnacle Face 12m Severe
Start as for the above route but continue up and right, pulling over a bulge into a recess. Go up and left to finish as for Falseface.

Middle Quarry

The next bay, some 150m to the left of Pinnacle Quarry. There are several other climbs here, mostly on loose rock.

3   The Slant   18m   Moderate
The obvious left-slanting line.

South Quarry

This is the deeply recessed section of cliff beyond middle quarry. It provides some good short routes on solid rock, and also contains the best bouldering in the area.

4   Black Chimney   15m   Severe   ★
The open black groove in the top right-hand corner of the quarry. Climb the steepening groove until it is possible to pull into a short steep corner. Continue past the left-hand side of a large projection to gain the top.

   To the right of Black Chimney, towards the arête, is a very steep black wall; a traverse is possible at 6b. A short route climbs straight up the wall to the left of some old bolts (5c).

5   Roofer Madness   12m   Hard Very Severe   5a
A somewhat loose climb through the roofs to the left of Black Chimney. Start 5m left of Black Chimney, just to the left of a roof. Go up a few metres until it is possible to move right into a groove. Up this to the roofs. Pull through a slight break to gain the top.

6   Sentry Box   12m   Severe
8 metres to the left of Black Chimney is a slab with a recess resembling a sentry box just below its top. Start to the left of an overhang directly below the sentry box. Climb a shallow groove moving right to gain the recess. Finish direct.

7   Rib and Mantleshelf   12m   Severe
Start just left of Sentry Box. Climb directly up a shallow, steepening rib. At the top mantleshelf on to a large hold and finish more easily.

8   Notch Climb   12m   Severe   ★
An interesting route. Start 6m to the left of Rib and Mantleshelf where two smooth grooves slant up the cliff from a large boulder.
   Climb the right-hand groove finishing up the arête on the right.
Variation: It is possible to climb directly up the right edge of Notch Climb, finishing on the last few moves of that climb (E1 5a).

9   Spike Fright   12m   Hard Very Severe   5a
In the centre of the rear wall, some 8m left of the previous route, is a large overhang with a square-cut recess on its right. Start below the recess.
Climb to the left of a down-pointing spike then up to a position just right of the overhang. Up and to the left is a spike; gain a standing position on this and finish up the slab above.

10   Black Slab   12m   Severe   ★★
An enjoyable climb, the best in the south quarry. Start 8m left of Spike Fright below the left-hand end of a black overhang. Climb a very shallow groove to a block below the overhang. Hand traverse right, surmount the bulge and finish up the exposed wall above.

11   Hyphen Route   12m   Hard Very Severe   5a
As for Black Slab to the block, then move delicately up and left on to a slab. Pull straight over the bulge above and finish up the black wall on the left.

12   Red Slab   10m   Very Difficult
The steep groove to the left of the previous route.

13   Initial Route   10m   Very Severe   4c
Start 2m to the right of the Lift.
Climb a smooth corner moving out left at the top. Go up and right to a small projection then finish up the wall above.

14   The Lift   10m   Moderate   ★
The obvious right-facing corner line some 20m from the left-hand corner of the quarry. A good descent route and a worthwhile climb in its own right. Climb a steep corner to gain some ledges on the right, move up and left to a steep corner which is climbed to finish.

15   White Slab   8m   Very Difficult
The white-flecked slab in the left-hand side of the rear wall.

16   The Long Stride   8m   Moderate
Start in the corner 2m left of the previous route.
Climb the corner for 3m then step left to a small ledge. Finish up the easy wall above.
Variation: A short jamming crack provides an interesting direct start (5a).

17   Original Route   8m   Moderate
Start in the left-hand corner of the little quarry.
   Climb to a shelf on the left, step up then traverse right across a bulge until it is possible to gain the easy wall above.

18   Wicked Lady   8m   Very Severe   4c
Left of the previous route is a shelf below a black overhang. Climb easily to gain the left-hand end of the shelf, the traverse awkwardly to the right until it is possible to get established above the overhang. Continue to the top on good holds.

19   Archie's Slab   15m   Hard Very Severe   5a   ★
As for Wicked Lady then move left to the base of a steep corner. Traverse left on to the bottom corner of the slab and continue to better holds and the top.

20   Harrison's Climb   17m   Severe   ★★
A steep route with some unusual moves. Start just left of a shallow cave. Climb the rib for 6m then move right on to a small ledge. Move up to a higher ledge and finish up the exposed wall above.

21   Doubledecker   20m   Mild Severe
Takes a line up the wall just to the right at the left edge of the quarry.

Western Buttress

This is the left-hand buttress of the South Quarry. A broad level ledge, the platform, runs across the base, and a broken ledge, the terrace, runs the length of the face just below the top.

22   Slab and Wedge route   25m   Very Difficult
Below the right-hand end of the platform is a steep corner.
1.   4m   The corner.
2.   21m   Up the left-hand side of the slab above, at its top go left then back right to easy ground and the top.

23   Wall Route   20m   Mild Severe
Start at the left-hand end of the platform at a steep corner.
   Climb the corner for 2m then go right to a small ledge. Easy rock leads to the top.

24 Groove Route 20m Very Severe 4c
Start as for Wall Route, but where that route moves right continue up
the groove turning the overhangs on the left.

25 Horne's Slab 12m Very Severe 5a
8m left of the left-hand end of the platform is a red slab with a groove on
its left, leading to a large ledge at 12m. Climb the slab to a layback hold,
step up then move left to finish up the groove. Short but bold.

26 Hewit's Groove 12m Very Severe 4c
Round the rib to the left of Horne's Slab is a short twisting groove.
Climb this to the ledge at 12m.

Beyond the Western Buttress the cliff rears up into a series of steep,
loose bays and buttresses. After 60m the cliff goes back into the Great
Quarry. To the right of this is a broad buttress, called The Great
Buttress.

27 Great Buttress 40m Very Difficult   ★★★
A fine route in a magnificent situation. The rock requires care. Start to
the right of centre at a broad pillar.
1. 12m Climb the pillar to a terrace at 4m. Follow the terrace up and
right to a belay.
2. 16m Follow a ledge round on to the front face at the buttress, at
its end climb a 3m corner (crux), then follow another ledge to the left,
past a mantleshelf to a flake belay.
3. 12m Climb the staircase above to a wide recess and escape up
this to the top.
   A direct start climbs directly up to the second stance.

The Great Quarry

This is the long line of cliffs to the left of Great Buttress. The central
section is split by a terrace at 25m. Towards the left-hand end of the
wall below the terrace there is a deep groove starting from a ledge at
3m. This is the line of Steeplejack's Staircase.

28 The Blackdance 25m E3 5c   ★★
Start 5m right of Steeplejack's Staircase below a curving groove with a
slim pillar to its right.
   Climb the groove (pr) to a sloping foothold on the right. Move up the
groove then out right (pr) and up the wall to finish.

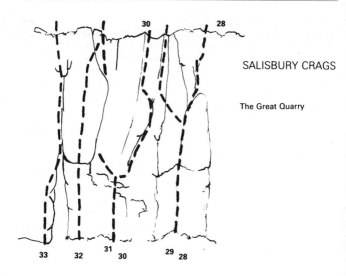

SALISBURY CRAGS

The Great Quarry

29   After The Axe   25m   E2   5b   ★
As for The Blackdance to the pr. Move left across the wall and round the
arête to the base of a shallow groove. Up this to finish.

30   Ginger Nymphos Lust   18m   E2   5c   ★
From the right-hand end of the ledge below Steeplejack's Staircase
move up and right (pr) to gain a shallow groove. Up this (pr) then
traverse left to the base of a smooth groove. This provides a technical
finish (2 pr).

31   Steeplejack's Staircase   15m   E2   5b
The deep groove. Quite technical and very badly protected.

32   Walking on Sunshine   20m   E3   6a   ★★★
The smooth arête to the left of Steeplejack's Staircase provides one of
the most enjoyable climbs in the area.
    Climb the smooth arête (2 pr) to gain a standing position on a long
narrow hold. Move up and right to finish in an easy groove.

33   Straight Satan   20m   E2   5c   ★★
This route climbs the vertical quartz crack to the left of the previous route. Climb the rib to the left of the crack until it is possible to step into the crack just below a pr. Continue up the crack to the top (pr).

34   Transatlantic Trip   30m   E2   5b   ★
The obvious right-facing white corner 50m left of Straight Satan. The route finishes on a ledge about 6m below the top, the final wall is fairly easy but as yet uncleaned and extremely loose.

The next important feature is The Cat Nick, an obvious deep gully about 100 yards beyond the Great Quarry.

35   Cat Nick Buttress   30m   Very Difficult
This climb ascends fairly sound rock on the buttress to the immediate right of the gully.

1.   10m   Follow easy ledges to gain a chimney which is climbed to the top of a prominent block.

2.   9m   Cross the slab on the left to a right-angled corner. Up this (crux) to a belay at the base of a shallow chimney.

3.   11m   Follow the chimney to the top.

36   The Cat Nick   30m   Easy   ★
The gully provides an interesting scramble with fine views. An early (c1950) guide to the climbs in the Park says of this climb, '(it) affords in good conditions the finest snow climb in the Park. In 1947 the cornice was some six feet thick, with an overhang of ten feet, and lasted for many weeks, despite much tunnelling'.

37   Cat Nick Arête   30m   Moderate
A rather vague climb up the ribs and corners just to the left of the Cat Nick.

To the left of the Cat Nick the cliff becomes looser and more vegetated. A short pinnacle, 'The Pic Robbieson', provides some interesting climbing at the extreme left-hand end of the cliff. A red slab just beyond this also provides some worthwhile climbing.

38   The Great Electrocardiogram Traverse   Mostly Severe,
often Very Severe
A traverse of the main section of the crags, starting 150m up the Radical Road from Pic Robbieson and continuing across Great, Little and Middle Quarries to the Hause.

The Long Row

This is the long line of cliffs overlooking Hunters Bay, the deep depression behind Salisbury Crags. The rock is good and there are many worthwhile climbs other than those described.

39   Fallen Column Climb   10m   Severe   ★
The 'Column' is a conspicuous feature of the left-hand end of the cliff. Climb the outside edge of the column and continue up the wall above.

40   Waverley Crack   8m   Difficult
The crack in the wall to the right of the previous climb.

41   Stomach Layback   7m   Mild Severe
Round the corner to the right is a steep crack which curls up and right round an overhang. Climb the crack.

The Dassies

Three small outcrops of excellent black rock, lying in front of the Long Row. The left and right-hand Dassies provide some interesting short routes and problems, the central Dassie contains two classic crack problems.

42   Black Heart   7m   Very Severe   4c   ★
The thin bulging crack splitting the central buttress.

   The vague arête just to the right of Black Heart provides a really fine top rope problem (6a).

43   Black Edge   6m   E2   5c
Start just left of the sharp arête to the right of Black Heart. Make a few bold moves up and right to better holds near the arête. Up this to the top. Unprotected.

44   Raeburn's Crack   7m   Severe   ★
The wide crack to the right of the central buttress.

Samson's Ribs

This is the large columnar cliff low down on the southern flank of Arthur's Seat. The finest cliff in the park, it is in such a conspicuous situation that no real exploration has taken place to date, except for a route by D.H. Haworth which climbs a ramp and groove line up the centre of the crag.

Moon Crag

This cliff is approached by continuing along the road that runs underneath Samson's Ribs, it appears on the left after 200m.

45   Evening Pillar   15m   Hard Severe   ★
Start below the obvious pillar on the left-hand side of the crag.
   Climb the pillar and the steep corner above, passing an overhang to a dirty finish.

46   Evening Crack   8m   Severe
The steep buttress to the left of the previous route is split by a crack. Pull through a bush to gain the crack, and follow it to the top.
   Further short routes can be found on the right.

Raven's Crag

This is the overhanging black cliff obvious from the road running above Samson's Ribs. It is 40m high and boasts some impressive lines; unfortunately it also boasts some impressively loose rock, and so far only one route has been climbed.

47   The Gutter   40m   Severe   ★
The long chimney/corner on the left side of the crag. An interesting experience!

Haworth's Crag

This small cliff lies to the right of Raven's Crag, almost directly opposite the summit of Samson's Ribs.

48   Wee Chokestone Crack   8m   Severe
The prominent corner-crack at the left-hand end of the cliff.

Red Craig

The long red buttress to the right of Haworth's Crag.

49   Pentland Slab   20m   Moderate
The obvious slab at the left-hand end of the cliff.

50   Red Buttress   18m   Severe   ★
At the right-hand end of the cliff is an ivy-filled chimney.
   Climb the obvious steps up the buttress on the right.

TRAPRAIN LAW

INTRODUCTION

Traprain Law is situated 6½km east of Haddington and 2½ km south of East Linton. The crags lie on the south side of the hill, facing the Lammermuir Hills, and consist of two high-angled slabs seamed with grooves, cracks and overlaps.

The rock is trachyte, a fine-grained volcanic rock which is generally very solid and well covered with holds. There is much good climbing, particularly in the lower and middle grades. This, in combination with the sunny aspect and rustic situation, makes for a very pleasant non-serious atmosphere.

ACCESS

By car the best way of approaching Traprain Law is to head for Haddington. From the town centre go east along Market Street and over Victoria Bridge. Follow the road out of town for 1½km or so to a hidden second turn right. Follow this road for a few km to a crossroad. Take the left turn and go past a farm. The crags are now visible on the left. The best parking place is beside a gate just beyond the farm. Several buses run along the A1 from Edinburgh. The most direct approach is to get off the bus at Overhails Farm, from where a tortuous trail leads over the river and across fields eventually leading round the hill to the crags (2km). A longer but more straightforward approach is to get off at East Linton from where a road can be followed southwards towards the hill (3km).

The climbs are described from left to right.

At the extreme left-hand end of the south face of the hill there is a high but loose cliff which gives one pitch routes of an easy nature. Above this is a short vertical wall which gives short problems.

1 Red Rib 20m Moderate
Starting from the lowest rocks, this route climbs the obvious rib in the centre of the high cliff.

Overhang Wall

This is the left-hand of the two main faces. Its main features are a band of overhangs at mid-height and some flakes which lie against the left-hand end.

2   Flake 1   5m   Severe
This route climbs the outside edge of the first flake.
   Climb up and over a bulge, moving right to gain the top.

3   Flake 2   5m   Difficult
Climb the left edge of the second flake.

4   Right Edge   5m   Very Severe
Climb the right edge of the second flake.
   An unprotected severe climbs the cleaned strip up the slab just right of Right Edge.

5   Steptoe   15m   Severe   ★
This route climbs the first clean rib, about 5m right of Flake 2.

6   Moss Groove   15m   Very Difficult
Climb the groove to the left of the obvious broad rib in the centre of the face.

7   The Shield   15m   Hard Very Severe   4c   ★
The broad rib gives an interesting and rather bold climb.
   Go up and trend right to a scoop. Go up this until it is possible to pull out left on to a ledge to finish.

8   Down my Street   15m   E1   5b
The mossy rib right of the shield. Bold.

9   Flake Wall   18m   Difficult
A poor climb up the wall above and right of Flake 3.

10   Flake 3   5m   Difficult
The outside face of the third flake.

11   Flake 4   5m   Severe
The outside face of the fourth flake.

12   Torque   10m   Hard Very Severe   5a
The blank-looking corner above flake 3. Move out right at the top.

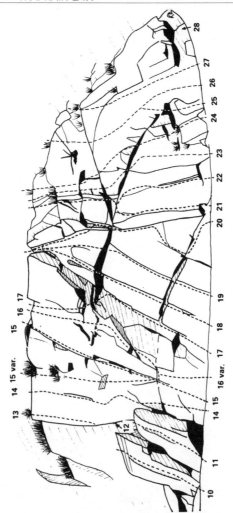

TRAPRAIN LAW. OVERHANG WALL

13 Swinging 15m Very Severe 4c
Follow Torque to a ledge on the right wall. Make an exciting move right round the arête to gain a sloping ledge. Follow the arête to the top.

14 Left Edge 18m Severe   ★★
A fine open route. Start just right of flake 4.
   Climb up until it is possible to move left on to a sloping ledge at 8m. Continue up the crack above to the top.

15 Via Macniven 18m Very Severe 5a
Start 4m right of Flake 4. (Arrow v.s.).
   Climb up to a small ledge. Go straight up the slim grassy groove above trending right to the top.
Variation: From the small ledge bridge up and move left to below a black bulge. Over this and go direct to the top. Easier than the original.

16 Wobble 18m Very Severe 5a   ★
Follow Via Macniven to the small ledge. Step right and go diagonally right to a small black overlap. Over this, then up and rightwards to a sloping ledge. Pull over a bulge to another ledge then finish more easily.
Variation: Gain the small ledge by the problematic wall on the right, recommended. This makes Wobble completely independent.

17 Piglet 18m Hard Very Severe 5a   ★★
A fine route climbing the deep groove and overhangs right of Wobble. Climb the groove to a polished rib below the overhang. Step left and pull over the overhang. Continue over the bulge above to finish up easy slabs.

18 Burp 18m Very Severe 5a
Start below the next groove to the right of Piglet.
   Climb the groove to a break in the overhang. Using a polished rib on the right, surmount the overhang and finish up an easy groove.

19 Chute 18m Hard Very Severe 5b   ★
Start below the shallow groove between Burp and Great Corner. Climb the groove to the overhang. Move left and make some committing moves to get established on the slab above the overhang. Finish easily.

20 Great Corner 18m Severe   ★★★
The obvious deep corner gives an excellent climb. Start below a shelf 2m left of the corner.

Follow the shelf up and right into the corner and continue up to a ledge on the right. Go up the groove until it is possible to move left. Finish up the corner crack above.
Variation: It is possible to start directly up the corner (4c).

21   Sabre Cut   18m   Very Severe   5b
A combination of two routes, this gives an interesting and varied climb. Climb the arête to the right of Great Corner to a ledge at 9m. Gain a short groove above. Up this to finish.

22   Staircase   9m   Very Difficult
Start 4m right of Great Corner.
   Climb a crack until it is possible to gain a slab on the right. Up this on good holds to gain the ledge at 9m. Finish up Great Corner.

23   Slab and Tickle   16m   Hard Very Severe   5b
A contrived route but with some interesting moves.
   Climb the slab right of Staircase, moving right at the top. Go back left to below a clean nose of rock. Pull over this and finish straight up.

24   Fake Route   16m   Severe   ★
The crack-line right of Slab and Tickle and left of an ivy recess.
   Follow the crack over an overlap at 8m to a steep flake crack. Go up and left to gain rib on the left. Finish straight up.

25   Cat's Paw   16m   Hard Very Severe   5b
Basically a variation start to Falseface.
   From a slab in the ivy recess pull over the overhang moving diagonally right on to slabs. Up these to finish.

26   Falseface   16m   Severe
The overlapping slabs left of the obvious twin cracks of Deception.

27   Deception   15m   Very Difficult
The obvious twin cracks, passing a large flake on the left.

   Between Deception and a large overhang on the right are some interesting short steep problems at a reasonable standard.

28   Wheech's Overhang   5m   Very Severe   5a
The large overhang at the right-hand end of Overhang Wall.

29   The Western Girdle   60m   Very Severe   4c   4c   4a   ★★
This is a left to right girdle of Overhang Wall, it gives some very good climbing but is best avoided when the crag is busy.

1.   20m   Climb Flake 3 and go up and right as for Swinging. Go horizontally right to a stance on the sloping ledge of Wobble.

2.   20m   Continue rightwards to below the overhang of Piglet and continue traversing underneath the overhangs to belay on the ledge at the top of the arête of Sabre Cut.

3.   20m   Continue rightwards to the end of the crag.

Between Overhang Wall and the right-hand crag, Lammer Wall, there are some slabby ribs, most of which have been climbed. There are two worth doing.

30   Ripple Rib   16m   Severe
A prominent clean rib. Climb up to a bulge at 3m, turn it on the left then go back right and follow the rib to the top.
Variation: Climb the bulge direct (4c).

31   Via Dolorosa   15m   Hard Severe
Start just left of the chimney bounding Lammer Wall on the left. Climb a shallow groove which trends rightwards across the steep mossy face.

Lammer Wall

This is the right-hand of the two main crags. Although it is small there are many climbs crammed on to its slabby face. In the interest of clarity only the main lines are described, but it is possible to climb anywhere.

Descent is by a chimney groove on the left or by some large ledges on the right, just left of Queue Corner.

32   Retard Arête   12m   Very Severe   5a
This is the right arête of the chimney groove.

The initial blunt nose can be climbed from several directions, the easiest being from the left. Continue up the groove above the nose to the top.

33   Tiger Wall   12m   Hard Very Severe   5b
The smooth wall below and right of Retard Arête is topped by a horizontal break and an overhung triangular niche.

The break can be gained by various boulder problem starts, the best being straight up the middle (avoiding a crack on the left). Gain the niche then pull over the overhang and finish direct.

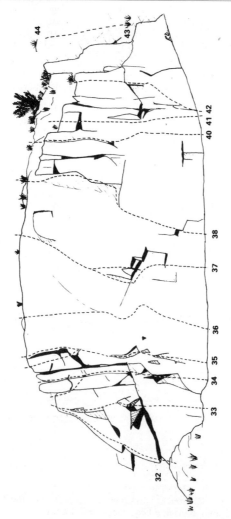

TRAPRAIN LAW. LAMMER WALL

34   The Vertical Ladder   12m   Difficult   ★
To the right of Tiger Wall is a wide crack/chimney jammed with blocks.
Climb this and exit either left or straight up.

35   Double Stretch   13m   Severe   ★
Start at a shallow left-facing groove just right of the last route.
   Climb the slab to the top of the groove. Go up to gain a crack and
follow it to the top.
Variation: Left of the top crack is a projecting rock rib. Gain it direct and
follow it to the top (Hard Severe).

36   The MS Route   15m   Hard Severe   ★★
An excellent route, giving sustained and delicate climbing. Start just
right of Double Stretch.
   Climb the rounded slab for 6m (crux) and gain a small ledge on the
left. Continue up the slab above to the top.

37   Pinch   15m   Hard Severe
To the right of the last route is a wide shallow groove topped by small
overhangs. Climb the groove to the overhangs, turn these on the left
then go up and trend right to the top.
Variation: Climb the overhangs (VS 5a).

38   Brute   16m   Severe
Start almost in the centre of the cliff, below the rib to the right of Pinch.
Go straight up to a ledge at 7m. Move right and up a crack and groove to
the top.

39   Pedestrian   15m   Hard Severe
Start 3m right of Brute and follow thin black cracks, trending right. Go
back left and up to gain the ledge on Brute. Finish directly up the slab.

40   Spider Route 1   12m   Mild Severe
Climb the faint crack-line right of Pedestrian trending rightwards, after
6m follow the rib on the left.

41   Spider Route 2   12m   Severe
Climb the slabs on the right finishing over a bulge at the top.

42   Shuffle   12m   Very Difficult
Start just right of Spider Route 2 and climb diagonally right then back left
to a niche. Continue up to a large ledge and the top.

There are a few short routes further right.

The right-hand side of the cliff ends in broken ledges to the right of which is a clean-cut corner.

43   Queue Corner   12m   Severe   ★
Scramble up ledges to the foot of the corner. Up this direct. A fine pitch.

44   Turf Trundle   26m   Very Severe   4b
To the right of Queue Corner is an expanse of mossy slabs.
  Climb the left-hand of two cleaned strips. The right-hand strip is slightly cleaner and better (VS 4c).

The next cliff to the right of Lammer Wall consists of a right-leaning cracked slab which runs into a band of overlaps which arch up and right.

45   Hexagon Wall   26m   Very Difficult   ★
Start just right of some small flakes which lean against the foot of the cracked slab. Climb the slab by the line of least resistance. Descend to the left, facing out.

46   Dangle   20m   Hard Very Severe   5a
Start below the left-hand end of the overhangs on a black and sometimes wet slab (arrow and VS). Go up the slab to gain a clean-cut right-facing groove. Go up the groove pulling over its capping overlap to gain Hexagon Wall. Up this to finish.

  The next three routes are gained by scrambling up and right below the overhangs from the start of Dangle.

47   Beatle Crack   9m   E1   5b
Start up and right of Dangle, about 12m above the path, below a flaky crack splitting the bulge. A short hard problem.
  Pull into the crack from the right and go up (pr) then left to easier ground.

48   Hanging Crack   10m   Very Severe   5a
Start further up and right from Beatle crack where a rib butts against the underside of the overhangs.
  Climb the right-hand side of the rib. Pull over the overhang and finish up the groove.

49   Utang   9m   Very Difficult
Climb the obvious clean-cut corner 3m right of Hanging Crack.

50   Pip's Pillar   Very Severe   4b
Below the band of overhangs there is an expanse of vegetated slabs.
An obvious semi-detached flake can be seen halfway up the cliff. Climb
directly up the outside of the flake. Cross the gap at the top and follow
the flake above.
Variation: It is possible to climb inside the flake to gain its top (Very
Difficult).

There are numerous lines up the slabs on the right, mostly climbable
at about severe.
The cliffs at the top of the hill have been climbed on and the
numerous outlying slabs provide further excursions for the
adventurous.

THE FASTCASTLE SEA-CLIFFS

INTRODUCTION

The cliffs of the Fastcastle area lie on the coastline between Cockburnspath and Coldingham, approximately 70km east of Edinburgh and 130km north of Newcastle.

The craggy coastline extends for 9½km in a series of rugged headlands and pebble beaches. Despite so much rock only three areas have so far been found which provide worthwhile climbing.

The first, Fastcastle Head, is a slabby headland on top of which sit the ruins of an ancient castle. At the tip of the headland there is the entrance to a large cave which runs deep into the rocks. From the castle a sea stack is visible about 1½km to the east. This is The Souter, around which are a series of fins jutting out into the sea. So far this area has provided the best climbing and the majority of routes. Further east is a huge pebble bay, beyond which a prominent ridge of rock runs far out into the sea. This is The Brander, and it is on this, together with the fins and ridges beyond, that the remainder of the climbing in the area has taken place.

A sea-level traverse linking all three areas provides an interesting excursion with fairly complex route-finding, much dependent on the state of the tide.

Due to the relatively low rainfall the coast is often dry when other areas are wet, it is also very sheltered from strong or chilling winds. Such a combination therefore makes this an ideal place for climbing from late summer right through the winter to early spring. The remaining months are affected by nesting sea birds, and unless one can put up with the noise, mess and smell it is probably best to go elsewhere during this period.

ACCESS

Travelling east from Edinburgh on the A1, take the A1107 left about 1½km past Cockburnspath, signposted for Coldingham and Eyemouth. Follow this for about 5km to the top of the hills and take a single-track road left to Dowlaw Farm. Park on the left just before a cattle grid leading to the farm. Travelling from Newcastle, take the A1107 right to Eyemouth just north of Berwick-upon-Tweed and follow this through Coldingham to gain the single-track road leading right to Dowlaw Farm, approximately 15 miles from Berwick. Approach to this area other than by private transport is not recommended.

Gradings
The grades and descriptions of routes in the Fastcastle and Brander areas should be treated with care, as these routes have not had known recent ascents. Very Severe in these areas should be taken as 'old' Scottish Very Severe, ie anything from Very Severe upwards.

Map: Sheet 67, G.R. 860 711

FASTCASTLE HEAD

ACCESS
At the farm a track signposted to Fastcastle leads down left past the end of some cottages and through a gate. Follow a vague path diagonally down to the right to reach the headland and the castle ruins in approximately 1½km.

There are two main sections: the most appealing and compact is about 60m high and lies directly beneath the castle ruins; the other section is more vegetated and lies to the south of the previous section — it is about 120m high.

To reach the foot of the climbs an abseil down the gully from the bridge can be made or the steep grassy slope to the south-east can be descended.

1   Abseil Gully   60m   Very Difficult
Climb the wall to the right of the chimney for 9m, continue up the right-angled groove, using many bridging moves, all the way to the bridge at the top.

A rather broken and scrappy route exists up the rock just to the left of Abseil Gully. It is about Very Difficult, but because of the loose nature of the rock is not worthy of description.

2   The East Arête   45m   Severe

1.   30m   Climb the slab and arête at the east end of the crag for 18m then trend left to a ledge and loose blocks. A poor spike belay and good stance can be found under the overhanging arête.

2.   15m   Go left on to the arête and continue for 5m traversing to the left of two cracks in the steep wall. Climb this to a stance and belay.

3   Atlanta   45m   Very Severe
This is a continuously interesting route. Start 5m right of the East Arête, at the foot of a holdless-looking corner.

1.   30m   Climb directly up the left corner of the wall (pr). At the overhang a thread can be arranged before going right for 1½m. Continue up the wall, trending back left on obvious holds. Spike belay and good stance below the arête.

2.   15m   Continue straight up the crack and wall for 6m then go left on to the arête and climb the right-hand of the twin cracks in the steep wall above.

Note: A large block has apparently fallen from this climb altering both its grade and its appearance.

4   Vertigo   55m   Hard Very Severe   4c   4b
This route follows the largest and most obvious line of weakness up the slabs. Towards the middle of the slab mass two cracks can be seen cutting through the folds about 6m up. The right-hand crack marks the route.

1.   15m   Climb the slab to the foot of the crack (pr). Climb the crack and continue to a small ledge and piton belay.

2.   40m   Continue directly up over three slight overhangs, separated by slab climbing, to the top. An easy and enjoyable pitch.

5   Urinal Wall   55m   Very Severe
1.   40m   Start at the very foot of the dièdre just to the right of the huge main mass of slabs. Climb the wall and groove to a ledge and peg belay.

2.   15m   Continue up the corner for 9m then move left on to loose blocks on the arête, and so to the top.

6   Castle Wall   45m   Very Severe
This route runs up the solid face which is separated from the slab mass by a cave and a 12m water strip at high tide. The foot of the route is reached by abseiling from the outermost tip of land beyond the castle ruins. On the first ascent a Tyrolean traverse was arranged between the two sections of crag over the water strip as an emergency escape route.
    Climb the crack in the middle of the face then traverse left towards the groove. Finish with an upward traverse to the right.

7   Gannet Groove   73m   Very Severe

This route follows the obvious crack up the bands on the east face of the crag. As soon as the route is started one is over the sea.

1.   15m   Step from the pinnacle at the left-hand corner into the groove. Move slightly downwards and to the right across the wall then up to a pointed stance in the groove. Climb the groove (crux) and the wall above into another groove which leads to a stance and piton belay.

2.   23m   Continue up the groove and round the overhang at the top to a large stance.

3.   35m   Traverse round a corner on the left and continue up a small gangway for 9m. Traverse right on to sound rock and then straight up to the top.

8   Cyclops   94m   Very Severe/A2

A good and continuously interesting climb, but loose and poorly protected on the upper pitches. The route lies on the high east-facing sea wall south of the main slab mass and descent gully, which is marked by a steep, solid 25m high wall above a cave. Start on the right-hand side of the cave below a diagonal overhanging crack.

1.   15m   Climb the crack using pegs, pull into a shallow groove and climb free to a stance and belay.

2.   14m   Continue up the corner to an overhang (pr), over this (1pa), and climb the corner above moving out right on to the arête. Use two pegs to move up to a big stance on the left.

3.   27m   Climb the black corner above the stance and follow the arête breaking left to the foot of a big grassy groove. Follow the shaly slab to the right of the groove until it steepens. Stance and peg belay.

4.   12m   Traverse left towards a steep solid wall of rock and climb this to a stance and block belay on the right side of a rightward-slanting loose grassy rake.

5.   26m   Climb steep loose rocks above the belay tending to the left until overhangs force a traverse to the right. Climb straight up to finish, and walk up the slope for 9m to a fence post belay.

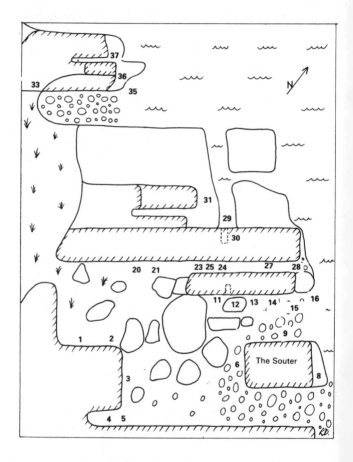

THE FASTCASTLE SEA CLIFFS. THE SOUTER

THE SOUTER

Map: Sheet 67, G.R. 868 708

ACCESS

Instead of going down left for Fastcastle Head follow the track right round the other side of the farm, through a gate, downhill through another and along to a wall where the track ends. Cross the field round the side of a small hillock to reach a fence, follow this downhill and descend a grassy ridge to reach The Souter, approximately 1½km.

On the right as one descends to The Souter is an undercut buttress. The following three routes climb this buttress. To obtain a satisfactory belay at the top it may be advisable to pull a rope up and tie it to the fence post at the top of the descent ridge.

1   Lightning Crack   15m   Hard Very Severe   5a
To the right of the undercut arête is a crack, climb this to the break, move left to the edge and follow a ramp to the top.

2   Moving like a Slug   15m   E2   5a   ★
Climbs the arête, gained by a left traverse from the base of Lightning crack.

3   Blockbuster   20m   E1   5a
Round on the frontal face is a break in the roof, climb this using the block and continue up the crack and wall above.

4   Pigeon Shit   6m   E2   6a
The entrance to the cave left of Blockbuster has a short crack running up its left wall, climb this.

5   Graddled   6m   E4   6a
Climbs the wall just left of the previous route.

The following routes all climb The Souter. Pegs and slings are in place for descent. These should be checked and replaced if necessary before use.

6   Landward Side   22m   Very Severe
Start in the middle of the face. Climb to a ledge at 7m and traverse 3m right on to the East Face. Move up to a ledge, traverse left to gain the top slab and climb this to an overhang which is turned on the right.

7 Direct Variant   22m   Very Severe
From the ledge 7m up, climb a smooth corner for 3m, break right and climb an overhanging wall to a ledge on the left of a small wall. Cross the wall and climb a sharp crack to the top slab. Finish as for the previous route or go straight over the overlap, nut and peg used for aid on the first ascent.

8 Ordinary Route   25m   Hard Very Severe   5a   ★★
Takes the seaward face starting from a raised platform.
  Climb the groove above with difficulty to a ledge, and move up and right, passing a peg runner. Go left and up a diagonal crack to finish up the wall above.
Variation: Follow the ledge above the initial groove round left to link up with the routes on the landward side (Very Severe).

9 Squid Vicious   25m   E5   6a   ★★★
This route climbs the crack-line on the north west face of The Souter. Climb the crack to a small roof at 8m. Traverse right and climb to two obvious pockets on the wall (pr up and right). Return to the crack and climb to the roof. Pull over on the right and climb to another roof. Pull over this on the left and climb up and right across a wall to reach an easy-angled groove. Block belay on left.
  Facing the Squid Vicious side of The Souter there is a small fin of rock running out to sea in front of the larger, main fin.

10 Shorty   8m   Severe
The crack and arête at the left-hand end of the wall.

11 Sweep   8m   Very Severe   4c
The cracks right of Shorty.

12 Sooty   8m   Very Severe   5a   ★
The obvious short chimney and crack.

13 Take it to the Limpets   10m   E3   5c   ★★
An excellent sustained wall climb to the right of Sooty.
  Climb the left-hand of two cracks to a jug in the centre of the wall, move right and follow a vague crack-line to the top.
Variation: From the jug go up left to gain the arête, move up and back right under a small roof before pulling on to the slab (E2 5c).

14   The Great Gonzo   10m   E2   5c   ★
This route climbs the crack in the arête to the right of the previous
climb. The crack is gained from the chimney on the right.

15   Chimp   10m   Very Severe   4c
The chimney to the right of the previous route. A short tricky wall gives
access to the chimney which is then followed more easily to the top.

16   Leech   6m   Hard Very Severe   5b
Climb the right-hand of two short cracks to the right of Chimp.

The Main Fin
On the left, descending to The Souter, is a long fin running out into the
sea. The south-eastern side starts as a short wall gaining in height to
where a short col links the fin to the smaller fin facing The Souter. At
this point a descent has to be made to the floor of a wide fissure
between the two fins. Although not as long, the north-western side of
the fin is of greater height. It can be gained by descending a gully beside
the fin.
    South-Eastern Side. The routes are described from left to right.

17   Walli   4m   Very Severe   5a
The short crack at the start of the fin.

18   Wallow   6m   E2   5c
The thin crack just right of Walli.

19   Wallette   8m   E2   5c   ★
The thin crack right of Wallow.

20   Zig Zag   10m   Hard Very Severe   5a
Start below a thin crack 6m left of the obvious diagonal fault. Climb the
crack then move up and right to finish up the fault.

Variation 1: Direct Start. Climb directly up the wall to the right of the
initial crack (E1 5c).

Variation 2: Direct Finish. Climb up and left to reach and climb a thin
crack (E2 5c).

21   Fraud Escort   10m   E3   5c   ★★
Immediately to the right of the diagonal fault is a steep bulge.

Surmount the bulge, moving right to the base of a thin crack. Up this to finish.

22   Mingy Metro   10m   E4   6a
Where the previous route moves right, continue up and left following a thin crack.

23   J.P.S.   8m   Hard Very Severe   5a
Climb the slim corner starting just above the col.

24   Plain Sailing   16m   E1   5b   ★★★
The fine crack in the wall to the right, starting from the floor of the fissure.

25   Orgasmatron   8m   E2   6a   ★
The short, thin crack opposite Plain Sailing.

26   Drunk and Disorderly   18m   E3   5c
A worthwhile eliminate up the wall between Plain Sailing and Walnut. Climb parallel cracks to the right of Plain Sailing to reach and pull through a roof, as for Walnut. Step left to finish up a thin crack.

27   Walnut   16m   E3   5c   ★★★
Climb the thin crack in the middle of the wall to the right of Plain Sailing. From the top of the crack move right then up to a small roof. Move left and surmount the roof, and continue to ledges and the top.

28   The Porker's Wall   16m   E4   5c
Though rather contrived this route provides some serious climbing.
    Climb the wall to the right of Walnut then go up and right, passing a pocket, to gain the arête. Move up and left to cross a bulge and continue to a ledge. Finish on the right.

North-Western Side

29   Fast Bleeder   18m   E3   6a   ★★★
The obvious central crack provides one of the finest jamming problems in the area.

30   Souterrain   18m   E3   5c   ★★
Climb the cul-de-sac chimney just right of Fast Bleeder, exit right to gain a ledge, move up to a recess and pull out left to reach the top.

Variation: Direct Start: Climb the crack to the right of the chimney (E3 6a ★★).

31   Stiff Bunnies   10m   E1   5b
This climb follows a thin crack up the prow of the small fin to the right of the descent gully.

32   Return to Sender   50m   E2   ★
This is a girdle of the main fin, start on the south-eastern side of the col.

1.   25m   5a   Follows the obvious traverse line across the wall and round the arête to belay on a ledge at the start of the north-western wall.

2.   25m   5c   Make the return trip along ledges to move up and finish up a groove right of Souterrain.

Immediately to the west is a small inlet beyond which is another fin, easily indentified by a prominent crack running up its prow.

33   Gull Talk   10m   Very Difficult
Climb the corner and slab at the left-hand end of the fin, walk right to descend a chimney. A useful means of access and descent when the tide is in along the base of the fin.

34   The Fish Business   10m   E2   5c
To the right of Gull Talk are three short corners. Climb the thin crack, just to the right of the corners, to gain an easy slab.

35   A Drop in The Ocean   12m   E2   5b
This route climbs the arête of the Prow. Start below second Sight.
   Move left to the arête and climb the wall just right of the arête on good holds. Swing round left to a small niche. Pull out of the niche and continue more easily to the top.
Variation: When the tide is out it is possible to climb a line of cracks just left of the arête (E1 5b).

36   Second Sight   12m   Hard Very Severe   5b   ★★
The prominent crack running up the prow of the fin. An excellent climb.

37   Bloodbath   10m   Hard Very Severe   5a
The short arête just right of Second Sight.

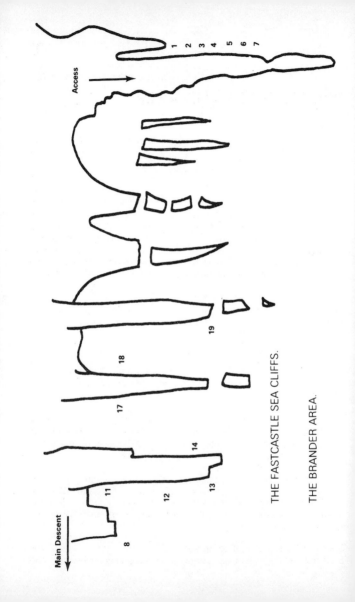

THE FASTCASTLE SEA CLIFFS.

THE BRANDER AREA.

Map: Sheet 67, G.R. 874 706

THE BRANDER AND AREA

ACCESS

From Dowlaw Farm follow the track round to the other side of the farm and instead of going left as for The Souter, go through the gate straight ahead and follow a track leading gently downhill beside a wall to a stream. For The Brander Slab follow the stream down its left bank to the shore, this point being easily reached along the cliff top from The Souter. For the area of fins beyond The Brander Slab, rather than following the stream down, the easiest approach is to follow the track gently uphill through a gate until the field on the left can be entered through another gate. Continue to an old pillbox and strike across the field to reach a fence on the clifftop. Follow this eastwards for a short way until a long grassy ridge can be descended to the shore and hence to the fins at the back of The Brander.

The Brander Slab

The Brander Slab is the obvious north-west facing slab jutting out into the sea to the east of The Souter, very much like Cornwall's Baggy Point, with some equally fine routes.

The following routes are probably best seen from a small promontory which lies immediately in front of the west face. Descents can be made either by abseil or by descending the seaward tip of the main slab to reach a ramp running back under the slab to the water. The climbs are described from right to left, facing the cliff.

1   Spring Shower   35m   Very Severe   4c   ★★★
This is the obvious continuous crack-line on the right-hand side of the slab, starting from the lower ledge. A classic route in an exciting position. Follow the crack throughout.

2   Jonathon Livingstone Shitehawk   35m   Very Severe   4c
Start on the lower ledge about 6m left of Spring Shower. Move up directly into the right-bounding corner of 'the shield' to surmount the overlap and move diagonally left to reach a thin crack-line leading to the top.

3   Blue Moves   40m   E1   5a   ★★
Start from a hanging stance under the sea level bulge at low tide. The

stance is directly below the centre of the obvious pink shield in the centre of the slab.

Make bold moves up and diagonally right to reach the lower ledge and then move up a shallow overlapped groove to reach the middle ledge. Climb through the overlap at the apex and go up the shield passing some shallow pockets. Poorly protected.

4   Sea Sprite   40m   HVS   5a   ★★
Good climbing up the thin disjointed crack-line in the left-hand side of the shield. Start as for Blue Moves and climb vertically up the lower slab to the halfway ledge. Climb through the overlap and continue up the cracks.

5   What have the Vikings ever done for us?   40m   HVS   4c
Start just left of Blue Moves directly below the left-bounding corner of the shield. Move up the slab to the corner and climb this to pull out rightwards at the top.

6   Rufus the Red   37m   E1   5a   ★
Start at the base of the ramp and follow cracks to the halfway ledge. Move up into the apex of the shallow overlap near the top; unprotected.

7   Sea Ahoy   37m   Hard Severe
Climb the crack-line left of Rufus the Red, bearing left at the top.

The next section, a fine slab right at the top of the Brander, is called The Seaward Slab. It is composed of a basalt bottom half overlayed by a shield of perfect sandstone on the upper half. There are about 5 routes on 'go anywhere' rock with grades varying between 4a and 4c.

The East Brander Bay
The following routes lie on the fins encountered after descending the long grassy ridge to the South-East of The Brander. The first fin is called the main fin and other fins lie just beyond this.

The Main Fin
8   Skate   90m   Severe
Start at the left-hand end.
Climb a vegetated ramp until broken ground is reached, follow this and trend right until the upper tier of rock is gained. A fine chimney is then climbed to the top.

9   Carapus   60m   Very Severe
The obvious chimney line to the right of skate.

10   Un-Named   no details available
Climb the crack left of Carapus until progress is barred by an overhang. Enter Carapus and finish by this route.

11   Guano Corner   61m   Hard Very Severe   4c
Climb the corner at the left-hand end of the main wall. A horror show, for reasons explicit in the name!

12   Cockle Shell Cracks   60m   Very Severe
Probably the hardest of the original routes in the area. Climb the thin crack system between the chimney of Carapus and the corner of Squid. Continue until the crack divides and then follow the left branch.

13   Squid   60m   Hard Very Severe   5a
The obvious corner in the edge of the fin. Climb straight up the corner passing a large bulge, pr (crux) and ascend a chimney to reach the top. An enjoyable route.

14   Sperm   18m   Severe
Climbs the chimney around the corner from the main fin.

15   Lucky Day   30m   E3   5b
The north face has an obvious right-leaning diagonal groove leading up to a block. Climb the groove past an ancient peg to pull on to the block with difficulty and traverse rightwards on the overhung ledge to a ramp. Climb this to a niche at the top of the wall. Dangerous.

16
A thin crack-line leading direct to the ramp and niche of Lucky Day, no grade available.

First Fin

17   Dayglo   18m   Hard Very Severe   5b
Follow the sharp crack in the middle of the wall until it fades out into a shallow groove leading to the top.

18   Quasi's Back   12m   E3   6a   ★★★
Climb the zig-zag crack in the middle of the north west face to finish up the crest of the buttress.

19 Purve 45m Very Severe
The thin left, seaward, edge of the second fin is climbed in one runout.
There is apparently no protection and the rock is loose.

OTHER CRAGS

Map: Sheet 66, G.R. 191 847

BELL'S ROCKS

The sandstone outcrops behind the first green on Aberdour golf course.
Approaching from the harbour along the beach two tors are passed,
each of which has a few interesting problems. Bell's Rocks consist of
three separate tors. The first has a dozen routes up to 15m long of
various grades on its seaward face. The second is disappointing, but
the third (the most north-westerly) has a dozen stiff leads and problems
on a pleasant sunny face.

Map: Sheet 65, G.R. 125 835

ROSYTH QUARRY

This small dolerite quarry lies just south-east of the junction of the M90
and the A92. There are nearly fifty routes here some of which are quite
worthwhile, particularly a series of deep cracks and corners in the
highest part of the quarry. These provide climbs of Very Severe
standard.

Map: Sheet 65, G.R. 043 735

BINNIE CRAIG

This small, natural dolerite outcrop lies to the north of the A71 in West
Lothian. The main cliff is rather loose and broken, but a smaller cliff
down and to its left (north) has some good climbs at VS to HVS
standard.

Map: Sheet 66, G.R. 863 202

DALOCHY QUARRY

This spectacular sandstone quarry provides the only worthwhile aid
climbing in the Edinburgh area. Most of the lines are quite obvious and
The Great Roof is absolutely unmistakable, a line of bolts leading up a
vertical wall and over a 16m roof.

BOULDERING

INTRODUCTION

Bouldering has always been an important aspect of rock climbing in the Edinburgh area. Traditionally it was carried out on 'natural' cliffs like Salisbury Crags, but Tiso's 1967 guide contained information on a significant departure — Haston's descriptions of bouldering on the Currie Railway Wa's, man-made railway embankments. Due to lack of imagination, or perhaps potential embarrassment at being thought exhibitionist, this practice was slow to be extended, but Edinburgh abounds with fine, man-made bouldering walls and there are now several areas regularly used by climbers. There are even some routes: the Newbridge Viaduct has at least one, the work of Ken Spence, Rab Anderson and Duncan McCallum, climbed using nuts in gaps in the masonry for protection. The route at Roseburn Viaduct was climbed by Derek Austin and Ewan Kellar, re-establishing interest in an area first climbed on by Jimmy Marshall, amongst others.

The more significant bouldering areas are described below. Where there is bouldering at or near one of the outcrops this is mentioned in the appropriate section. There are certainly more potentially suitable walls in and around the city, but it is to be hoped that any walls chosen for this are such that a little minor damage to the odd bit of crumbling masonry will be of no consequence.

As ever, the comments of uncomprehending passers-by or impudent youth remain one of the most trying objective hazards.

An Edinburgh City Street Plan will be of more use in finding these places than an O.S. map.

Map: Sheet 66, G.R. 109 723

NEWBRIDGE VIADUCT

Follow the A8 from Edinburgh to the Newbridge roundabout and take the A89 (Bathgate) exit. Follow this for about 1½km, and turn left for Birdsmill (signposted) immediately before the road goes under a small viaduct. The west end of the main viaduct is gained by following the road, turning left at a T-junction, to park under the viaduct itself.

The viaduct carries the main Edinburgh — Stirling railway line. This should be borne in mind when taking a belay at the top.

The only route described lies on the south west face of the western embankment of the viaduct, up a line past obviously cleaned gaps in the masonry (E3 5c/6a).

The embankment walls and pillars all give good bouldering. Traverses of the latter can provide excellent stamina training for the fingers, and the number of pillars makes overcrowding rather unlikely.

NEWHAVEN/GRANTON WALLS   Map: Sheet 66, G.R. 245 771

These sea-walls lie adjacent to McKelvie Parade, which itself lies at the other side of the railway line which runs along the north side of Lower Granton Road. Pass on to McKelvie Parade through a subway from Lower Granton Road at the west end of the blocks of flats. Turn left and walk along until it is possible to descend to the base of the wall via a line of iron spikes. The faint-hearted can approach from the new sewage outfall system at the east end of McKelvie Parade.

There are two distinct walls, a vertical one on the left and a slabbier one on the right. The latter provides the best climbing, a traverse being possible at a fairly low level. All the hardest moves are apparently near the ground, so a fall on to the sloping ramp at the base should not result in permanent injury. The complete traverse of this wall has been done at least once, and provides a fine expedition.

Map: Sheet 66, G.R. 251 763

BONNINGTON WALLS

These are gained by following Ferry Road to the eastern edge of Goldenacre Sports Ground. A disused railway cutting runs under Ferry Road here. This is gained and followed north for a couple of hundred metres, to reach the pillar of a long-demolished bridge. There are many straight-up problems, and the pillar can be traversed at different levels.

Other bridges over the disused railways in the area also provide good bouldering. It is possible to climb in the rain under one or two of these, always useful in the Scottish summer.

Map: Sheet 66, G.R. 241 738

DEAN WALLS

Turn left off Queensferry Street on to Belford Road, just before the Dean Bridge (travelling north). The walls are found on the right a short distance down Belford Road, and face north across the Water of Leith on to Dean Village.

There are some short straight-up problems on the steep wall and up the corner, and some longer straight-up problems and a traverse on the slabby wall on the left.

Map: Sheet 66, G.R. 231 734

ROSEBURN VIADUCT

Opposite the Roseburn Bar, Roseburn Terrace, billboards face the road. Climb through a gap between these and across waste ground at their rear for about 100m to reach a disused railway viaduct spanning the Water of Leith. Good bouldering can be had on the pillars, although many may prefer top-rope practice. One climb is described.

Slotter Alley   20m   E2   5b
Looking from the downstream side, the facing wall of the left-hand pillar. Climb this to a small ledge at 10m, then straight up to parapet.

Map: Sheet 66, G.R. 264 735

PLEASANCE WALL

Travelling down Holyrood Road towards the Palace, turn right into Viewcraig Gardens and carry on until a fine steep wall appears on the right, opposite a block of flats. A complete traverse of this wall is very strenuous, and excellent finger training.

BLACKFORD QUARRY   Map: Sheet 66, G.R. 258 703

CORBIE'S CRAIG   Map: Sheet 66, G.R. 256 704

These crags are found on Blackford Hill on the south side of the city. Both have very attractive and sunny situations, particularly the latter. Follow Blackford Glen Road off Liberton Brae to its far (west) end (car parking). From here a popular footpath leads along to the Hermitage of Braid. Follow this for a couple of hundred metres until the path forks; take the right fork into the quarry bowl. There are numerous walls in the quarry, the highest and best being the west-facing wall. This reaches some 20m in height, and provides several routes in the lower grades climbed on slabby rock well-provided with holds. This wall is popularly used for training beginners in abseiling and rock climbing.

For Corbie's Craig, instead of taking the right fork into the quarry described above, take the left fork and continue for a further 100m by the Braid Burn. Before a bridge the path branches once more; take the right fork and the crag comes into view immediately, on the right. It is steeper and more complicated than the quarry walls, and also reaches some 20m in height. The rock runs to lots of flat and incut holds and several lines exist, up to about Hard Very Severe. Unfortunately detailed descriptions for any routes here do not seem to be available.

Both crags can also be reached by following paths south from the car park at the Royal Observatory.

Map: Sheet 66, G.R. 180 675

THE CURRIE RAILWAY WA'S

The original, but no longer the best. Follow Lanark Road and Lanark Road West into Currie. A road leads down left opposite Riccarton Mains Road; follow this to reach the Water of Leith Walkway – the Railway of Haston's day. Travel west along the path towards Balerno. After about ten minutes the Bowling Green Walls are reached — the Lower Bowling Green Wall has several routes and a traverse, all made more interesting by the penalty clause. Further walls and bridges along the path provide several straight-up problems and traverses. The last bridge, Balerno Bridge, provides the two hardest traverses on the Wa's.

Map: Sheet 66, G.R. 237 662

CAERKETTON HILL

This is the hill in the Pentlands with the Hillend Ski Slope on it. Although hardly worth a visit purely for the climbing, the situation is highly attractive and a visit could be combined with walking the dog, or any other pleasant pursuit which might otherwise be felt to be a little tame. The climbing is on the most continuous mass of rock to the west of the ski-slope. Routes have been climbed here by some of the great names of Scottish climbing, so it is hoped that would-be explorers will bring a suitably reverent approach. Modern rock gymnasts may find the experience good for the soul, if not for the fingers.

THE SOUTH WEST

INTRODUCTION

This is the first guide book to bring together the collective experience of the rock climber in the South West. The reason for the vague term 'collective experience' is that word of mouth, as opposed to the written word, has been the method of communication. This guide may be seen by some as breaking the spirit of these earlier explorations but it is to be hoped that the opposite will be the case.

The function of this guide then, is twofold: firstly, to alert local climbers to existing and potential routes; secondly, to show those interested from further afield that there is excellent, year-round climbing available.

The climate is drier and sunnier than that of Northern Scotland or the near-by Lake District. Therefore, the bedraggled rock climber late in his season, or the frustrated ice climber waiting for his to start, might find that a sojourn on these warm, sheltered, quick-drying crags is just the fillip he needs.

Since the first recorded climbs at Meikle Ross in 1972, activity and standards have been steadily rising. While the climbs have not reached the standards of the Central Belt, this guide comes out at a period of increased interest in this area. The discovery of Burrow Head is the most important event of recent times and it is on this cliff that the hardest and most impressive lines are waiting to be climbed. For the future . . . who knows what a casual coastal walk might un-cover; perhaps another crag X?.

HISTORY

Investigating the development of climbing in the South West does not yield any dramatic results nor any complete heritage. Rather the early history is one of possibilities than events: the few articles from the turn of the century, though they mention all the crags in the Galloway Hills, give no real climbing. Indeed, in the S.M.C.J. 1906, which gives the first comprehensive round-up of walking and climbing in this area, the Climbs section points the prospective climber to the steepest and most continuous crags, but records no routes.

Perhaps in character, rock climbing in the South West is given an obtuse start when E.C. Thomson and company, discovering Benbeoch, soloed the easiest line in the centre of the crag, in 1932.

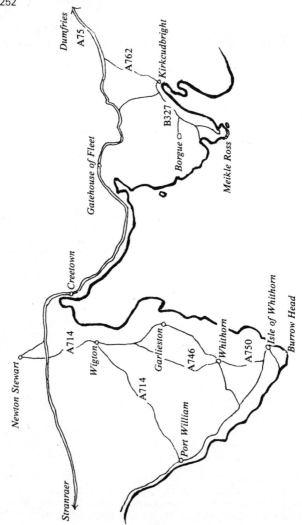

The general tone of the early articles is apologetic and pleading. This follows, perhaps, as the South West has always been something of an unknown quantity. The pleas having been largely unheeded, this tone is still apparent in 1958 when A.G. Waldie wrote of the first climbing in the district:

> The disconsolate climber, enervated by the balmy climate of Galloway and preserving his nails on its lush vegetation, might well consider selling his rope to the Solway boatmen.

Waldie nevertheless goes on to give a series of reasons, in the shape of sea-cliffs, and outcrops, as well as the crags of the Galloway Hills, that might persuade the climber to hold on to his rope. Recording the first routes in the Galloway Hills, Waldie tells of climbing on most of the major crags including the Cooran Buttress, the Flesh Market and the Clints of Dromore. From this time on, local knowledge has it that climbing continued, though without any recording of routes or any direct contact between those taking part. The lack of a tradition or the relative youth of the climbers is perhaps the reason for this.

Waldie notes a further area of development — what is now known as the Dumfries Outcrops. Again, the inquisitive climber can only discover the number of routes that were climbed, as opposed to locating any one of them. Sixteen climbs are mentioned at Clifton, from Easy to Very Severe. This means progress has to be gauged in numbers and grades: there are now 48 routes on this cliff, up to E4. This increase in activity started in 1976, when C.A. and G.Macadam were pointed to the cliff. Technical standards began to move and the following year the first extremes were climbed. Jugular Vein was the first to fall, then Wall Street was exposed from behind a tenuous line of ivy on the first ascent. Finally, the Toddamundo arête was soloed, after a quick brushing. 1978 saw the first 5c in The Arête, and in 1979, the first 6a's — Fingerlust, and Lemur. However, unknown to the local climbers, and predating the first climbs at Clifton, the larger sea-cliffs south of Kirkcudbright were being developed. W.Cheverest had started climbing at Meikle Ross in 1972. His first route, Limehouse Blues, climbed in April of that year, is not the most obvious when an entire cliff is available. Limehouse Blues, however, was climbed in the days before pre-cleaning was common-place as it is now, and this route stays naturally clean. This was the same with K.9, Cheverest's other major climb, which also has a similar structure: from a straightforward, slabby start, the route steepens to an exposed and technical crux finish. These routes were the first advance in standards for twenty years.

Cheverest, significantly, wrote the first article on climbing in the

South West since A.G.Waldie. This was published in Rocksport, and brought the attention of a number of other climbers to this area.

After a two-year lull, J.F.Kerry, a pioneer Welshman who sought new rock, was brought south from Glasgow by the Rocksport article. He gardened and climbed a series of major routes in the period from March 1975 to September 1977, which were recorded in the Glasgow Outcrops, Volumes 1 & 2. Initially, Kerry's attention was focussed on the eye-catching crack-lines, which are a feature of these cliffs. Salty Dog, H.V.S. 4c, was climbed on March 3rd 1975 — the same day as Kerry led the twin bulges of Mellow Yellow, in Little Zawn. However, excellent as these routes are, Kerry's real interest was in the longer, layback grooves of the main cliff. Galloway Corner, climbed in early 1975 by Andy Hunter, though favoured at the time, is not of the same quality as Side Track, which, by climbing direct to the first stance, avoids a 15m walk and gives the route a more sustained interest and difficulty. The first pitch of Side Track is part of a natural groove line, 60m high. Kerry returned in May 1977 and completed this route, Back Track, E1 5a — the boldest in the area at that time.

C.Macadam was alerted to these sea-cliffs through the Glasgow Outcrops guide. However, as an inexperienced climber, these more intimidating cliffs proved more of a test than the local outcrops. Kerry's technical high-point — Bloody Crack, E1 5b, climbed in January 1976 — was not surpassed in the seventies. Excellent routes were found by a thorough examination of the cracks and spaces on Limehouse Blues Cliff, but the hardest and best of these, the wall of Finesse, climbed in October 1978, is only just inside the extreme category.

Late in 1979, the discovery of Burrow Head turned attention away from the locally established crags. The steeper, smoother greywacke has meant that the routes are more strenuous and more sustained than those of the Ross. Conquistador, climbed in January 1980, was the first E2 on the Southern sea-cliffs. However, the pace of development, while constant, was never quickened by the threat of competition. Seven months later, Naked Fun, another sustained E2, was climbed on the best-looking face in the South West.

The period from 1975 to 1980 was one of great activity, with the discovery of four new crags and the consequent surfeit of unclimbed rock. The same has not been true of the years from 1981 to 1985. For this, there are a number of reasons: a lack of information deterred potential first ascenscionists from further afield; and, as most of the major lines had been climbed, there was not the same scope for the few that knew of the latest developments.

These years did see major new additions on all the main crags, and a small increase in the number of active climbers. Two years behind Clifton, Macadam climbed the first E3's at Meikle Ross in 1981. The smooth corner of Fil d'Or', with its difficult initial bridging, is particularly of note. Burrow Head was visited the following year by Ian Duckworth and Macadam, then Stirling-based. The result was Mirror, Mirror, E3 5c, by a direct start — a bold on-sight lead by Duckworth.

A border raid by P.Whillance and J.Fotheringham was the only activity of 1982. Of their three routes, The Highwayman had been climbed by G.Little in 1968, exemplifying the recording problems in this area. Of the other routes, Saddle Tramp, at E2 5c the hardest route in the Galloway Hills, makes excellent use of the terraced buttress it climbs.

Nothing of any importance was climbed in 1983, but 1984 more than compensated for this. After a four-year gap, the first new routes were put up on Clifton. D.I.Austin climbed through the curving overhang of Moonshine to make Beyond the Terminator, and Macadam, after one fall, completed Toddamundo by forcing the headwall above the initial arête, the first E4 in the South West.

Meikle Ross was closely scrutinised, and a number of possibilities were spotted. Austin climbed the deceptive crack of Corridor of Power, E3 5c. This climb is unusual as it is formed by the edge of the bedding planes — the first climb to do this, but surely not the last. Catalysed by this activity, Macadam returned to the Ross and forced the smooth wall right of Mellow Yellow. Called Sunshine Superman, E4 6a, this is the boldest climb in this section.

The future seems likely to produce several further discoveries as this part of the world is by no means climbed out. As with the Rocksport article and the Highrange Guides, this publication will in turn yield its fruit.

THE SOUTHERN SEACLIFFS
INTRODUCTION

The coastline along the Solway Firth has a considerable number of sea-cliffs, rocky islands and inlets. This section is only concerned with those that have been extensively explored — Meikle Ross and Burrow Head. Other cliffs are mentioned in the Minor Crag section.

It should be pointed out that a voluntary ban is observed at these cliffs from May until late August. The reason for this is not only one of conservation but of the condition of the guano-covered rock. However, Fox Craig and The Red Slab are unaffected.

MEIKLE ROSS   Map: Sheet 83, G.R. 652 433
INTRODUCTION

Meikle Ross is the collective name given to the south-east facing sea-cliffs on the tip of the peninsula on the west side of Kirkcudbright Bay. The cliffs hold the sun until late afternoon in all seasons. This welcome information, allied to the sheltered aspect of the cliffs, presents climbers with the opportunity of climbing through the winter and early spring.

The rock is Silurian Greywacke, which, though it does not appear so, is a form of hard sandstone. The friction is excellent and, although the rock had a covering of loose material, ten years of climbing and the now ubiquitous abseil gardening has stripped this down to reveal the firm grey rock that is presently climbed upon. It is prudent, however, to treat some routes with care (this will be noted in the text). Recent developments have increased the range and quality of routes from mainly good cracks to excellent slabs, walls and corners: Scared to Dance, Finesse and Fil d'Or respectively representing the best of these routes.

Camping is possible at Ross Bay, but is basic. However, there is a luxurious site at Brighouse Bay, immediately west of the cliffs. In Kirkcudbright, the usual post-route necessities — chip shops and a good local bar can be quickly located.

ACCESS

From the north or the south, turn off the A74 and make for Dumfries. From Dumfries, take the A75 Stranraer road, turning left for Kirkcudbright, on the A711. Reaching Kirkcudbright town centre, turn right, crossing the river, then left and follow the B727 Borgue road. Turn

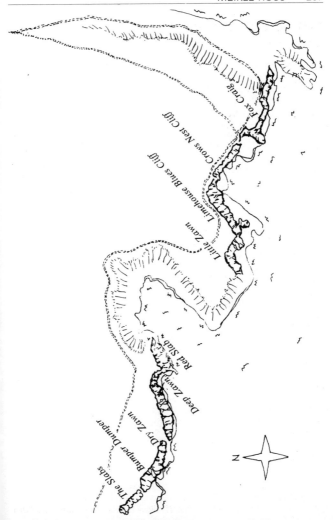

Fox Craig

Crows Nest Cliff

Limehouse Blues Cliff

Little Zawn

Red Slab

Deep Zawn

Dry Zawn

Bumper Dumper

The Slabs

N

left at the signpost for Brighouse Bay and left again, at a fork, to Ross Bay. Parking and camping are at the far side of the bay. The track over the hill leads to the headland and the cliffs, taking about ten minutes.

The climbing is split into two areas: that to the east and that to the west of Slack Heugh Bay; the eastern section is the first to be encountered, and, if the sea level path is taken, Fox Craig the first cliff.

Fox Craig

This cliff (marked by a pronged stake on its summit) is below the promontory which allows an excellent view of Limehouse Blues Cliff, and access to that cliff at low tide. Fox Craig can be gained from either side.

At its left-hand side, a number of cracks and ribs, formed by the bedding plane, extend steeply upwards for 30 metres. The cliff then decreases in height and a soaring but easier-angled arête seen. The arête marks an angle in the cliff, round from which are two walls, the first as high as the second is long. These walls are the first to be seen if the lower path is taken. The routes are described from right to left, facing the cliff.

1   Shark's Tooth   9m   Very Difficult
On the right of the longer wall — the cleaned cracks.

2   Alligator Crawl   9m   Very Severe   4c   ★
Start in the middle of the wall and climb straight to the top. Good, slabby wall climbing.

3   Fats Waller   14m   Very Severe   4c
This route climbs the higher wall, left of the previous routes. Move up a crack for 7m. Traverse right 1½m, and up over the small overhang (crux) to the top.

4   Curving Arête   15m   Severe   ★★
Climbs the bounding arête of the last route. One small leap . . .

On the left, the main section of cliff now protrudes as a large, square tower, with a clean-cut ledge at two-thirds of its height.

5   Dolphin Groove   20m   Hard Very Severe   4c
Start on the right of a distinct crack.
Climb to a ledge on the right. Follow a shallow groove on the left, then a steep groove on the right (pr) to a ledge. Climb an overhanging groove to the top.

6   Crack and Corner   30m   Very Severe   4b   ★
Climb the distinct crack to the right-hand side of the ledge. Climb the
corner on the left of the top. A characteristic Ross route.

7   Ken's Groove   30m   Hard Severe
Climb a shallow groove, left of Crack and Corner, to its ledge. Follow it
to the top.

Left again is the steepest section of the cliff, constantly overhanging
for 22 metres, brought to a focus in the prominent central lamination, a
hanging arête. To its right is an obvious concave crack line.

8   Corridor of Power   30m   E3   5c   ★★
A strenuous climb, taking the impressive first-sized crack. A good
selection of Friends, including a No.4, is advisable.
    Climb the crack and, as it steepens into the crack-cum-groove of its
crux, wonder where the jamming might be. Move right at the top of the
crux section. Finish up a groove on the left.

9   Promontory Wall   16m   Severe
At the left extremity of the crag a wall juts into the sea. It has a corner at
mid-height on its right. Start 5m left of the corner.
    Climb the wall to a ledge. Move into the corner and finish directly.
Better than it looks.

Crow's Nest Cliff

This is the very steep and loose cliff, west of the promontory, which
forms a right-angle with the smooth bedding plane of Limehouse Blues
Cliff.
    It is marked by a broken diagonal fault line, crossing the cliff from
bottom left to top right, above a large cave. The left-hand section of the
cliff contains a large pinnacle. Though not for the purist, much remains
to be discovered.

10   The Battle of Osfrontalis   45m   Hard Very Severe   4c   4b
An impressive expedition — care is needed with protection on pitch 1
and the rock generally. Start left of the cave where a small promontory
meets the cliff.

1.   20m   Climb left of a chimney to a ledge. Make a precarious move
up the wall and continue to a large bower, pb in situ.

2.   25m   Move right to join the diagonal fault. Follow this to a finish up
a short groove. Not for the nervous!

MEIKLE ROSS — LIMEHOUSE BLUES CLIFF.

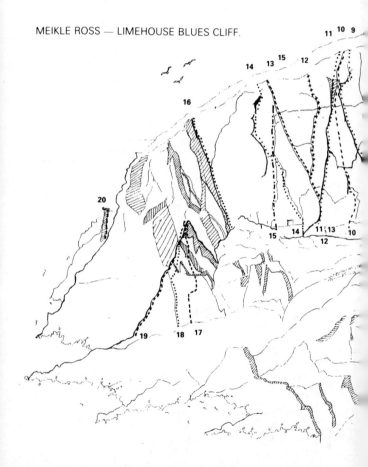

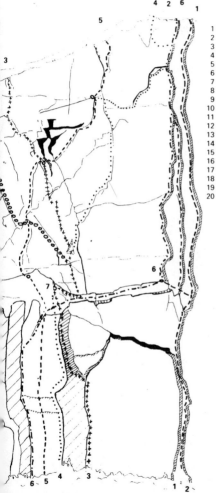

1 Back Track
2 Side Track
3 Maple Leaf Rag
4 Crack Track
5 Limehouse Blues
6 Galloway Corner
7 Bluefinger
8 Finesse
9 Sorcerer's Apprentice
10 Accutrac
11 Salty Dog
12 Akela
13 Dogleg
14 Argus
15 Sea Dog
16 Exit Groove
17 Zugsfang
18 Compulsion
19 Groove Y
20 Orange Chimney (Little Zawn)

Limehouse Blues Cliff

The highest and most impressive cliff on the peninsula. The most obvious feature is a terrace splitting the cliff. It narrows on the right to a sloping ledge, above a large cave recess. This recess is flanked by narrow slabs, left and right. The tier above the terrace (on which the best climbing is found) is a smooth-looking wall, with a pear-shaped outline. At its right-hand section, in contrast, there are a series of layback grooves, set out from the wall.

The first climbs are affected by high tide. It is possible, if the sea is calm, to sea-level traverse to the starts, or they can be joined at pitch two by descending Access Groove and moving right, along the terrace.

11   Back Track   60m   E1   5a   5a
Takes the good-looking natural line of the continuous groove right of the cave recess. Start at the first level above the recess.

1.   22m   Move up the slab to the groove line and follow it until a traverse line to the terrace is found. Piton or horizontal nut belay.

2.   38m   Regain the groove and follow it to the top. Care is needed with the rock and the protection — a hard lead.

12   Side Track   60m   Hard Very Severe   5a   5a   ★★
A fine, sustained route.

1.   22m   As for Back Track.

2.   38m   Move right 2m and climb the groove until it peters out.
   Join the groove on the left (Galloway Corner) and follow it to the top. Enjoyable laybacking!

13   Maple Leaf Rag   60m   Hard Very Severe   4b   5a   4c   ★★★
A classic route with a surprising last pitch. Start in the cave recess, just right of the left-hand slab.

1.   20m   Climb the slab to the roof, move left, and climb a groove to the terrace. Flake belay.

2.   20m   The wall on the right has a steep crack. Climb steeply on the right of the crack to the right-hand of two niches. From the top of the niche, climb thinly up the slab to a good resting place. Step left, and climb the front face of a large flake to belay in a large niche.

3.   20m   Move left from the niche. Gain and climb a curving crack to a ledge with a horizontal crack; climb the wall above with whatever it may or may not conceal!

14   Crack Track   65m   Hard Very Severe   4a   5a   5a   ★
A route with delicate climbing in a good situation. Start at the base of
the slab left of the cave recess.

1.   18m   Climb the right edge of the slab to a flake belay on the
terrace.

2.   20m   As for Maple Leaf Rag to the second niche. Traverse right to
a crack and follow it past a small spike to a ledge and belay on the left.

3.   20m   Traverse right to the base of an edge and follow this, boldly,
to a junction with a groove (Galloway Corner). Move up, traverse left 2m
and climb on good holds to the top.

15   Limehouse Blues   60m   Hard Very Severe   4a   4b   5a   ★
The original route on the cliff, which builds to an airy and bold finish.
Start at the slab at the left of the recess.

1.   18m   Climb the middle of the slab to the terrace. Flake belay.

2.   20m   Gain and climb the obvious flake crack to the large niche.

3.   22m   Step down 1 metre and climb the fine slab right round the
edge to a short crack, then a thin ledge. From the right-hand end of the
ledge, climb a crack to gain a small ledge on the right (crux). Up the wall
above to finish.

16   Galloway Corner   70m   Hard Very Severe   4c   5a
Start at a chimney, in the left edge of Limehouse Blues' slab.

1.   30m   Climb the chimney and the groove above, moving right to
the terrace. Walk right for 13m to a belay below the first layback groove.

2.   40m   Climb the stepped corner to the top with hard moves at the
start and three-quarters height.

   The area of rock left of pitch one of the last route has given two minor
routes: Belemnite Groove, which climbs a groove in the wall left of
Galloway Corner, quitting it when it overhangs to the left; and Limpet
Arête, the good edge left again. They are graded Severe and Very
Difficult, respectively.

   The next group of climbs start from the terrace. This can be gained in
one of three ways: by descending Exit Groove (ironically this poor
route's main function); by abseil from the fence; or, easily across the
bay at low tide.

19   Bluefinger   30m   Very Severe   4c
Starts as for Maple Leaf Rag, pitch 2.

Climb into the left-hand niche and follow a crack left to a junction with Limehouse Blues. Move up and left to gain a leftward-slanting crack which is taken to the top.

The section of cliff to the left of Bluefinger has the distinguishing feature of a capital 'A' the full height of the cliff, formed by two prominent cracks. The next route starts 1m right of the right-hand crack and climbs the sweep of wall above.

20   Finesse   30m   E1   5b   ★★
A superb slab of rock, giving bold balance climbing.
    Climb over a small overlap to a ledge. Up past a hinged spike to an inverted-V overlap. Then climb the fine wall above, moving right to an indefinite crack which leads to a ledge. Step left and follow a crack to the top.

21   Sorcerer's Apprentice   27m   Very Severe   4c
The right-hand crack of the 'A' climbed to within a few feet of Salty Dog. Then traverse right past a small ledge and climb direct to the top.

22   Accutrac   26m   Hard Very Severe   5a
Climb directly to the apex of the 'A' starting at a crack right of centre.

23   Salty Dog   26m   Hard Very Severe   4c   ★★★
A fine, strenuous route with the hard moves in the first 4m.
    Climb the left-hand crack of the 'A'.

24   Dogleg   25m   Hard Very Severe   5a   ★★
Good steep crack climbing with the crux high on the crag.
    Start as for Salty Dog, but move immediately left and follow the left-slanting crack to the top. A fitting companion route to Salty Dog.

25   Akela   27m   Hard Very Severe   5a   ★
Takes the crack between Dogleg and Salty Dog.
    Climb Dogleg for 3m. Traverse right for 1 m to a good jug. Follow the crack direct to the top.

26   Argus   25m   E1   5b
A parallel line to Dogleg, starting 1m left of that route.
    Climb, strenuously, to a rectangular niche. Then take the continuation crack leftwards to a shallow recess. Climb the left edge of the recess or, better, the finger-crack in the recess, to a roof, then the top.

27   Seadog   24m   Hard Very Severe   5a
A good route, starting 1m left of Argus.
   Gain a thin crack and follow this and its wider continuation to a junction with Dogleg.

28   Exit Groove   16m   Very Difficult
Left of the main face, the cliff tapers into a groove, which starts at an easy angle. Where the groove splits follow the left-hand branch.
   Good for quick access to the top or bottom of the cliff.

29   Rhythm n' Blues   60m   Hard Very Severe   5a   5a   ★★
An enjoyable girdle with considerable atmosphere of its own. Start 6m up the right branch of Exit Groove, at a ledge and thread belay.

1.   30m   Traverse right, passing a small roof to a spike. Then, either climb a further 3m and descend Dogleg to a ledge, or, harder, descend immediately a finger-crack then traverse right to the same point. Step down, and traverse right to a crack. Climb until a traverse line which leads to Salty Dog can be gained. Continue in this line to a ledge and horizontal crack.

2.   30m   Move right to the ledge on Limehouse Blues, then follow Crack Track pitch 3 to Galloway Corner, finishing up this.

Pinnacle Face

Left of the upper tier is an obvious pinnacle, which forms a chimney with the main face. Its own front face is sportingly smoothed.

31   Pigeon Chimney   20m   Difficult   ★★
Climbs the chimney, going below a huge chockstone and thence to the summit.

32   Groove Y   15m   Very Difficult   ★
The left edge of the pinnacle — pleasant.

33   Compulsion   15m   E1   5b
Climb the left-hand crack in the front face for 8m. Move right, and climb right on pockets to the top.

34   Zugsfang   15m   E3   6a   ★
A good problem, climbing thinly on pockets at the hardest point. Start 1m right of Compulsion, at a thin crack.

Climb the wall, right, then left of the crack, until forced right to a good pocket, crux. Continue direct to the top.

35   White Out   14m   Hard Severe
Climb the groove in the right-hand arête of the pinnacle.

Little Zawn

These steep walls and corners of excellent rock are found to the left of the main cliff. It was said initially of this area that it was justifiably popular — so it has now proved to be. To reach the cliff continue down the hill above Limehouse Blues Cliff to a flat area of grass on the left. This is directly above the zawn. The climbs can be approached either by abseil or the grassy bank on the left of the cliff, then making an airy traverse, right above the water. This traverse finishes below a short wall which ends at a chimney. The first route starts 4m left of the chimney.

36   Steve's Route   12m   Very Severe   4b
Start at a square recess, where the traverse ends.
    After a long reach, climb direct to the top.

37   Orange Chimney   14m   Very Difficult   ★
The chimney mentioned above, with a finish either on the left or, better and harder, direct over the bulge.

38   Spectrum Wall   12m   Very Severe   5b
Start 1m left of Orange Chimney, at an inverted-V recess.
    Climb through the recess (crux) then up the wall above.

39   Green Wall   15m   Hard Severe   ★ ★
An excellent climb taking the wall right of Orange Chimney. Start 2m right of the chimney.
    Climb the leftward-sloping crack to a horizontal break. Move right and climb the rightward-leaning niche until a step left can be made. Finish up the wall above.

40   Clockwork Orange   15m   Very Difficult
Right again is a corner-crack which is climbed on the left wall to a finish over loose blocks. May improve with traffic.

41 Pinking Sheer 18m Hard Very Severe ★★
The right-angled arête, right of Clockwork Orange, gives an enjoyable route with surprisingly good protection. Start 1m right of the corner.

Climb up to and over the first bulge. Then make a move left to a ledge. Over the second bulge at the left, move right up a crack and finish by the wall above, on good holds.

42 Mellow Yellow 18m Very Severe 4c ★★★
A climb that looks and is a classic, which climbs the clean-cut crack splitting the yellow wall right of Pinking Sheer.

43 Sunshine Superman 18m E4 6a ★★
A sustained eliminate which gains independence with height. Start 1m right of Mellow Yellow.

Climb the short wall to the roof, move over this, then make a hard move up the wall to a small spike. Move right, then left to gain a crack above the bulge; move right and continue to the top. The use of runners in Mellow Yellow reduces the seriousness to the extent that the grade is E3 6a.

44 Stepped Corner 18m Hard Severe
The corner that bounds the Mellow Yellow wall. It requires large nut or Friend runners. Better than it looks.

45 Bloody Crack 16m E1 5b ★
A good strenuous effort, taking the crack right of Stepped Corner.

46 Fil d'Or 16m E3 6a ★★
Beside Bloody Crack is an alarmingly smooth corner. It has a pr at half-height. A technical test-piece.

The following two routes are found by scrambling up to the back of the zawn.

47 Left Corner 12m Severe
The left-hand corner crack, left of a band of shale. Good but short.

48 Right Corner 12m Severe
Not surprisingly, the right-hand corner crack.

49   Amnesia   23m   Very Severe   4c
The right wall of the zawn has an obvious, long, stepped corner. The start is just right of a green tongue of moss. One peg runner, used low down on the right wall, can be eliminated by a cleverly cammed 'Rock'. An interesting route — whatever it's called!

50   Headcase   15m   Very Severe   4c
The steep corner right of Amnesia; swing out right to finish.

51   A Walk on the Wild Side   48m   E1   5b   5b   ★★★
This girdle traverse makes good use of the natural lines on the crag. Start as for Steve's Route.

1.   27m   Climb the initial steep section of Steve's Route, then follow a rising line right, past Orange Chimney, until an overhanging arête blocks progress. A hard move round the arête leads to Mellow Yellow. Continue in this line to a small spike; descend into Stepped Corner. Belay.

2.   21m   Climb the pocketed rib on the right, then hand traverse right under a roof to Bloody Crack. Follow this, over its crux, to a ledge. Move right on excellent incuts, round a corner to a foot traverse which leads into Left Corner. Hence the top.

The Western Slabs

The following routes are found on the headlands and inlets west of Slack Heugh Bay. They are best approached by taking the right-hand path after the barn (see diagram.) The cliffs are described as they would be approached along this path, moving westwards.

The Red Slab

This cliff, over 30 metres high, contains the area's finest slab routes and the climbing, though rarely desperate, is enjoyable and highly recommended. Access to the climbs is by grassy bank on the right of the cliff. The routes are described from right to left and the first two routes are on the smoother right-hand section.

52   Scared to Dance   27m   E1   5a   ★★★
This satisfying slab route starts 1m left of the right-hand corner of the crag.
    Climb a brushed strip for 15m, traverse left 4m, then go straight up to a break. Move up and left to the top. Protection from numerous small wires.

53   Dolce Vita   27m   Hard Very Severe   4c   ★
Start left of Scared to Dance, below a lyre-shaped mark in the rock.
   Climb up to the mark, move diagonally for 5m, then continue direct to
the top.

54   Grand Central Couloir   34m   Very Severe   4c
Climbs the central depression, immediately left of Dolce Vita. good
climbing in its first half.

55   Cairn's Cream   34m   Very Severe   4c
Giving good slabby crack and groove moves, this climb starts 1m right
of an obvious tongue of rock.
   Climb a crack to the right-hand side of the tongue. Follow it until it
becomes an overlap. Move over it to a ledge. Finish up the blocky rib on
the left.

56   Bad Medicine Waltz   34m   Hard Very Severe   5a
Start below the tongue, 3m right of Cairn's Cream.
   Climb a crack to the left side of the tongue. Step right on to the
tongue and climb boldly up its centre to a ledge. Finish up the twin
cracks above.

57   Mental Block   30m   Very Severe   4c   ★★
This route starts at a higher level than the previous ones, at a long ledge.
Climb in a direct line, past a break, to gain the strange block. Move left,
up 3m, and right to below a corner, up which the route finishes.

58   Demolition Tango   30m   Hard Severe   ★★
Climbs a good thin crack between Mental Block and a larger, dirtier
crack (Tinman). Start 2m left of Mental Block.
   Make hard moves up the slab to below an overhang. Step left and
climb the crack to a ledge. finish on the right.

59   Tinman   30m   Severe
The large, dirty crack on the left. Follow it to the ridge and finish up it.

60   Coffin Crack   30m   Severe
Start 2m left of Tinman, below a coffin-shaped recess.
   Climb the recess and the overlap above to the ridge.

61   Access Ridge   29m   Very Difficult
The left edge of the slab.

Meikle Ross — The Red Slab and Deep Zawn

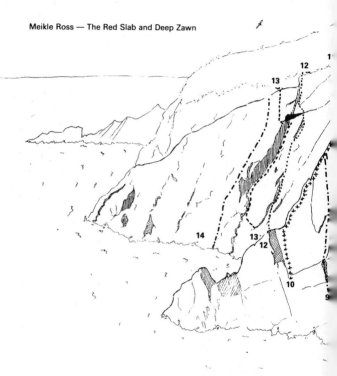

1 Scared to Dance
2 Dolce Vita
3 Grand Central Couloir
4 Cairn's Cream
5 Bad Medicine Waltz
6 Mental Block
7 Demolition Tango

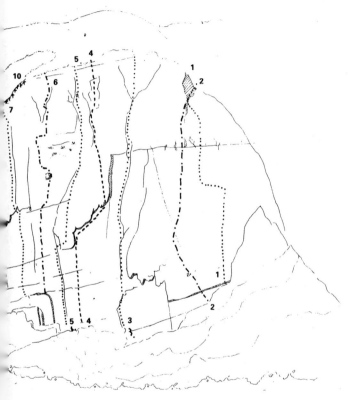

8 Tinman
9 Coffin Crack
10 Access Ridge
11 Rift Route
12 Yellow Dog
13 Dog Walk
14 Avernal Buttress

Deep Zawn

The climbing on this, the only truly tidal cliff, is at its best on a sunny, spring afternoon, when a sense of 'splendid isolation' adds atmosphere to the routes. The cliff is best seen from the rocks left of Access Ridge. It is split by a huge gash (The Rift) almost the height of the crag. Though the angle is generally pleasantly slabby, the top 15m steepen dramatically. The routes are described from right to left.

62   K.9.   50m   Hard Very Severe   ★★
A route with an exciting and exposed finish. Either abseil to the lowest ledge, or better, traverse from Access Ridge to the same point, (Difficult).

1.   18m   Climb steeply past a large ledge until a traverse right can be made to another ledge.

2.   32m   Move left to a small groove bordering The Rift. Climb delicately up this to a resting place. Continue in the same line, through the bulges, to the top.

It is possible from the position below the final bulges to traverse right, on to a slab and finish up this — easier but greener than the original finish.

The next climbs start to the left of The Rift. Though they may be reached by abseil, the best way to reach them is by an enjoyable sea-level traverse which is gained from the ramp left of the cliff. Either method leads to a ledge system in the middle of the crag.

63   Rift Route   50m   Severe
From the ledges, traverse right to the edge and follow it to the top. Stances and belays as required.

64   Eminence Grise   40m   Hard Severe   ★★
From the ledges, climb right to a deep recess. At the top of the recess pull out right to a ledge. Climb the thin crack in the slab above and pull over the overlap on the left. The cleaned strip leads to the top. To traverse to the foot of Eminence Grise and climb it is one of the best experiences the Ross can offer in the lower grades.

65   A Sop for Cerberus   40m   Hard Severe
Move into the recess on the left and exit 2m left of the previous route.

Climb slabs, moving left, to a ledge below the barrier. Climb the overhanging wall from left to right, on huge holds, to the top.

66   Yellow Dog   39m   Hard Very Severe   4a   4c
Start from the left side of the ledges.

1.   21m   Climb the slab, trending left to a ledge and nut belay 3m below the barrier.

2.   18m   Move right to the first overhang; climb this, moving left to a ledge. Move left and layback the second bulge; continue moving right along grooves to the top. Stake belay.

67   Dog Walk   30m   Difficult
Start at the left side of the ledges.

1.   20m   Traverse left to a corner and climb it to a roof, exiting left to a ledge and belay.

2.   10m   Climb direct to the gangway.

68   Avernal Buttress   30m   Very Difficult
The arête left of Dog Walk, climbed 1m left of the edge. Good.

Dry Zawn

To locate this small cliff, follow the rocky ramp that forms the left-hand crest of the previous cliff to the sea; climb the rib on the left to the floor of the zawn. The fact that this cliff forms three sides of a rectangle makes for still conditions on even the windiest days. The following routes are on the left-hand wall as you face the back of the zawn.

69   Route One   11m   Severe
The cracks at the left-hand end of the cliff. Good.

70   Route Two   11m   Mild Very Severe   4b
A worthwhile line which climbs the wall in the centre of the cliff.

71   Route Three   11m   Very Difficult
The right-hand corner.

   The next climb is found most easily by following the cliff tops westward, until a stake is located at the top of a pointed headland. The cliff below is extensive but, in the main, loose. Abseil is the quickest approach but it is more entertaining to traverse the rocks leftwards from Dry Zawn.

72   Bumper Dumper   28m   Hard Very Severe   5b   ★
At the right-hand side of the cliff is a smooth, sound face, split by two cracks.
   Climb the left-hand crack to a ledge; step right to a crack and follow it to the top. Suprisingly good, well-protected face climbing.

   The main cliff, left of Bumper Dumper, after major archaeological activity, gave up an unsatisfactory route: climb a crack (4m left of Bumper Dumper) and then the gardened trench to the top — shale delight!
   Looking west from the last route, there is a large area of slab which is easy-angled, but blank. Immediately below the headland is the best slab. This is bounded by a steep wall on its right and is split by an east-angled groove which gives the best access to the next route.

73   Titan's Corner   40m   Hard Very Severe   5a   ★
A good route, with delicate and bold climbing. It takes a line up the slab 1m left of the wall, climbing the overlap to finish.

74   Marie Celeste   40m   Mild Very Severe   4b
Start midway between the descent groove and Titan's Corner.
   Follow the prominent cracks up the slab, moving right to finish as for Titan's Corner.

75   Blistering Barnacles   40m   Severe
Takes the middle of the slab left of the groove. Pleasant, relaxed climbing.

BURROW HEAD

INTRODUCTION

Burrow Head is the name given to the group of sea-cliffs on the tip of the peninsula south of Newton Stewart. The rock is Silurian Greywacke which is similar to that of Meikle Ross. However, there are important differences: the bedding planes are set at a higher angle — the climbing on the main cliff is vertical or overhanging; the rock is sounder, though on early ascents some holds will alarmingly shed their outside edge; and, in general, the holds are smaller and more widely spaced than at the Ross: the consequences are that the climbs are harder, more athletic and more exposed than those, for instance, of Limehouse Blues Cliff. In fact, the verticality combined with the right-angled shape of the main cliffs gives it something of the atmosphere of Mother Carey's Kitchen. Fine sweeps of face catch the eye, and a number of routes (such as Naked Fun) combine a variety of features and moves that typify the climbing.

The caravan site nearby is remarkably well-equipped with showers, a chip shop, general store and a large pub. The draw-back is that camping is expensive and only possible from March until mid-October. Out of season, it is still possible to park here and camp elsewhere.

ACCESS

From Dumfries the A75 leads to Newton Stewart. At the by-pass roundabout, take the first left and make for Isle of Whithorn. From here, turn right following the signs for Burrow Head Caravan Site. The circular road round the site should be left at a sand quarry, where it is possible to park.

Walking east, a path is taken round several rocky inlets: the cliffs start where the path turns right-angled to the left (see diagram). A stake is seen above Diamond Buttress, and, to the west, a series of blocks marks the top of the first cliff. The foot of the cliff is reached by scrambling down the west-facing grassy bank behind the cliffs and moving right (as you face the bank) round a corner where the rock becomes more continuous.

The first cliff is recognised by a slim corner-groove leading to the right-hand end of a long thin roof. Below and left of the roof is a smooth wall. The first route starts left of this wall, below a short groove leading to a corner.

BURROW HEAD — GENERAL

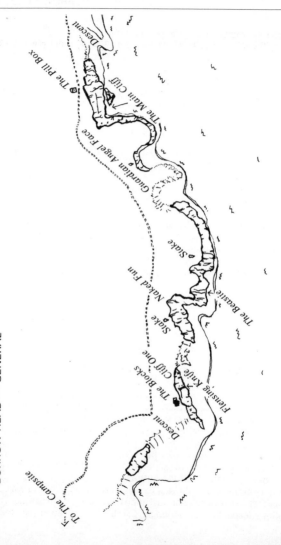

Descent

The Pill Box

The Main Cliff

Guardian Angel Face

Slake

The Beastie

Naked Fun

Slake

Cliff One

The Blocks

Flensing Knife

Descent

To The Campsite

1   Run, Rabbit, Run   20m   Hard Severe
Climb a juggy wall to the groove, climb it (crux) moving left to a longer,
easier groove. Difficult to protect the crux. A good steep finish.

2   Lemming's Wall   20m   Very Severe   4c
Climb the off-vertical wall immediately right of, and, in its top section,
over-looking, Run, Rabbit, Run. So called as it was first ascended by a
part of seven!

3   Watership Down   20m   Very Severe   4c   ★★
An inviting wall climb which needs some small wires low down. Start 1
m right of Lemming's Wall, below a crack high in the wall.
    Climb up 7m, past an undercling, and right to a ledge; regain the
original line at the crack, then straight to the top. Possible in the rain, as
the first ascent proved.

4   Prometheus (on his crag)   20m   E1   5b   ★★
Unprotected and delicate climbing leads to a strenuous roof on this
sustained climb. Start 3m left of the corner.
    Move left over quartz-flecked rock to gain a shallow scoop; up and
right to a ledge. Climb the roof, on the left, by twin cracks to finish.

5   Flensing Knife   22m   Very Severe   4c   ★
Climb the corner, to a bulge; either layback left (strenuous) or bridge
right (technical) to gain a ledge. Follow a diagonal line of flake holds left
to finish.

6   Yellow Crack   18m   Severe
The wall right of the corner has a good crack. Finish up a shallow scoop.

Diamond Buttress

The next climbs are marked at the top by a stake. They are found right of
the previous cliff. The wall itself is shaped like a giant, elongated
diamond and both of the climbs on it are among the best in this guide.

7   Naked Fun   36m   E2   5b   ★★★
A physical pleasure, well protected and sustained. Start at a grooved
ramp left of the toe of the buttress.
    The ramp leads right to a foothold on the edge of the wall. Make a
hard reach to a horizontal crack then traverse right 3m to a jug. The ramp
above leads to a small ledge. Climb left to a good jug, then hand

traverse right 2m into a strenuous position. Go directly up the wall to a ramp (crux) which leads to the finishing cracks.

8   Adventures in the Skin Trade   30m   E3   5c   ★★
Another excellent route with a thin, bold crux. Start at the toe of the buttress.

Climb direct to the small foothold on Naked Fun; move up to the horizontal crack, step left and climb straight up (crux) to a line of good holds.

Follow these right (not without interest) until a flake line leads back left and up to a finishing crack.

Round the corner on the right, at higher level, is a triangular face (unclimbed as yet). To the right of this are twin chimneys, both Very Difficult. The left-hand chimney splits into two: the left-hand variant is Boozer's Chimney and is shaped like an upside down bottle; the better right-hand variant, The Newt, gives good laybacking to finish. The wall between the twin chimneys is a pleasant Severe (The Changeling).

Forming a right-angle with this cliff is a large, impressive wall-cum-chimney as yet unclimbed; the cliff turns a right-angle again and there is a long face seamed with grooves, 20m in height. Only one route has so far been recorded. This route (The Beastie) starts at the left-hand end of the cliff and climbs a crack through a small roof and the groove above, E1 5b, an amusing divertissement.

Guardian Angel Face

This tall, grey cliff of solid rock has four quality routes. It is found 75m right of the previous routes, mid-way between the first cliff and the pillbox. A solitary stake marks the top of the cliff. Descent is on the left facing the cliff.

9   Mephistopheles   22m   Very severe   4c
Climb a crack left of the cut-away corner, with a hard move above the corner to a ledge; up and left to the top.

10   Wild Horses   22m   E1   5b   ★
Up the cut-away corner with an excursion on the right-hand wall to gain a crack at its top. Continue directly for 10m, stepping right to a ledge below the final wall. Climb this using an edge on the left — precipitous and piquant.

11   Guardian Angel   22m   Hard Very Severe   5b   ★★★
Very well protected, this route has a sharp start and finish. Start immediately right of the cut-away corner.
   Make a strong pull-up right to a ledge. Climb the steep crack above to a circular bulge, which forces the climber left then right, crossing the slab above to a ledge. Step left and climb the fingery wall to the top.

12   Devil's Daughter   22m   Hard Very Severe   5a   ★★
Start 1m right of Guardian Angel, below a steep finger-crack.
   Climb the rightward-sloping crack, step left then up to a ledge. The groove on the left is climbed to its finish, then direct to the top.

The Main Cliff

This is found below the pillbox, 75m east of the Guardian Angel Face. It is split into three sections. The highest is the most impressive, with a huge hanging curtain of stone, 20m by 5m but only 2m thick. This is flanked on the right by a sweep of wall, cut by a long ledge. Descent is by a grassy bank 50m east of the pill-box.

13   Conquistador   45m   E2   5b   5a   ★★
This energetic performance starts at the left end of the flanking wall, below the right-hand edge of the crag's highest point.

1.   28m   Climb a distinct finger-crack for 3m, move left and climb a deceptive crack to the ledge. Above is an overhanging finger-crack. Climb this rightwards to a ledge and belay. A strenuous pitch.

2.   18m   The cleaned arête above.

14   Mirror, Mirror   45m   E3   5c   5b   5a
A serious climb, with a good first pitch; care should be taken with the protection on the first pitch and the rock on the second. Start in the centre of the wall, 1m left of a left-sloping flake crack.

1.   16m   Climb the wall with increasing difficulty until a hard move right leads to a block (runner) at the foot of the flake edge. Follow this to the ledge and belay. A pulse-quickening pitch.

2.   11m   Climb parallel cracks above to a good Friend placement. Move right over a bulge and up to a ledge.

3.   18m   As for pitch 2 Conquistador.
   Direct start: climb the twin cracks in the lower wall to a junction with the original route at the long ledge.

BURROW HEAD — MAIN FACE.

1 The Shootist
2 Bright Eyes
3 Waiting For Godot
4 The Cutter
5 Mirror, Mirror
6 Mirror, Mirror, Direct Start
7 Conquistador

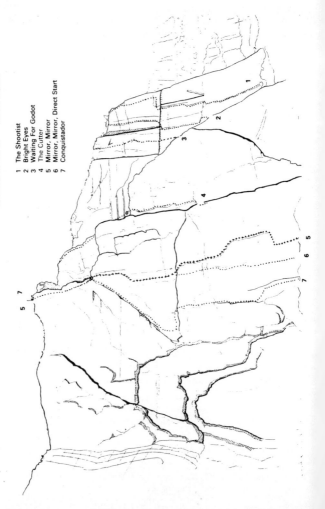

15   The Cut   33m   Severe
The chimney-cum-gully which separates the main face from the next face on the right — in need of a good sweeping!

16   The Cutter   45m   Hard Very Severe   5a   4b

1.   26m   Climb the flake in the steepening slab, right of The Cut, to a ledge. Move up left, then right to the foot of a corner which is followed to a ledge and belay.

2.   19m   Climb the slabby arête on the left.

Another gully formed by the edge of the bedding planes, filled with detritus, is best avoided completely. On its right a large white wall, patterned with vertical cracks, is seen.

17   Waiting for Godot   30m   Hard Very Severe   4c
Start 1m right of the gully.
Climb the wall above on large holds to a ledge. Starting right of centre, climb the next wall to the top (crux).

18   Bright Eyes   30m   Very Severe   4c
Start below a V-chimney, 3m right of the previous route.
Climb a crack to the chimney and avoid this on the left by a flake edge.
Climb twin finger-cracks in the wall above to finish. Improves with height.

19   The Shootist   32m   Very Severe   4c   ★
An enjoyable climb, with an exposed finish. Start 1m right of Bright Eyes.
Climb a good steepening crack to a ledge. Traverse right for 2m to a small foot-ledge; climb directly to the top on good holds. Strenuous for its grade.

THE GALLOWAY HILLS

INTRODUCTION

Tucked away in the south west corner of Scotland lies this rounded and extensive range of hills. The particular area that has been of profit to the rock climber is the chain of granite hills that are found between the Merrick in the west, and the Rhinns of Kell to the east. Relatively unfrequented and unspoiled, one of the attractions of this remote area is the large, unexplored granite crags which await those prepared to step off the beaten track and risk a day's climbing.

To date the best climbing has been found in two distinct groups: the first is the remote crags of the Dungeon of Buchan, secondly, the friendly and accessible crags of Cairnsmore of Fleet. This section will document the best climbing that has been found so far and conclude with a pointer to the area's untapped potential.

On a more technical note, no star ratings have been included as there is no consensus from which to work. Where possible an indication of a climb's quality is given in the introduction.

ACCESS

From Glasgow or Edinburgh, follow the A74 and turn right for Thornhill on the A702. Continue on the same road to New Galloway. From the South, follow the A75 to Dumfries. At Dumfries, change direction and take the A712 to New Galloway. This is the general access for all the crags in this area.

Map: Sheet 77, G.R. 462 848

THE DUNGEON OF BUCHAN

INTRODUCTION

Dungeon Hill, set above the Silver Flow, is the highest and best set of cliffs in Galloway; however, to complete this trio of superlatives, it also has the longest approach in this guide. The climbs are worth the walk.

ACCESS

From New Galloway, follow the A712 to Clatteringshaws Loch. Turn right past the loch and park at Craigen callie. From here follow the forestry road for two miles, turn right and continue to Backhill of Bush — an excellent base for this crag. Opposite the bothy, select an appropriate break in the forest, cross the marsh and climb to the crag (10½ Km). Alternative approaches are from Glen Trool (Sh.77 G.R. 416 804) via Loch Neldricken (6½ Km) or, from the north and west, by Loch Doon (Sh. 77 G.R. 482 924) via Backhill of Bush (13½ Km).

The main cliffs face east, overlooking the Dungeon Lochs, and are slow to dry, taking two days. The Cooran Buttress is the largest cliff and is found towards the left-hand side of the escarpment; above the Round Loch of Dungeon, on the right-hand side of the escarpment is a large slabby cliff climbed by Saddle Tramp. Most of the smaller crags are as yet unclimbed.

1   Saddle Tramp   72m   E2   5b   5a   5c
A fine route with a good final pitch. At the right-hand edge of the cliffs is a concave white wall, split by horizontal heather ledges. Start at the foot of a large, clean slab, directly below an obvious diagonal crack at 45m.

1.   18m   Climb directly up the middle of the slab to a grass terrace and belay on the right.

2.   24m   Step right and follow an obvious crack-cum-groove in the slab, over a bulge to a grass ledge. Belay below a rightward-slanting crack in the steep upper wall.

3.   30m   Climb a groove left of the crack to a horizontal break; move right to a large, triangular niche. From the top of the niche, a crack leads to a large sloping ledge. Move left to a thin curving crack to finish.

The Cooran Buttress

2   Cyclopath   120m   Hard Very Severe
On the right of the buttress is a steep, unclimbed dièdre. This route starts at a steep slab on the right of the dièdre.

1.   42m   Climb a groove in the slab; move left on to a wall and up flakes to the start of a crack. Follow this widening crack to a ledge and belay on the right.

2.   45m   Climb the wall behind the stance; follow a thin crack through a bulge, past a spike to grass ledges; easily to the final wall.

3.   33m   The most obvious crack-line, in the centre of the wall, leads to an awkward finish.

3   The Highway Man   120m   Hard Very Severe
The classic of the crag. Start 10m left of the dièdre.

1.   45m   Take the obvious crack-line for 12m; traverse right to a groove, which is followed to a ledge. Continue up a crack, beside a rib, over a bulge to heather ledges.

2.   45m   Trend right to the central crack to heather ledges. Easily up to a belay.

3.   30m   A crack and groove in the left side of the final wall leads to the top.

Moving further left, one encounters a long, grassy fault — Roraima, Very Difficult; left again, there is more broken ground — Cooran Buttress, Very Difficult, meanders in this area. A series of clean, inter-locking slabs and walls is found on the left of the broken ground — this is taken by Traitor's Gait.

4   Traitor's Gait   107m   Mild Severe
Continuously interesting climbing on impeccable rock. Start 5m right of the left toe of the buttress (arrow).

1.   28m   Climb the crack to a ledge on the left at 8m. Traverse back right and climb to a large heather ledge.

2.   28m   Climb the slab on the right to a ledge.

3.   18m   Climb the short steep crack above; an arête and slab lead to the final headwall.

4.   33m   Parallel cracks lead to a large ledge on the left edge of the buttress.
    Climb the arête above to a large ledge and easy ground.

CRAIGNAW
Map: Sheet 77, G.R. 463 833

Craignaw is formed by many large and rambling cliffs, which may be concealing better things. So far the best the hill has to offer is Galloway's one classic gully.

ACCESS

The climbs can be reached in two ways: either by following the Glen Trool approach to Dungeon Hill, when the cliffs are reached over the summit of Craignaw, or, by using the Backhill of Bush approach and traversing south from the Dungeon Lochs.

1   Drainpipe Gully   100m   Very Difficult
A wet day classic of the genre. On the east face of Craignaw, directly below the summit, are three prominent and narrow gullies, start below the central gully.
   This is climbed in five pitches. Delights include scenic cascades, chimneys, caves, a through route, as well as the inevitable crux groove.

Map: Sheet 83, G.R. 502 671

CAIRNSMORE OF FLEET

INTRODUCTION

South of the Dungeon and south of the A712 New Galloway to Newton Stewart road, Cairnsmore of Fleet is an extensive hill which has several areas that have proved profitable to the rock climber. The crags, in general, are less serious and quicker to approach than those of the Dungeon, a fact that may make these crags the most popular in this section. The first crags to be described are in the Craignelder area, at the north end of Cairnsmore of Fleet.

Big Gairy

This crag, within easy reach of the road, offers good, granite slab climbing. To date, only one climb has been discovered and more seem inevitable.
   The slabs are split by a grassy gully.

ACCESS

Follow the A712 from New Galloway and park at Murray's Monument. Cross the stream and walk through the forest on to Craignelder — the crag is approached in one hour.

1   Pale Face   63m   Mild Very Severe
This is a good slab route, especially if the easier variations are avoided.
Start immediately right of the gully.

1.   13m   From the right toe of a band of light slabs, climb easily to a ledge beneath a short crack.

2.   15m   The wall above is climbed, leftwards (crux) to a ledge and belay. A delicate pitch.

3.   7m   Climb twin cracks to a ledge.

4.   28m   Climb the slabs on the right to a bulge; move left and climb a short corner. A final slab and bulge are taken direct to easier ground.

Map: Sheet 83, G.R. 499 696

CRAIG-AN-EILTE OR, THE FLESH MARKET

This is the companion crag for the Big Gairy. It forms an escarpment which is notable for a prominent tower at its right-hand end.

ACCESS
The same approach is taken as the Big Gairy, but continue past these slabs until the tower is seen.

1   Gloom   25m   Severe
An atmospheric route. Start at the left edge of the tower.

1.   10m   Climb the arête and the chimney above to a ledge beneath a pronounced roof.

2.   15m   Climb the chimney to the roof then move left to an arête which leads to a ledge on the left. Climb a short corner, then a chimney followed by a corner to the top.

2   The Original Route   22m   Severe
An obscure gem. Start on the right of the tower's roof.

1.   14m   Follow the prominent groove system to a ledge.

2.   8m   Move right and climb a short steep crack to the top.

CLINTS OF DROMORE

This quick-drying crag boasts a number of fine routes in the easier grades and some good bouldering.

ACCESS

Take the A75 from Dumfries to Gatehouse of Fleet; turn right and follow the B796 for 9½ Km, past Upper Rusko Cottage, and park near the old railway station. Walk along the disused railway line, north — the crag is easily approached in twenty minutes.

The left side of the crag is marked by the two largest buttresses, the following route is on the steeper, left-hand buttress.

1   Central Buttress   45m   Very Difficult
Start at the right side of the buttress, beside some quartz flecks.

1.   12m   Climb easily to a ledge.

2.   32m   Climb the steep scoop above with difficulty. Slabs then lead to a crack in the crest of the buttress. Follow this to easy ground.

In the centre of the crags is a large slab, black-streaked, with a large boulder resting against it. The next route uses this slab.

2   Black Streaker   35m   Very Difficult
Climb the slab to a fault line and follow it left, stepping right at the top.

This slab can be climbed anywhere at Severe — an enjoyable experience.

LOCH GRANNOCH CRAG

Another worthwhile crag in a remote situation. Two routes have been recorded, as well as some good bouldering.

ACCESS

Follow the Clints of Dromore access, walking past these cliffs to the Big Water of Fleet viaduct. Turn left and take a forestry road past Meikle Cullendoch. Then take the next left and left again to Loch Grannoch Lodge. The slab is reached in 1½ hours from the road.

The crag consists of two groups of slabs: the first climb is on the right hand area.

1 Goat Grooves 45m Severe
Pleasant slab climbing. Start left of the main slab in the right-hand area, at a clean, white slab.
1. 22m Climb the deceptive slab in the middle to a heather ledge.
2. 23m Move left and climb the easier upper tier.

2 Captain Madman 25m Very Severe
A fine route — easy for the grade. Start, in the left-hand area, at a large right-leaning crag.

From the centre of the crag, gain and climb a rightward-sloping crack-line.

Minor Crags

Benbeoch — Sh. 77 GR 495 083 — Basalt columns which give short routes.

Mullwharchar — The Slock — Sh. 77 Gr 459 895 — large but vegetated.

The Tauchers — Sh. 77 GR 460 872 — Some hard lines, all apparently unclimbed.

Craignaw — Snibe Hill — Sh. 77 GR 466 814 — Clean and very worthwhile outcrop.

North Gairy Top — Sh. 77 GR 522 869 — A steep, metamorphic cliff, possibly unclimbed.

Craigencallie — Sh. 77 Gr 500 782 — A clean, granite outcrop which has seen some attention.

Craigdews — Sh. 77 GR 497 722 — Granite crags near the road.

The Spout of the Clints — Sh. 83 Gr 509 668 — Large, remote and rambling — but has a strange appeal!

THE DUMFRIES OUTCROPS

INTRODUCTION

Within twenty miles of Dumfries, there are a dozen crags that local climbers have investigated over the past ten years. Of these, Clifton, Lion's Head, and Powillimont are the best, meriting outside attention. As these crags are both close together and near the road, a trip round all three is not only possible but recommended.

The other crags, though by no means worthless, are of more use to climbers based in the South West. Some of these could also be investigated by outside climbers in the course of a round of the crags. Most of the crags are quick drying: Sandy Hills has nature's idea of an indoor crag, a fact which can salvage a wet day.

Map: Sheet 84, G.R. 909 571

CLIFTON CRAG

These sound granite crags lie modestly behind Upper Clifton Farm, fronted by some scree of often quite massive boulders. Facing south west, with an open prospect of the Solway, the Lakes beyond and the Galloway Hills away to the north, it is particularly pleasant on sunny afternoons and evenings, which it not infrequently experiences. The climbing for such relatively short cliffs (about 13m) has an intensity, variety and high quality which has made them a popular venue for more than the local cognoscenti. Protection is uniformly good.

ACCESS

Approach picturesquely along the A710 south from Dumfries to Dalbeattie, beyond the narrow bridge of Caulkerbush, turn right 2km to Upper Clifton Farm. Permission should be sought and tact is appreciated.

Hollowstones Wall

This is the leftmost extremity of the crag. It has a hawthorn on its left and a large grass ledge halfway up on its right.

THE DUMFRIES OUTCROPS

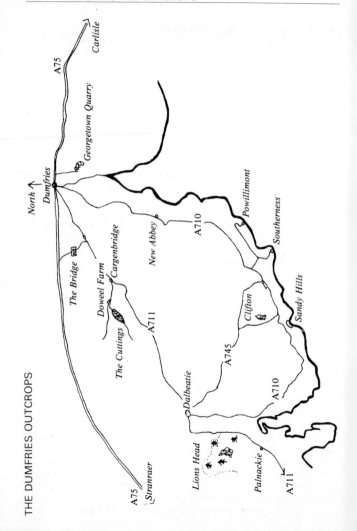

1   Sideshoot   15m   Very Severe   4c
Climbs the slab and corner which marks the left boundary of the area.
  Start just left of the tree; the undercut is the crux. Good.

2   Sidekick   15m   Hard Severe
The groove behind the tree. Finish up the crack right of Sideshoot.

3   Jeune Ecole   16m   Severe   ★★
Right of the tree, climb a vegetated crack till a line of jugs leads left to a
crack, to a ledge. Move to the arête. A fine, airy route.

4   Aquiline   15m   E2   5c
Start as for Jeune Ecole, but move directly up the left side of the arête
to a crack, then move on to the right side of the arête to finish.

5   Overground   10m   Severe   ★
Start right of the vegetated crack. Climb a wall to the ledge, then the
corner above. Popular.

6   Hollowstones Chimney   10m   Severe
Climb the V-groove right of Overground. Then the chimney. Good,
honest 'no-star' material. It is better to take the right edge of the
chimney, moving left at the top.

7   Outcast   10m   Hard Very Severe   5a
Start up the wall right of the V-groove, which leads to an overhanging
crack right of Overground's corner.

Dirl Chimney Area

The next climbs are found up and right of the last — in a bay behind an
oak. The first route takes the bottomless, roofed chimney on the left
which gives the area its name.

8   Dirl Chimney   13m   Mild Very Severe   4b   ★★★
The classic of the crag. A precise and continuously interesting route.
The dictionary gives 'dirl' as : 'A tremulous stroke; a sharp blow; a
resonating sound; an anxious haste or hurry; a twinge of conscience;
an exhilarating pleasure of mind or body.' (Or both). All this can happen
when you tap the walls of the chimney . . .
  The start is a crack, below the left side of the chimney.

9   Gibbon In Wonderland   13m   Hard Very Severe   5a
Start 3m right of Dirl and climb right across a slab to below a fist-sized crack. Up this.

10   Lemur   13m   E3   6a   ★
Between Dirl and Gibbon. Climb a sharp arête to a roof. Through the roof, moving right, then left. Strenuous and sensational.

11   Blazing Apostles   16m   E1   5b   ★★
Takes the large overhang below Gibbon's slab, and the overhanging groove right of its crack. A good strenuous climb.

12   Tour De Force   17m   Very Severe   4c   ★★
A high quality climb. Start as for Blazing Apostles, but traverse right below the overhang for 2m; go straight up, over a bulge and up a corner.

13   Owl Cave
So called because of its occupant, who forced and intrepid explorer to retreat fast (aided by gravity). It is found in the scrub right of Tour de Farce. A convenient descent.

Jigsaw Buttress

Round from Owl Cave is an undercut wall.

14   Lipstick   10m   Very Severe   4b
The crack on the extreme left. The start is the crux.

15   Lip Service   11m   Very Severe   4b
Start as for Lipstick, but move right and climb a chimney.

16   Hotlips   11m   Very Severe   4c   ★
3m right of Lipstick. Climb right, past a thread, to a ledge. Go up past an undercling, finishing by a thin crack. Good.

17   Labrum   12m   Hard Very Severe   5b
Start 1½m right of Hotlips. Climb directly on to the wall at an obvious plate of rock. Move right, then left, via flakes to the top. It is possible to traverse on to the plate, making the climb 5a. Interesting.

18   Liplet   10m   Severe   ★★
The roofed corner, turned on the left. Good but short.

The Main Area

This is defined by a steep corner on the left; and a fine arête (the outstanding feature of the crags) on the right; the whole area is dominated by a large beaked roof.

19   Ratten's Rest   8m   Hard Very Severe   5a   ★
The steep corner — not to be under-estimated.

20   Wall Street   13m   E1   5b   ★★★
Climb the crack right of Ratten's Rest and finish up the groove left of the roof. The hard classic of the crag.

21   The Groove   13m   Very Severe   4c
Beneath the roof, the V-groove. A good feature.

22   Novice Crack   12m   Severe
Start as for The Groove, but climb right, to the chimney.

23   Kenny's Chimney   8m   Mild Very Severe   4b
The chimney mentioned above, the grade depending on your thickness. (Don't they all.)

24   The Arête   16m   E2   5c   ★★★
A superb climb with an exciting, blind reach on the crux.
    Start 8m lower than the chimney, and 2m right of the edge. Climb to a block then traverse left and turn the arête. Go directly up to a spike, finishing by a short crack.

25   Elder's Crack   16m   Very Severe   4b
Start as for the crack of The Arête, but move right at the block, to reach the crack.

26   The Esplanade   20m   Difficult
The gangway on which the previous two routes finish, starting 9m to their right. A good descent route.

The Red Slab

Bound by the Esplanade on the left and a leaning tower on the right.

27   Pegasus   18m   Hard Severe
Starts 2m right of the Esplanade. Climb to a crack that rises from the

right, halfway up the crag. Follow this to a ledge, and finish up a groove with jammed blocks. (Named after the interaction of the first known ascentionist and a transient block, now nestling in the scree.)

28   Red Slab   13m   Very Severe   4c
Climb left of the slab, to a tree. Take the headwall and traverse sharply right to finish. Two fine contrasting sections.

29   D.I.Y.   16m   Hard Very Severe   5a   ★
Takes the corner-crack of the slab, moving left and then right to a pleasing hand traverse. Finally up an awkward break in the roof. An unusual and satisfying climb.

30   Toddamundo   16m   E4   6a   ★★★
Climb the blunt arête right of D.I.Y. to the break. A thought-provoking reach, from a sharp fingerhold on the roof's lip, gives access to a strenuous and exposed head wall. A further hard move (crux) leads to a jug at the top of the crag. A Friend 4 is advisable.

Variation: From the break, as for D.I.Y. (E2 5b ★★★).

31   Nebula   19m   E1   5b
The corner right of Toddamundo; then traverse right beneath the roof to finish. Loose.

32   Crosswires   12m   E1   5b
The thin groove, starting just left of the Fingerlust buttress.

33   Fingerlust   12m   E3   6a   ★★
In the leaning tower there is a finger crack. Strenuous and very substantial.

The Twin Cracks Area

This area is 100m right of Fingerlust, and is marked by an angular tree at its top and a detached pinnacle below it. Revolver's pouch also takes the eye.

34   Twin Cracks   16m   Very Severe   4b   ★★
Starts at the large pinnacle. Climb a crack to a niche, then follow the cracks above left. Fine layback moves.

35   Revolver   15m   E1   5b   ★★
To the left, round the arête, climb the flake crack to the tree. Make a hard reach left, move right then go direct to the top. Fine delicate climbing.

36   Crackshot   16m   Hard Very Severe   5a   ★
Companion to Revolver, taking the slender buttress 2m to its left, with a delicate start, to Revolver's ledge, then left to the top.

37   The Direct   13m   Hard Very Severe   5b
The crack parallel to Crackshot. A jamming problem.

38   Wiggle   14m   Hard Very Severe   5a
The curving crack, starting and finishing on The Direct.

39   Crawl Wall   13m   Very Severe   4b
The wall left of Wiggle.

40   Horner Corner   8m   Severe
The crack, up left of Crawl Wall.

Jugular Vein Buttress

The next substantial crag on the right.

41   Beyond The Terminator   14m   E3   5c   ★★
Climb as for Moonshine to a rest at the top of the initial slab. From here swing out left and gain the obvious good hold. Continue directly to the top surmounting a small roof.

42   Moonshine   17m   E2   5c   ★★
At the left side of the buttress is a slab topped by a crescent-shaped roof. Climb the slab, moving right to a junction with Jugular Vein at about mid-height. Continue across this route for 3m and finish up a short crack. A meaty expedition.

43   The Slash   13m   Very Severe   4c
The obvious crack right of Moonshine.

44   Jugular Vein   13m   E1   5b   ★★★
Takes the wall and then the high crack starting slightly right, round the buttress from the Slash. Very fine and sustained.

45   Loneliness of the Long Distance Runner   10m   E4   6a
The blunt arête 3m right of Jugular Vein. A short but serious undertaking.

46   Little Wall   14m   E1   5b
The crack-veined wall right of Jugular. A little Marie Celeste?

The Slab
Another 200 metres to the right, flanked by flying buttresses.

47   Crack-Up   16m   Hard Severe
There is an obvious crack on the left. Climb to this, make an awkward move, then easily to the top.

48   Sunset   18m   Very Severe   4c
Start in the middle of the slab at its lowest point. Climb to a horizontal break. Trend right to the top with increasing difficulty.

The little corner on the right gives 'scrambling plus a move.' Or alternatively, to give the first ascentionist's description: 'it gives a major route with extreme difficulty, high objective dangers and mixed climbing in an haute montagne setting.'

LION'S HEAD
Map: Sheet 84, G.R. 822 581

This schist buttress stands clear of the forest mane that surrounds it. Though over 30m high, the cliff is split by a terrace which forces the climber's attention to the upper tier. The open aspect of the crag, with its changing backdrop of pastoral scene, busy marina, open water and Lakeland hills, makes climbing on the rough rock of Lion's Head particularly enjoyable on spring afternoons.

ACCESS

From Dumfries, follow the A711 through Dalbeattie, heading for Palnackie. When the road passes Kirkennan House, the crag can be glimpsed through the wooded hillside on the right of the road. It is possible to park at a gap in the hedge fence, 20m before the wood gives way to open farm land. To reach the crag, follow the path behind the gap in the fence first left, then back right for 200m. The crag is then seen through the thinning forest.

The left-hand section of the crag, a loose, steep, side wall, has two routes, both unsatisfactory. However, on the right of this wall, there is a grassy bay which marks the left-hand end of the terrace. It contains the best climbing on the crag.

1   The Slant   18m   Hard Very Severe   5a
This climbs the line of holds on the left side of the bay; finish up an inverted V-chimney.

2   Catspaw   18m   Hard Very Severe   5a   ★
Start on the left of the obvious corner, below a small sapling. Climb the wall past the sapling; finish sharply by the groove above.

3   Twinkletoe Wall   24m   Hard Very Severe   5a   ★★
An excellent climb taking the corner that froms the right-hand side of the bay. Some small wires needed.

4   Sheer Can   26m   Hard Very Severe   5a
Start on the right of the corner.
Climb the right wall of the corner to a ledge. Traverse right, 4m; move left up the groove to a large spike. Climb the wall above to finish.

5   Claustrophobia   25m   E2   5b   ★
Climb the arête right of Sheer Can to the ledge on that route — bold. Move right and follow a crack to a roof. Make a hard move over the roof and climb the groove above and left to finish.

6   Snout Direct   32m   Very Severe   4c   ★
A varied and interesting route, spoiled by a dirty first pitch. Start at the bottom of the crag, behind a large pinnacle.

1.   15m   Up the pinnacle, by its right edge. From the top, step across to a groove on the main crag and follow it to the terrace. Tree belay.

2.   17m   Traverse left to a small spike in the middle of the wall, left of the tree. Climb directly to a ledge. Climb the flake crack above, past a first ledge to a second. From the left-hand side of this ledge climb steeply to the top.

From the ledge on the second pitch, it is possible to climb the cracked face on the right — no change in grade.

An alternative second pitch has been climbed, starting on the right of the tree and taking the wall and layback crack above.

Map: Sheet 84, G.R. 993 568

POWILLIMONT — THE THIRLSTANE

The Thirlstane is a triangular-shaped, sandstone outcrop, found on the shore, east of Southerness. It offers excellent bouldering and has numerous short routes of all grades. As the crag is not extensive it is best used on summer evenings, or as part of a tour of these closely grouped outcrops.

The main section of cliff faces inland, and is 10m high: the rock on the seaward side presents a gentle, slabby incline to the sea. However, the most interesting feature (and the reason for the crag's name) is the roofless cave that splits the cliff. It provides two overhanging faces, devoid of the sandstone jugs that are characteristic of the outside walls.

ACCESS

The approach is along the A710 Solway Coast Road, which is followed for about 18km. Turn left to Southerness, first left again, following this road for about 2½km until a right-angled bend is seen. Turn right 10m further on at a road with the farm sign 'Powillimont'. Follow this to the sea, turn left, and park. The crag is a short walk in this direction, along the shore.

Climbs are described from left to right, facing the crag.

1 Left Arête   9m   Very Difficult   ★★★
Climb the wall immediately right of the left-hand edge of the crag. Steep and juggy.

2 Goodnight Irene   10m   E3   5b   ★★
Start 2m left of the cave. Pull over the initial small roof, then follow the line of the larger roofs to a finish in a short groove.

The Thirl Walls

These are extended boulder problems and hence have only been given a technical grade.

3 Route 1   8m   5c   ★
On the left side of the cave, 2m inside, is a smooth groove formed by a series of sloping holds.
Start with difficulty, balance, finish with difficulty!

4   Route 2   6m   6a   ★★
At the sea entrance to the cave, on the left, is a low-level roof. Start with both feet on the slab. Fun.

5   Route 3   9m   5a
On the right side of the cave, at the mouth, is an open corner.
   Climb this steeply past a protruding block to a chockstone; finish up the wall above.

6   Route 4   9m   5c
Start 2m left of the previous route, below a niche.
   Climb in to the niche and finish up a crack on its right.

7   Route 5   11m   5b   ★★★
From the niche of Route 4, break out left and climb the gradually steepening wall on dramatically improving holds. Strenuous and extended.

8   Route 6   6m   5c   ★★
Climb the wall opposite Route 2 on pockets to a rounded finish.

8a   Cave Route   14m   Severe
Start on the right of the cave mouth.
   Climb a groove and move left to bridge across the cave. Swarm into the constriction and emerge hopefully on the other side.

9   Zig-Zag   12m   Mild Very Severe   4b   ★
Start as for Cave Route, but continue directly into the recess above. From this point, either traverse the slab on the right and finish up the large, rippled groove, or, climb the crack above and left to the top.

10   Catechumen Groove   10m   Mild Severe
The well-defined groove right of the cave. A good lesson in bridging.

11   The Overhang   10m   Hard Very Severe   5b
Start below the obvious ramp and 3m right of the previous route.
   Climb the overhang from right to left to a ledge; finish up the overhang above. Many variations are possible.

12   The Ramp   10m   Difficult
The obvious ramp.

13   Colourful and Carefree   8m   Very Severe   4b   ★
To the right of the Ramp, a prow is visible. Start below this prow.
    Climb to the prow, swing left and climb the arête to finish. it is also
possible to climb the slab below the prow to the arête — this raises the
technical grade to 4c.

14   Short and Curly   8m   Hard Very Severe   5a
To the right of The Ramp is a small roof. Climb this to join Colourful and
Carefree.

15   Rough Buttress   7m   Very Difficult
Start at a fence post and climb the buttress to the top.

    To the right, the crag is overgrown. However, there is good
bouldering.
    A short wall with a circular pocket is particularly good; the undercut
slab on the right gives easier bouldering routes.

MINOR CRAGS

From Powillimont, following the A710, there are a number of rocky
bays and headlands. The best are noted here. Map references must
serve for access.

LOT'S WIFE, SOUTHWICK   Map: Sheet 84, G.R. 910 558

On the east side of the Sandy Hills bay, dotted along the shore, are a
number of slabby outcrops which terminate at two pinnacles. Though
limited, the climbing ranges from bouldering to 30m routes, with
grades from Very Difficult to Very Severe.

SANDY HILLS   Map: Sheet 84, G.R. 891 547

This is the bouldering centre of the South West. The best climbing is
found on the west side of the bay. The large crag at the spectacular
Needle's Eye (G.R. 916 561) is disappointing — loose and vegetated.
However, there is some sounder rock by an ivy mass that is as yet
unexplored.

GUTCHER'S ISLE   Map: Sheet 84, G.R. 864 527

This tidal island has good, longer boulder problems but needs at least two days to dry. It is found 1½km east of Rockcliff.

The following climbing areas are found north and west of Dumfries.

GLENWHARGEN CRAG   Map: Sheet 78, G.R. 763 031

Perched above the Scar Water, this crag has so far given up no worthwhile climbs, though it has not been subjected to the intensive exploration that has been seen, for example, at Clifton. The local opinion is that this is doubly disappointing as the valley of the Scar Water is secluded and ideal for a quite, meditative day's climbing.

GEORGETOWN QUARRY   Map: Sheet 84, G.R. 998 742

This under-developed quarry (the only one in the South West worthy of recording, so far) is only two miles outside Dumfries. It has two good but hard bouldering walls and one route Geronimo (E2 5b) taking the crack in the right wall.

The main wall has been top-roped but awaits a fresh climber to give it respectability. The walls, 20m high, take two days to dry in summer.

Two other areas of interest to local climbers are the rough-cut sandstone bridge on the Dumfries side of the I.C.I. works (Sh 84 G.R. 947 751); and some disused railway cuttings (Sh 84 G.R. 938 739), on the opposite side of the I.C.I. Works.